TRAVELERS' TALES BOOKS

Country and Regional Guides
America, Australia, Brazil, Central America, Cuba, France, Greece,
India, Ireland, Italy, Japan, Mexico, Nepal, Spain,
Thailand, Tibet, Turkey; American Southwest, Grand Canyon,
Hawai'i, Hong Kong, Paris, San Francisco, Tuscany

Women's Travel
Her Fork in the Road, A Woman's Path, A Woman's
Passion for Travel, A Woman's World, Women in the Wild,
A Mother's World, Safety and Security for Women
Who Travel, Gutsy Women, Gutsy Mamas

Body & Soul
The Spiritual Gifts of Travel, The Road Within,
Love & Romance, Food, The Fearless Diner, The Adventure
of Food, The Ultimate Journey, Pilgrimage

Special Interest
Not So Funny When It Happened,
The Gift of Rivers, Shitting Pretty, Testosterone Planet,
Danger!, The Fearless Shopper, The Penny Pincher's
Passport to Luxury Travel, The Gift of Birds, Family Travel,
A Dog's World, There's No Toilet Paper on the Road Less
Traveled, The Gift of Travel, 365 Travel, Adventures in Wine

Footsteps
Kite Strings of the Southern Cross, The Sword of Heaven,
Storm, Take Me With You, Last Trout in Venice, The Way of the
Wanderer, One Year Off, The Fire Never Dies

Classics
The Royal Road to Romance, Unbeaten Tracks in Japan,
The Rivers Ran East, Coast to Coast, Trader Horn

TRAVELERS' TALES

TURKEY

TRUE STORIES

TRAVELERS' TALES

TURKEY

TRUE STORIES

Edited by

JAMES VILLERS JR.

Series Editors
JAMES O'REILLY AND LARRY HABEGGER

TRAVELERS' TALES
SAN FRANCISCO

Art Direction: Michele Wetherbee
Interior design: Kathryn Heflin and Susan Bailey
Cover photograph: © Nigel Hillier/gettyimages. Yeni Cami (New Mosque), Istanbul.
Map: Keith Granger
Page layout: Cynthia Lamb, using the fonts Bembo and Remedy

Distributed by: Publishers Group West, 1700 Fourth Street, Berkeley, California 94710.

Library of Congress Cataloguing-in-Publication Data

Turkey: true stories / edited by James Villers, Jr.—1st ed.
     p. cm. — (Travelers' Tales guides)
Includes bibliographical references and index.
    ISBN 1-885211-82-1
  1. Turkey—Description and travel. I. Villers, James, 1966– II. Series

DR429.4.T87 2002
956.1—dc21   2002008737

First Edition
Printed in the United States
10 9 8 7 6 5 4 3 2 1

For my father.

Everything you see has its roots
in the Unseen world.
The forms may change,
yet the essence remains the same.

—RUMI

Table of Contents

Part Two
SOME THINGS TO DO

Part Three
GOING YOUR OWN WAY

Part Four
IN THE SHADOWS

Part Five
THE LAST WORD

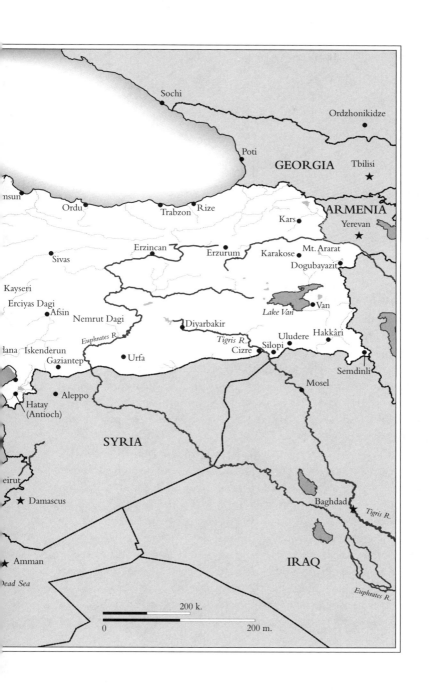

Turkey: An Introduction

I tell you truly,
everything you now see
will vanish like a dream.

—RUMI, "From Box to Box"

RUMI WAS NOT A TURK BY BIRTH, BUT HE WHIRLED TO spiritual fame in Konya, an ancient Turkish Islamic capital. He is recognized as a mystic (the founder of the order of dervishes) and poet, and, as such, his verse is meant to touch the spiritual voyager in all of us. His words on the intangibility of dreams strike me as paradoxical, a reminder of the illusory nature of time and of the impermanence of human creation, but also of the importance of the immediate. Never mind these mundane struggles, Rumi seems to be telling me; but pay close attention to your surroundings, nevertheless.

His words seem particularly relevant to the subject of these stories: Turkey and its inhabitants. Journeys so often lead us to profundities, in any case, deeper ways of thinking than we're accustomed to in the everyday. Why not flip the process? Let's begin this journey with Rumi's universal truth in mind, a truth that's applicable to the subject in more ways than one.

Turkey is shockingly timeless; all around the country, from mountains to plains to coastline, it's impossible not to step into the currents of past, present and future. It is ancient, young, and not yet born. The cradle of civilization lies within its borders; countless cultures have trod its shores and plains, leaving behind no more than layers of crumbling ruins and echoes of whispered voices. Modern Turkey, however, born as recently as the 1920s, still struggles to find its true nature; positioned at the crossroads between Europe and the Middle East, it teeters from one way of life to the other, swayed by the forces of politics, religion, tourism, and television. And this precarious balance gives rise to a question pertaining to Turkey's unknown future: Which way will the country swing in the coming years, and how will this color the lives of its inhabitants, world neighbors, and curious visitors?

I didn't know much of Turkey before I left to go there. Nor did my friends or family. When I shared the news that I'd gotten a job in Istanbul and would soon be moving, the most prevalent comment made by people was, "Have you seen *Midnight Express*?"

The question was never asked in genuine fear for my safety. At least I don't think it was. Still, there's something a bit strange in the question coming up at all, because many of those who asked the question hadn't even seen the film. I certainly hadn't, and, what's more, I absolutely refused to see it before I left. I didn't want any sort of nightmarish Hollywood vision clouding my perception of a place I hadn't yet seen.

The point seems to be this: enough people I talked to had long-lasting negative impressions of Turkey based on the 1978 film, whether they'd seen it or not, that I refused to see it. How many others in the West have avoided Turkey based solely on this film?

Turkey is not the land of *Midnight Express*. As certain of these stories attest, brutal acts have been perpetrated within its borders, but Turkey's shadows are no different from any other country's, developed or not.

I had been in Turkey—in a strange suburb near Istanbul—for exactly fourteen days when the first major 1999 earthquake hit; my new job as a teacher was to start that very week. It was approximately 3 A.M., and I was awake when the shaking started. As habituated to earth tremors as I am after nearly a lifetime in California, I wasn't ready for the violence of this upheaval. The rocking was long and strong, and it gathered in force over a full forty-five seconds. I leaped from the sheets, and stood, shakily, in my bedroom doorway until the trembling stopped.

Even with the intense fright—deeper than any I'd ever known—I still might have climbed back under my covers; it's what I always did back home, whenever we felt tremors.

The voices of my neighboring Turks, however, lifted up from the outside and in through my open window. Looking out, I saw them filing out from our apartment building and the ones nearby, to huddle together in and around the playground. I watched the growing crowd, heard the incomprehensible murmurs (nothing in view had crumbled—unlike the devastation in Izmit and Avcilar, thirty or so miles away—and so the crowd didn't seem at all panicked), and became convinced that the people down there knew something I didn't. I descended to join my neighbors, to await any aftershocks or news.

After two years in their midst—as friend to some, stranger to most, observer of all I came across—I'm now positive that Turks know many things that I do not. How to make the most of any open patch of grass, for example, or how to profit from a sunny day (first step, go outside, no matter what kind of landscape you find yourself in). Lingering over breakfast is an art, particularly on a weekend. Soccer is a religion (albeit, a gender-centric one; but men also embrace warmly, and kiss each other on the cheeks when they meet). Bread is considered sacred, and never thrown out (in Istanbul, the hard, inedible ends are left outside for the numerous street cats and dogs, both of which share a shaky, often perilous existence with the vast city's human inhabitants). And children come first, for all Turks. In each of these aspects of daily Turkish existence, there seems to be an echo of Rumi's admonition that the present moment matters. It matters very much.

Two years wasn't enough to begin to know Turkey in its entirety of place and people. I even came back to California with the vague and uneasy feeling that, despite my daily wanderings in Istanbul and frequent travels around the country, I hadn't let much inside of me. The research I've done for this book, however, has changed that feeling, revealing to me faces and sites that I easily recognize, even ones I've never actually seen.

Turkey is exactly what you'll read here. Ancient. Diverse. Hospitable. Harsh. Stunning. Paradoxical. A little nutty. And timeless. But the pieces you'll read here—for all their color and character, for all their diversity and depth—certainly can't do complete justice to the country. I hope that these stories, though, will give you just enough of a taste of the place that you'll decide to go there and sense for yourself, before the Turkey of today vanishes like Rumi's dream.

—JAMES VILLERS JR.

PART ONE

ESSENCE OF TURKEY

STEPHEN KINZER

A Dazzling Kaleidoscope

*Raki, like Turkey, involves every one
of the senses.*

THE FIRST FRIENDS I MADE IN TURKEY TOLD ME THAT IF I really wanted to understand their country, I would have to drink a lot of raki. These were wise people, so I took their advice. Every year the annual level of raki consumption in Turkey rises by slightly more than 1 million liters, and my contribution to the increase has not been inconsiderable.

In the bottle raki is absolutely clear, but it is rarely consumed that way. Instead it is mixed with water, which turns it translucent. Drinking it has the same effect on one's perception of Turkey. After a glass or two, what at first seemed clear becomes obscure. By the time the bottle is empty, everything appears murky and confused. Yet through this evocative haze, truths about Turkey may be most profoundly understood.

Many countries have national drinks, but raki is much more than that because it embodies the very concept of Turkey. The mere fact that a Muslim land would fall under the spell of a powerful distilled drink is enough to suggest this nation's unexpected and tantalizing appeal. Do not speak to a Turk about ouzo or other anise-based drinks supposed to reflect the characters of other lands. The careful mix of natural ingredients in raki and the loving process by which it is distilled, they believe, make it gloriously unique.

3

History books say that Mustafa Kemal Atatürk died from the effects of overindulgence in raki. That is only partly true. In fact he died from an overdose of Turkey. His involvement with Turkey, like his involvement with raki, was so passionate and so intense that it ultimately consumed him.

The same almost happened to me. I had admired Turkey from afar, but it was only after long nights drinking raki with friends that I came to understand the true audacity of the Turkish idea. Its grandeur and beauty filled me with awe. My excitement rose with each glass as I realized how much Turkey has to share with the world, to give the world, to teach the world.

I should have stopped there, but you never do with raki. That is its blessing and its curse. As months and years passed, raki began to work subtly on my mind. Slowly the delight I had found in discovering Turkey became mixed with other, more ambiguous emotions. No longer did my evenings end with the exhilarating sensation that I had found a jewel of a country poised on the brink of greatness. Raki led me inexorably toward frustration and doubt. It never shook my conviction that Turkey is a nation of unlimited potential, but it did lead me to wonder why so much of its potential remains unrealized. Turkey is undoubtedly the country of the future, but will it always be? Can it ever become what it hopes to be, or is it condemned to remain an unfulfilled dream, an exquisite fantasy that contains within it the seeds of its own failure?

There are as yet no answers to those questions, and therein lies the Turkish conundrum. This nation is still very much a work in progress, a dazzling kaleidoscope of competing images and ideas. Born of trauma and upheaval, it remains deeply insecure, shrouded in old fears and uncertain which direction it should take.

This identity crisis led to a near-collapse of the raki tradition in the 1960s and 1970s. Turkey was opening itself to the world, and a class of educated and sophisticated Turks was emerging. These people considered raki anathema because it symbolized the primitive mentality of rural peasants. If illiterate hillbillies wanted to drink it in their broken-down shacks, that was one thing, but no modern Turk would do so; much better to sip wine, cognac, or some other drink with a European pedigree.

Fortunately, those days are past. Turks no longer feel embarrassed to embrace their heritage and identity. Drinking raki is an ideal way to do so while at the same time enjoying a sublime pleasure.

Raki is the key to Turkey, not because of the drink itself but because of the circumstances in which one consumes it. This is not a drink like whiskey, useful for solitary reflection; not like beer, good for drinking in a noisy bar while munching on pretzels; and not like gin or vodka, lubricants for cocktail-party chatter. Bars and cocktail parties are, in fact, mortal enemies of the Turkish drinking tradition. Resistance to these pernicious influences is centered around the *meyhane*, a sort of bistro created especially for raki drinking. The *meyhane* is a temple of Turkish cuisine, but it is also a place where people meet, talk, debate, embrace, and lament. Turkey's diversity is most tangible at the *meyhane* because it is spread out on tables for all to see.

An evening at a *meyhane* is centered around raki, but raki never stands alone. It is only one component, albeit the essential one, of a highly stylized ritual. With raki always come *meze*, small plates of food that appear stealthily, a few at a time. Theoretically, *meze* are appetizers leading to a main course, but often the main course, like Turkey's supposedly great destiny, never materializes. No one complains about that because eating *meze* while sipping raki is such a supreme pleasure in itself. The path is so blissful that the idea of a destination seems somehow sacrilegious.

Meze usually come in waves. The first will include salad, thick slabs of white cheese, smoked eggplant purée, and honeydew melon. What comes next depends on the chef's whim. There might be a selection of cooked, cooled vegetables in olive oil, each presented on its own miniature platter, or small dolma, which are peppers stuffed with rice, currants, and pine nuts. And their close cousins, *sarma*, made from grape or cabbage leaves. After the next pause might come spicy red lentil balls, mussels on the half shell, mashed beans with lemon sauce, puréed fish roe, yogurt seasoned with garlic and dill, raw tuna fillets, poached mackerel with hazelnut paste, or an explosively flavorful dish made of baby egg-plants stuffed with garlic cloves, tomatoes, sliced onion, and parsley. This last is called *Imam Bayildi*, meaning "the Imam fainted."

After these come piping-hot *börek*, delicate pastries filled with feta cheese and sometimes also spinach, diced chicken, ground lamb or veal, pistachios, walnuts, or whatever else is lying around the kitchen. Some are layered, others triangular and still others cylindrical or crescent-shaped. Often they are served with squid rings fried in a light batter, which are to be dipped in a white sauce made from wine vinegar, olive oil, and garlic.

Turkey's ethnic vitality shines through as the evening proceeds. Kebabs and other *meze* made from meat recall the Central Asian steppes from which nomadic Turkic tribes migrated to Asia Minor, now called Anatolia, a thousand years ago. With them come hummus from Arabia, shredded chicken with walnuts from the Caucasus, diced liver from Albania, and cooked cheese thickened with corn flour from coastal villages along the Black Sea. Then comes the crowning glory, the seafood, a gift from the Greeks, who for millennia did all the cooking along what is now Turkey's Aegean coast. Raki sharpens the taste of all food, but its magic works best with fish. An old proverb calls raki the pimp that brings fish and men together for acts of love.

The variety of fish in Turkey seems endless. It changes according to what body of water is nearest and also according to the season. Always the fish is very fresh, and always it is prepared very simply, grilled or pan-fried and served with no sauce, only a lemon wedge and perhaps a slice of onion or sprig of parsley.

Such a meal is a microcosm of Turkey. It is an astonishingly rich experience but yields its secrets slowly. Patrons at the *meyhane*, like all Turks, confront an ever-changing mosaic, endless variations on a theme. Each *meze* tastes different, has its own color, aroma, texture, and character. The full effect is comparable to that of a symphony, complete with melodies, different rhythms, pacing, and flashes of virtuosity, all contained within an overarching structure.

Meze makes a feast, but drinking raki with them raises the experience to a truly transcendent level. "All the senses are involved," my friend Aydin Boysan, an architect and bon vivant who had been drinking raki for more than sixty years when I met him, told me during a long night we spent at a *meyhane* overlooking the Bosporus. "First you watch the water being poured into the glass and mixing with the raki. Then you pick up the glass and inhale the aroma. When you drink it, you take a small sip, feel the pleasure of it flowing down your throat, take another small sip, then put the glass down."

Aydin demonstrated this ritual to me, seeming to enjoy it every bit as much as he might have half a century earlier, and then closed his eyes for a moment. "The best part is feeling it go down your throat," he said lovingly. "A giraffe—that's an animal ideally made to appreciate raki."

The *meyhane* culture tells a great deal about Turkey. Like the country, it offers almost infinite possibilities because it blends the heritage of so many different peoples. It encourages discourse and deepens friendship, but because the food is brought unbidden by a waiter instead of ordered from a menu, it does not require any action, any decision, any act of choice other than turning away dishes that do not strike one's fancy. Raki can evoke either determination or resignation, a desire to rebel or an acceptance of the inevitability of submission.

At a *meyhane*, the world can either be invited in or shut out. Turks have not yet decided which is the wisest path. By the time they drain their final glasses and step out into the darkness, they have often concluded that their country is either the "golden nation" destined to shape world history or a hopeless mess certain to remain mired in wretched mediocrity.

Stephen Kinzer is a veteran foreign correspondent who has covered more than fifty countries on four continents. In 1996 he became the first New York Times *bureau chief in Istanbul; he is now that paper's national culture correspondent, based in Chicago. He is the author of* Blood of Brothers: Life and War in Nicaragua, *and* Crescent and Star: Turkey Between Two Worlds, *from which this story was excerpted.*

Above the Ruins of Ephesus

*On the trail of John Turtle Wood, amateur archaeologist
who unearthed Ephesus and the temple of Artemis,
the author walks a sacred road toward her own
encounter with Turkey's hidden past.*

SO I, A FOREIGN LADY DRESSED IN A LARGE SUN HAT AND
sensible Reeboks, started one morning in the early sun, at the single
standing column that is all that is left above ground of the hundreds
of columns that were once the great temple of Artemis. I set out on
the main road until I saw that there was a dirt road, more direct, that
ran at an angle through farm fields and up the mountainside.

I dodged invaders in tour buses and private cars on their busy
ways, and in a few minutes I had found a path through country
silence, headed toward the mountain that is on the north side of
the ruins.

I walked past orchards and farmhouses. The little path grew faint
beyond the last farmhouse. I began to climb the hill, watching the
shadow of my hat on the ground. Nobody had climbed there for
so long that weeds had grown high in the middle of it, but it was
still marked, if only by the slight dip in the otherwise weedy cover
and tangled vines. I began to thrust my way through them.

In the middle of what had become a ghost path, I saw the bones
and a little of the torn pelt of a large animal—a cow, a deer—eaten
there by wild things, and I knew that I had found something of
what that world was like when there was no civilized modern

overlay. I told myself that whatever beast it was, wolf or wild dog, it was asleep. At least I hoped it was well-fed and asleep.

I went on climbing in the sun that was getting heavier, searching the ground and the undergrowth. At the crest of one of the lower foothills, I looked, and looked again, afraid of being fooled. There it was, a fragment of marble that had been exposed by years of weather, and beyond it, a long straight edge of white marble that glistened in the light.

I had played at being Wood and I had found it, the sacred road. I went all blithe and brave in the morning, a nice lady in a big hat. I parted weeds, and struggled through vines, and when I parted two small saplings I found that I had walked to what I first thought was a cliff. It was not.

Down below me, still far away from the ruins of the ancient city within its fence and with its guides and crowds, was the small marble atrium of a lost suburban house. Weeds grew in an empty shallow pool. On either side of marble steps, there were still two dolphins that had once been fountains that poured water from their mouths into the pool. I slid down the hill to the level of the floor, and I walked a short path of marble to its door, where the two truncated columns on either side still showed the grooves where, at night, they would have closed the house to marauders.

But one night the marauders had come to this house, and it had been so long abandoned that nothing of any world was left there but a Roman atrium, a little pool, two dolphins, a threshold, and silence in the sun.

I went on past it, up along the crest of the hill again. I slipped and slid and felt a fool, and at one point thought, if I break an ankle or my leg on this hill, I won't be found until I am a lady skeleton in a big hat, picked clean. I parted the underbrush and looked down upon another atrium, this one large and complete, with a fountain base in the center, and roofless rooms beyond it. The wall looked about ten feet high, and I skirted the top of it, holding onto small trees for balance, to look for a way down.

I hadn't heard anything move, yet he stood there in front of me, smiling, quite silent, a large strong Turkish man, holding in his

hand a small bunch of sweet wild thyme. He held it toward me, saying nothing, still smiling. There was something so gentle about him
that I could not be afraid. I took the wild thyme, and I thanked
him, in Turkish. He smiled again and touched his mouth and his
ear. He was deaf and dumb. I still have the wild thyme, pressed and
dried, kept like a Victorian lady's souvenir of the Holy Land.

Dumb was the wrong word for him. There was no need for
speech. He was an actor, an eloquent mime. I pointed to the
atrium below and held my hands apart to show I didn't know how
to get down into it. He took my arm, and carefully, slowly, led me
down a steep pile of rubble.

He mimed the opening of a nonexistent door and ushered me
through it. He showed me roofless room after roofless room as if
he had discovered them. He dug and threw imaginary earth over
his shoulder to show that it had been dug up.

I think that he had scared people before, and he was happy that
here was someone who would let him show his house, for it was
his house. Maybe he did sleep there. I don't know. I only know that
he treated me as a guest in a ruin ten feet below the level of the
ground, and that he took me from room to room where once
there had been marble walls and now there was only stone, where
he was host and owner for a little while.

He showed me a small pool, held out his hand the height of a
small child, and then swam across the air. All the time he smiled.
He took me to a larger pool and swam again. Then he grabbed my
arm and led me through a dark corridor toward what I thought at
first was a cave. It was not. He sat down in a niche in the corridor,
and strained until his face was pink, to show me it was the toilet.
Then he took me into the kitchen where there were two ovens.
They were almost complete, except that the iron doors were gone.
The arches of narrow Byzantine bricks were graceful over them,
and the ovens were large as if there had been a large family there.

For the first one he rolled dough for bread, kneaded it in air,
slapped it, and put it in the oven. Then he took it out, broke it, and
shared it with me. I ate the air with him. The other was the main
oven, and he picked vegetables from the floor of the cave kitchen,

hit air to kill an animal, made a stew, and placed it in the stone and brick niche. We ate it and then we walked out into the sun of the larger atrium. Behind it, in the hill, he gestured that it had not yet been dug up, and then he pointed to a marble votive herma, whose head was missing, and knelt behind it, grinning, and set his own head there, to show me what it was. The grin was ancient, a satyr's grin.

We stood beyond his house on the edge of the hill, looking down on the buses and the crowd in the distance. Across and behind the noise and crowds, in a field looking abandoned too, was the church of the Virgin Mary. The house where we stood had looked out over that and the harbor, and although it has not been found, I knew that it was near where the Corresian Gate had been.

When I gave my friend, my *arkadash*, some money, he kissed my hand and held it to his forehead, and then, pleased with the sun and me, and the fact that someone had not run away from him who lived like Caliban in a ruin, he put his arms around me and kissed me on both cheeks. Then I went down the hill to Ephesus. When I looked back to wave he had disappeared.

Mary Lee Settle lived in Turkey for a number of years, and returned there to write, Turkish Reflections: A Biography of a Place, *from which this piece was excerpted. She is also the author of* The Beulah Quintet, Addie: A Memoir, I, Roger Williams, *and* Blood Tie, *for which she won the National Book Award.*

* ✴ *

In the Hearts of
God's Children

*The ancient verse of a mystic poet pulls this author
onto a contemporary pilgrimage.*

THE SUMMONS, I FOUND, WAS IRRESISTIBLE, FALLING AS IT
did on a spirit and a mind made weary by the insistent claims of
the orthodox, impervious defenders of the "true" faith and a cata-
logue of prophesies I had encountered on a host of pilgrimages. I
had none of the fire worshiper, perhaps a bit of the pagan, and
everything of the mortal who has violated his vows a hundred
times, and more.

And so I journeyed to ancient Anatolia, where those tolerant
words were dictated in exemplary and erudite Persian nearly eight
centuries ago. The author was born Jelaluddin Balkhi; he would
later earn the title of Mevlana, "Our Master," but most readers simply know him as Rumi, the founder of the Sufi order of whirling
dervishes known as the Mevlani. It was to his tomb in Konya,
Turkey, that I went to pay homage, not as I would have to that of
a prophet or a savior, but with all the reverence due to the Sufi
whose mystical poetry and message of love is a paradigm of the
spiritual heights of which humankind is capable.

In fact, Rumi didn't want a venerated tomb. "Look not for my
grave in the earth, but in the hearts of my devoted seers," he said

before his death. His followers, evidently, thought otherwise. When Rumi died on December 17, 1273, his funeral procession along the streets of Konya attracted a multitude. In a gesture telling of the mystic's ecumenical appeal, his coffin was alternately borne by his Muslim dervish disciples, Christians, Zoroastrians, and pantheists. He was buried alongside his father, Bahauddin Walad, also a theologian and mystic, in the gardens of the Seljuk sultanate. The sultan Velad was his son.

A mausoleum was built above the tombs of Rumi and his father, and it was here that the members of the Mevlani order came to pray, dance, play music, and pore over the Mevlana's words. Soon annexes were added, a mosque, and a monastic center, or *tekke*, for the dervishes. In time, the Mevlani complex became one of the most dynamic spiritual centers of the Ottoman Empire and a font of Sufism. The brightest young men *and* women knocked at the door of the *tekke*, seeking admission to the dervish order. Sultans and travelers, emirs and philosophers, the poor and the enlightened bowed before Rumi's tomb, and the Mevlani dervishes danced their whirling dance of prayer.

> The "tolerant words" the author refers to are Rumi's:
>
> Come again, come again,
> whoever you may be,
> come again, even though
> you may be a pagan or a fire
>   worshiper.
> Our Center is not one of
>   despair.
> Come again, even if you may
>   have
> violated your vows a hundred
>   times,
> come again.
>
> —JV

I stood in the courtyard of the Mevlana Mausoleum, blinded by the light reflecting off white marble and limestone. There were roses blooming in neat parterres, fountains filling reflecting pools, and Muslim pilgrims snapping pictures of domes, minarets, and Ottoman portals. Above the threshold that led to the mausoleum, a Persian inscription in gold relief was carved into the lintel:

> This station is the Mecca of all dervishes.
> What is lacking in them is here completed.
> Whoever came here unfulfilled,
> Was here made whole.

A Mecca for the mystics. I was glad to hear it, especially since, as a non-Muslim, I had been barred from making the hajj (pilgrimage) to the Ka'ba shrine at Mecca, arguably the world's most emblematic pilgrimage. Still, there was something sad about the inscription as well. There were no dervishes about, the *tekke* had been turned into a museum, and when the *sema* dance of the dervishes was performed once a year on the anniversary of Rumi's death, the dancers were no longer dervishes whirling in ecstatic prayer, but government employees engaging in a well-scripted pantomime under the guise of folklore. The 700-year history of monastic discipline and mystical rites of the Mevlani order came to an abrupt end in 1925 when Kemal Atatürk, father of the modern Turkish Republic, which emerged from the crumbling foundations of the Ottoman Empire, decreed the mystic orders banned and their *tekkes* closed. Since then, the Mevlani Center has been a museum and a monument, but a thoroughly lifeless one, and I found no more tragic or telling an image than that of a wax dummy Mevlani dervish, clad in his brown cloak and high, tube-shaped hat, set up as a display in one of the former monastic cells.

When the cry of the muezzin called the faithful to their midday prayers from the nearby Selimiye Mosque, Muslim pilgrims and tourists poured out of the mausoleum. I left my shoes with a stooped guard and made my way to Rumi's tomb in stocking feet and alone. I passed through a small domed chamber that had once been used as a Qur'anic reading room. The walls were crowded with inscriptions and calligraphic panels of rare beauty. In a display case were a series of heart-shaped leaves decorated with passages from the Qur'an rendered in gold. I continued on through silver doors and entered the central hall of the mausoleum. The room stretched beneath three massive domes, and velvet- and silk-draped sarcophagi lay in rows on raised dais to the left and right.

Here were the tombs of Rumi's most devoted followers and descendants and, according to tradition, those of the Horasanian dervishes who accompanied Rumi, his father, and family on their flight from Balkh in Persia and the Mongol hordes under Genghis Khan. A panel bore an inscription by Rumi: "Appear as you are or be as you appear."

When I reached the corner in which Rumi's tomb lay, I found a young woman crying, but when she saw me approach, she covered her face with her scarf and fled, sobbing as she went. Behind a low gate of silver latticework rose the marble sarcophagus of Rumi and that of his son, Sultan Velad, draped in a black silk shroud embroidered with Qur'anic verses. The tomb of Rumi's father stood at the foot of those of his sons. Atop the sarcophagus were the stone renditions of the Mevlana's tubular headdress (symbolizing the tombstone of the ego) wrapped in the turban of the order. Above soared a pyramidal dome. The walls were decorated in a dizzying composition of tiles and carved reliefs with floral motifs, passages from the Qur'an, and the words of Rumi. Everywhere there were candelabra

---

I am seated on a shaded bench near the entrance of the tomb, waiting for it to open. The path leading to the entrance is lined with shining white tiles and a fountain bubbles beside me creating a state of near-tranquility. A hollow sound resonates from behind the locked doors, they swing open to expose a ticket stand and a guard. I wait, not wanting to be the first person to rush in, and as I wait a lone figure hobbles slowly past me and toward the guard.

The figure is an old man wearing a tired *salwar kameez* under a beat-up navy-blue blazer. He stops in front of the guard and touches his forehead, bowing slightly. The guard points to the ticket stand. The old man tilts his head to the left and then to his feet which are spilling out of broken shoes. The guard tuts, shakes his head, and waves the old man through. They have not exchanged a single word.

—Joseph Gelfer, "Rumi's Tomb"

of gold and silver, precious oil lamps, and crystal chandeliers, all donated by admirers of the Mevlana who wished to give back to Rumi some of the light which he had instilled in them.

I wandered through the rooms that had once served as the Mevlani's dance hall and mosque and gazed at illuminated manuscripts and Mameluk vases, ivory and mother-of-pearl lecterns, and priceless carpets. One display case was devoted to the Mevlana's clothes and contained, in addition to his turban and nightcap, some silk and cotton gowns and cloaks of an elegance that would make any contemporary fashion designer flush with envy. In a gallery exhibiting countless Qur'ans, each more beautiful than the last, I watched two gentlemen praying around a display case. When they moved on, I stepped over to see what it was they were venerating. Beneath the glass was a mother-of-pearl reliquary chest; the plaque read: "Muhammad's Beard."

When I emerged from the mausoleum, the courtyard was bathed in a warm, autumnal light and a young couple was drinking from the fountain whose water is said to bestow blessings on newlyweds. They were very proper and formal with one another, no groping or silly chatter, but they were clearly very much in love. I could see it in their eyes. The Mevlana was right, I thought—his legacy didn't lie in a tomb, but in the hearts of God's children.

For days, I divided my time between a shoddy hotel and the mausoleum courtyard, where I spent hours sitting on a stone bench and reveling in the mystical writings of Rumi. His output was immense. The six-volume *Mathnawi*, Rumi's most celebrated work, consists of 5,618 couplets and took a full forty-three years to complete. There are volumes of odes and quatrains, letters and sermons, and a collection of discourses with the enigmatic title of *In It What Is In It*. I stuck mostly to the *Mathnawi* and *The Diwan of Shams of Tabriz*, a work Rumi dedicated to the mysterious dervish who changed the Mevlana's life, inspired him to write his greatest mystical poetry, and was subsequently murdered by some of Rumi's disciples in an act of fatal jealousy.

The scope of Rumi's field, I discovered, was virtually limitless. He could treat the mundane and the esoteric with equal subtlety and imbued all of his writing with a wisdom illuminated by the Sufi's notion of love and the continuous quest for union with the divine. Here is Rumi on "Quietness":

> Inside this new love, die.
> Your way begins on the other side.
> Become the sky.
> Take an axe to the prison wall.
> Escape.
> Walk out like someone suddenly born into color.
> Do it now.
> You're covered with thick cloud.
> Slide out the side. Die,
> and be quiet. Quietness is the surest sign
> that you've died.
> Your old life was a frantic running
> from silence.
> The speechless full moon
> comes out now.

Although Rumi was firmly rooted in the Islamic faith (his family descended from Abu Bakr, Muhammad's companion), he, like other Sufi mystics, was always striving toward a communion with God that clearly superseded the doctrines and dogmas of organized religion. To me, Rumi's message of tolerance and his ecumenical spirit in matters of faith seemed prophetic and, at the same time, thoroughly contemporary. Creeds, theology, debate, and exegesis interested him little; it was the inner journey that counted:

ONLY BREATH

> Not Christian or Jew or Muslim, not Hindu,
> Buddhist, Sufi, or Zen. Not any religion
>
> or cultural system. I am not from the East
> or the West, not out of the ocean or up

from the ground, not natural or ethereal, not
composed of elements at all. I do not exist,

am not an entity in this world or the next,
did not descend from Adam and Eve or any

origin story. My place is placeless, a trace
of the traceless. Neither body or soul.

I belong to the beloved, have seen the two
worlds as one and that one call to and know,

first, last, outer, inner, only that
breath breathing human beings.

Or this:

Cross and Christians, end to end, I examined. He was not
on the Cross. I went to the Hindu temple, to the ancient
pagoda. In neither was there any sign. To the heights of
Herat I went, and Kandahar. I looked. He was not on
height or lowland. Resolutely, I went to the top of the
Mountain of Kaf. There only was the place of the 'Anqa
bird. I went to the Kaaba. He was not there. I asked of his
state from Ibn Sina: he was beyond the limits of the
philosopher Avicenna...I looked into my own heart. In
that his place I saw him. He was in no other place.

I was beginning to wonder if all my incessant wandering of the
pilgrimage trails had been in vain.

As I was sipping tea one morning in a rather bleak cafe, I was
approached by a young stranger.

"You have been spending a great deal of time at the Mevlana's
tomb," he announced without introduction.

I nodded.

"And what have you found there?"

"A very lovely museum."

"But you are not here to visit museums."

"Not exactly."

He handed me a piece of paper with an address. "You will

come this evening after prayers," he stated roundly. "Do *not* be late. Come alone."

And with that he turned and walked out before I could so much as ask to what I had been so graciously invited and by whom.

I lurked in front of the house at the appointed hour. It was very dark and cold. I felt, I must admit, a tinge of fear. I thought of turning back. And then a man appeared from the shadows.

"Why do you not enter when you know we await you?"

"I wasn't sure I had the right house," I said by way of an excuse.

He motioned to me to follow him, and we walked into a dimly lit courtyard. In front of a door of a small house, there were dozens of shoes in neat rows. We took off ours silently and went in. We entered a room where perhaps fifty men, young and old, were engaged in prayer, bowing toward Mecca. I took a place in the last row at the back of the room.

I wasn't quite sure what to do. I thought I would be a mere observer, but an old man at my side pulled me down to my knees. I found myself bowing my head to the ground and mumbling something vaguely Arabic sounding, following along as best I could. The room was very hot and close and smelled of men. I recognized one of the guards from the museum and a pharmacist who had sold me aspirin. Some of the men were well dressed and distinguished looking, others appeared more humble. When the prayers were over, I was approached by the young man who had invited me.

"Welcome, brother," he said, embracing me.

"Good of you to ask me," I said, still not sure exactly where I was.

"Come. I will introduce you to the sheik."

I knelt before a wizened man with sparkling eyes. He offered me his hand to kiss. I obliged. He spoke in Turkish to my mysterious escort.

"He wants to know why you have come to Konya."

"To find Rumi," I answered. My response was translated for the sheik, and he nodded and said something else, smiling.

"He says that you have come to the right place."

Again, I thought of the Mevlana's words: "Look not for my grave in the earth but in the hearts of my devoted seers."

We sat in a wide circle. A place was made for me beside the sheik. Tea was served and *lochum* sweets. Everyone seemed to be watching me. I smiled unconvincingly. Into the room walked a young dervish dressed in his black cloak, white skirt (his ego's shroud), and his high, felt headdress (his ego's tombstone); behind him filed musicians bearing flutes, drums, and a sort of large tambourine. I was, I suddenly realized, about to witness a clandestine *Sema* ceremony.

We began with a prayer, the *Nat-i-sherif* in praise of the Prophet Muhammad. Then a drum sounded, followed by a high-pitched whining from a reed flute, which, my escort whispered, represented "the Divine Breath." The dervish dancer then rose, bowed to the assembled, prostrated himself before the sheik, and kissed his hand repeatedly. The music began to pick up pace and a chant rose up from the circle, *"Allah hu Akbar"* ("God is Great"). Ever so slowly the dervish began to whirl. He lowered his arms from his shoulders to his waist and raised them again outstretched. His right palm was turned heavenward to receive God's beneficence, his left palm to the ground, giving his divine gift to humankind. His skirt seemed to take flight and undulated like a wave as he whirled. His eyes went blank, his head tilted, and he seemed lost in ecstatic union.

It is not dancing and it is not performing, although there are elements of both. More than all these things, this is a transfiguration of the human body into a vessel of prayer. It is the transformation of the physicality of all of us into the beauty of the spirit.

And there is something utterly compelling about the whirling. Although there are perhaps fourteen or fifteen dancers, all of them have a slightly different tilt, one hand raised up to God, the other hand pointed down, bringing God to earth. On their faces, pure unadulterated rapture as if they have entered a trance, forgotten their bodies, and become pure spirit.

—Joanne Ellison, "Sailing to Byzantium"

A small boy stood up from the circle, followed the same sequence of salutations, and began to whirl as well. He couldn't have been more than eight or nine years old. The chanting grew louder and more feverish, and the circle swayed and jerked in unison. Others joined the dancing. The chant then shifted to "Al-lah, Al-lah, Al-lah…" Men beat their hearts and wailed. The music reached a crescendo. I grew delirious. And then the dancers suddenly whirled to a stop, the music ceased, and everyone murmured *"Hu,"* which is all the names of God in one.

There was a brief intermission and then the prayers, music, dancing, and chanting started up again. Four times we chanted and the dancers whirled, and each time the ceremony grew more frenzied until eyes rolled, sweat poured down ecstatic faces, and the chanting became hoarse. If Rumi chose the *Sema* as a vehicle designed to bring the seeker into contact with the mystical current, I thought, by the look of it, it worked.

We ended with a reading from the Qur'an: "Unto God belong the East and the West, and wherever you turn, there is God's countenance. He is All-Embracing, All-Knowing." Then we prayed for the peace of the souls of all prophets and all believers.

There was more tea and sweets and some informal discussion, the center of which, it appeared, was me.

"Why," asked one of the men seated near me who had bellowed above all the rest in his wild chanting, "did you refuse to chant 'Allah'? Are you an unbeliever?"

"I am a believer, but I was unfamiliar with the rite. I remained silent out of respect."

"We revere Jesus as a prophet," said another. "Why can't you Christians accept Muhammad as a prophet?"

"My sacred book, as you know, ends with Christ's resurrection. Muhammad came later; he does not figure in the Bible."

"But God sent Muhammad with a new message because Christians had corrupted Jesus' words. Islam is the more perfect faith. Surely you must see that."

"Very few sacred words have not been corrupted by someone. The extent to which Christianity has corrupted the words of

Jesus is open to debate. Still, I believe in the Christian message which, in the final analysis, is a message of love, not unlike that of the Mevlana."

"But the Mevlana was a Muslim!" someone shouted.

I was beginning to feel just a bit intimidated. It was more or less fifty faithful against one infidel. I looked to the Mevlana for defense.

"'When will you cease to worship and to love the pitcher? When will you begin to look for the water?'" I said, quoting Rumi. There was no reply, but the sheik was smiling and nodding his head. "We all seek God's salvation," I continued. "If on Judgment Day a good and pious Muslim and an equally good and pious Christian stand before God, would it be in the nature of the Almighty to reject the Christian?"

More nodding of heads.

The sheik pronounced the gathering over. We stood up and the modern-day Mevlani formed a line to bid the Christian good night. I kissed fifty men on both cheeks and the sheik on his hand.

"You must come to see us again, young Christian," he said. "We will study the Qur'an."

"And the Bible," I insisted, "and St. John of the Cross, and Gerard Manley Hopkins, and Emerson."

I walked back to my hotel in the dark, past the street sweepers and the last merchants closing up shop. When I got to my room, I drew the shades and began to whirl, but after a few brief turns I became hopelessly dizzy, lost my balance, and hit my head on a lamp. I settled into bed and turned to Rumi:

> One went to the door of the Beloved and knocked.
> A voice asked, "Who is there?"
> He answered, "It is I."
> The voice said. "There is no room for Me and Thee."
> The door was shut.
> After a year of solitude and deprivation he returned
> and knocked.
> A voice from within asked, "Who is there?"
> The man said, "It is Thee."
> The door was opened for him.

I had been knocking, I realized, until my knuckles were raw and swollen. It was Rumi who showed me that I had been knocking from inside and that all along the door had been open.

Nicholas Shrady was born and raised in Connecticut, and received a philosophy degree from Georgetown University. He has written for The New York Times Book Review, Travel & Leisure, Town & Country, *and* Forbes. *This story was excerpted from his book,* Sacred Roads: Adventures from the Pilgrimage Trail.

PIER ROBERTS

Waiting for *Gözleme*

In a race against time they lost,
but won, thanks to the kindness
and determination of strangers.

WE'D BEEN EXPLORING THE WONDERS OF CAPPADOCIA IN Central Turkey, marveling at the man-made and geological beauty of the area. Bright, colorful frescoes adorned the walls of churches, the oldest carved from the rocks more than 1,300 years ago. Beautiful rock formations known as fairy chimneys filled valleys with their strange forms. From the soft porous rock of the area emerged Zelve, a whole village of troglodyte dwellings that had been inhabited until quite recently.

Throughout the long day, my friend and I had forgotten about eating, distracted by the sights around us. Finally, as we headed to the bus stop in Zelve to catch the last bus back to Ürgüp, due in at six o'clock, we remembered that we hadn't eaten since breakfast. A typical Turkish breakfast offered massive amounts of food—bread, cheese, olives, tomatoes, cucumbers, hard-boiled eggs—and was usually enough to tide us over. But not today. When the hunger pangs hit we immediately started to talk about what we'd eat for dinner once we arrived.

We got to the bus stop with little time to spare, and that's when we saw two women sitting on the side of the road, a mother and daughter team, selling fresh *gözleme*. Both were beautiful, with long dark hair, loosely covered with a simple beaded headscarf. They were wearing the traditional dress of the area—a gauzy peasant blouse on top and baggy colorful pants on the bottom. They smiled at us and pointed to a large griddle by their side, offering to cook us some *gözleme*. I'd never tasted *gözleme*, a mixture of cheeses and spices wrapped in fresh dough and cooked over a hot griddle, but Kenan had, and he said that we should try it. I looked at my watch; I looked at the women and the griddle, a bowl of dough sitting next to it. I told Kenan that we didn't have time, but in the spirit of adventure, he said, "Let's try. We'll pay the women anyway if it's not ready when the bus comes."

Kenan explained to the mother that we had to catch the six o'clock bus back to Ürgüp, and immediately I saw something sparkle in her eyes when she met his gaze. I saw that she was determined to take on the challenge, to work against the clock. She looked back at him, intensely, gravely, seriously—the way that Turks can often look—and told him, "You will have your *gözleme*." Then she stood up and ordered her daughter to a shack a hundred or so feet away, and the daughter went off like a gazelle.

The mother turned up the heat on the griddle and took out two clumps of dough from the bowl. She began to roll out the dough, an expert at the task, this way and that, back and forth, a miracle before my eyes: in seconds, the thinnest, most perfectly round pieces of dough I'd ever seen. Just as she finished rolling, the daughter returned, panting, with a bowl of the filling—fresh cheese, parsley, red pepper, other spices, salt and pepper. The mother quickly flipped the dough onto the griddle, turned it once, sprinkled the filling over the dough, and I saw it beginning to happen: the birth of my first *gözleme*.

And then we heard it, all of us, in the distance, the *dolmus*—a minibus whose name means stuffed—on its way to Zelve. We all looked up to see it, rattling over the narrow road, working its way down to where we stood, suspended in the moment. It still had a few curves to take, a hill or two to climb and descend before it would arrive. But we all knew in an instant that we wouldn't make it; that it was a good try, but it wouldn't work; that the filling in the *gözleme* wouldn't melt just right; and the raw dough over the filling wouldn't cook just right in the amount of time that we had left before the bus arrived in Zelve.

As the bus approached, we tried to stop the women, tried to give them money anyway, tried to thank them for a valiant effort. But they wouldn't hear of it, and they insisted on continuing, the *gözleme* beginning to sizzle on the griddle. When the bus driver opened the door, Kenan and I stood still for a moment, not sure what to do. But the mother, she knew. *Maybe she has done this before*, I thought. She jumped up and asked the bus driver to wait for a moment.

He resisted.

She begged.

He resisted some more.

She implored. *"Lütfen, lütfen."* Please, please, she nearly wailed. Wouldn't he please, *lütfen*, hold on, rest a moment, wait until the *gözleme* was finished. It wouldn't be a huge problem now, would it? "And look," she pointed to us, "the visitors are starving."

We put on sad faces and tried to look really hungry, while I added in the best Turkish I could, *"Çok aç"* (very hungry) as the bus driver roared and moaned, protested profusely, claimed that he couldn't wait at every bus stop on his route for meals to be made. But she argued her case well, and she argued it long, and all the time she argued, the *gözleme* sizzled and sizzled, and the aroma from the griddle rose up from the side of the road, wafted through the open doors of the bus, and made its way slowly and purposefully down the aisle. Suddenly, I heard a sympathetic voice rise up from the back of the bus: "Oh come on, I don't mind waiting a little bit. Let them have their *gözleme*." And soon another voice joined that voice. Until eventually we had the support of everyone on the bus to wait out the cooking of the *gözleme*. "What's the big rush anyway?" someone from a front seat asked.

The bus driver turned to face the mutinous crowd of passengers behind him, and finally shrugged his shoulders, turned back to the mother, and said, "Okay. Okay. *Tamam*. But don't ask this of me again."

And so the bus waited at the Zelve bus stop while the women finished cooking our *gözleme*. The mother folded the dough over the filling as if she were sealing an envelope with a secret message inside. When it was all done, the dough was perfectly cooked, light brown spots dotting the outside, the cheese soft and warm, the spices just beginning to send out their flavor. The daughter wrapped up one and the mother wrapped up another as we paid for the food and then jumped onto the bus. Someone on the bus cheered as we sat down, and a few other passengers joined him. I smiled at everyone on the bus, a little embarrassed, but happy too to have my *gözleme*. We turned and waved to the women on the side of the road, now settling back down, squatting next to their hot griddle.

We sat on the bus, and the sun sank further into the Cappadocia landscape as we ate our *gözleme*, one of the best, and certainly one of the hardest won meals I had in Turkey.

Pier Roberts lives in Los Angeles, California. Her stories have appeared in Travelers' Tales Spain, A Woman's Passion for Travel, Her Fork in the Road, Escape *magazine, and* Atlantic Unbound.

TONY PERROTTET

* * *

From Troy to Gallipoli

*These war-torn shores are strewn
with blades, bullets, and bones.*

TRUVA, OR TROY, IS TODAY WIDELY REGARDED AS ONE OF
the Mediterranean world's greatest disappointments; guidebook
after guidebook insists that it's not worth the effort to visit. In fact,
the ancient ruins are so notoriously abject that desperate locals
have built a giant wooden model Trojan horse—just to give baf-
fled tourists something to photograph.

Apparently even this wasn't working, but it was irresistible to me.

After all, the mystique of Troy is as potent now as ever—thanks
as much to cinematic versions as to Homer's thunderous verse.
Today, Homer's screed is admired but rarely read; for modern
tastes, its 15,600 lines of mythological digressions, genealogy, for-
mulaic combat, and bombastic rhetoric comprise an all but im-
penetrable quagmire. It's an effort for us to imagine how utterly
revered the *Iliad* was in the Roman era, when it was considered the
ultimate text, as profound as Scripture and as insightful as
Shakespeare. I was carrying an extraordinary new translation by
Stanley Lombardo, which was more approachable: His terse,
clipped lines made the narrative crackle again, and the heroes'
speeches fluid. But even for those who have never read a line of
Homer, the stories of the siege remain brilliantly alive, embedded

deep in the Western psyche. In the nineteenth century, the quest to discover "lost Troy" became one of the great historical adventure stories of modern times. And the site can grab headlines: The war of words about the factual basis of Homer's account is as emotionally charged as when the redoubtable "father of field archaeology," Heinrich Schliemann, dug his first spade here in the 1870s. And then there are those endless reruns of *Ulysses* and *Helen of Troy*, circa 1955...

How could you be in Turkey and *not* make the pilgrimage to Troy?

So noted the poet Marcus Annaeus Lucanus, who visited the site around A.D. 60, in the reign of Nero, and used his impressions to describe the tour of Julius Caesar.

> He walked around what had once been Troy, now only a
> name, and looked for traces of the great wall which the
> god Apollo had built. But he found the hill clothed with
> thorny scrub and decaying trees, whose aged roots were
> embedded in the foundations.

The sightseeing Caesar in the poem doesn't pack up and leave in disappointment, or wish he hadn't bothered. To Romans, the disappearance of Troy's famous fortifications was logical and expected—after all, the city had been caught in a "whirlwind of doom," as Aeschylus said in one play, its glories "ground to dust." So the absence of major ruins actually added an extra poetic dimension to a visit, allowing visitors to poignantly muse on the fragility of human endeavor. Empires pass; fame and memory endure. "Every stone had a name," notes Lucanus, and Caesar's guide sardonically warns him not to tread on Hector's ghost.

This, I had a feeling, was something that modern visitors might need to keep in mind; standard tourist expectations might have to be left by the wayside.

The nearest town for visits to Troy today lies directly above the pebbly shore of the Dardanelles Strait. Çanakkale—pronounced *cha-knuckle-ay*—is yet another of Turkey's mysteriously faceless cities. It exists to the tune of high-pitched drilling, with every

street and building in a perpetual state of renovation from earthquake damage. Its fractured hotel balconies provide ringside seats
for the parade of supertankers on their way to the Black Sea;
down below, car ferries break loose of the Asian shore and plow
through the syrupy waters, describing a wide parabola as they defy
the powerful current. On both sides of this two-mile wide passage—one of the great strategic bottlenecks of history—Ottoman
fortresses squat like bloated gargoyles. Turkish air force jets regularly buzz overhead, naval recruits fill the streets, and worried
neighbors still rattle sabers over Turkey's dominance of crucial oil
shipping lanes.

On our own visit, the weather remained resolutely English. Day
after day, walls of rain and fog advanced and retreated in subtle tactical maneuvers.

Les wasn't getting any healthier in this damp northern climate,
but at least she seemed to be enjoying the view, staring in mes-
merized prenatal bliss at the eddying currents. As for me, I wandered the sodden streets of the town, meeting up with provincial
scholars at the museums, watching Turkish navy drills, returning
with lamb kebab dinners and bottles of Troy Pilsner, the local brew
with—of course!—the silhouette of the Trojan Horse on its label.

We'd been trapped in industrial outposts before, caught by bad
weather, and accepted our lot; gloomy Çanakkale was almost a welcome punctuation in the regime of constant travel. But then, on the
fourth morning, the skies cleared up without warning. It was like
the opening credits of *The Simpsons*. By noon, not a cloud was left
in the pearly blue sky. Down below, Turks were blinking at the bril-
liance with the expressions of coal miners emerged from the pit.

I left Les wrapped in a blanket, pondering the same dark waters
that Lord Byron had once swum (tour companies now help swimmers emulate the feat at a mere $550 a pop), and headed out into
that "whirlwind of doom," birthplace of Western civilization's most
cherished tales.

From the Çanakkale bus station, a crowded *dolmus* was carrying
cotton farmers into the fields. It already felt like a serious step back

in time. The men sat silently in peaked caps and woolen suit jackets; the women's gold teeth sparkled in the sun as they belly-laughed.

I sat with my knees against my chest, watching the driver work his way, cigarette by cigarette, through the pack. He passed me some Turkish delight ("Turkish Viagra—with cashew flavor"). Outside, it might have been French wine country; the pastures were filled with canary yellow wildflowers. But inside the bus, this was definitely Asia. Manic music clawed its way out of the radio. Piled boxes full of fish and cheese swayed in the aisles. Now I knew why one of the infatuated British expats I'd spoken to down south had compared rural Turkey to Spain fifty years ago. It felt a million miles away from the coast with its English pubs and ATMs.

The driver stopped outside the Helen Restaurant, which was nearly obliterated by plaster sculptures, and directed me down an empty agricultural road. A glossy black snake slithered in the thickets nearby. Overhead, a pair of Turkish F-111s shot past like Apollo's silver arrows; they tore the sky open as they broke the sound barrier. Then it was back to millennial silence, broken only by the scuttling of beetles on the stones.

So this was it—*the high road to Troy*. I couldn't quite believe it. The approach to the most famous city in history—symbol, in a way, of all man's cities—the place where the ancients felt the historical enmity between East and West had begun.

The entrance to the site was announced by a ranch house, where the guards were sipping tea from tall glasses, too pleased with the weather to bother charging me the entrance fee. I gathered I was the only visitor that afternoon. A shady path wound onwards directly to the main attraction—a wooden horse standing above a trimmed rose garden.

Today's Trojan horse isn't quite the "steed of monstrous height" sung by the poets; in fact, it's a bit of a dwarf. It had been lacquered with a staunch dark gloss; the mane was trimmed into a brittle mohawk. You could climb inside its belly and play Ulysses; windows were inserted for a better view of the flowers. The reconstruction wasn't an entirely risible effort, though. After all, even the guidebook writers who cruelly mocked it had included pictures.

It filled a need, obviously, as much as ancient Ilium's guides had needed imaginative props like Paris' lyre.

Naturally, I took several photographs.

A rocky path led out to the hill now called Hisarlik—a spearhead of land jutting above an apple-green plain, which runs five miles out to the indigo sea. Only after drinking in the space and light did I realize that there were some archaeological trenches around my feet. A few haphazard mounds of excavated earth rose like refuse heaps. I'd passed through the legendary Scaean Gates of Troy—or at least their foundations—and hadn't actually noticed.

Yes, it was undeniably a far stretch from the standardized visions of the city's grandeur—not only Homer's grandiose epithets, but all those chintzy film versions. In the execrable *Helen of Troy*, for example, the ancient towers look taller than Babylon's, giant gates swing back and forth, while 30,000 extras and war chariots charge in and out. Kirk Douglas himself had been needed to get past them in *Ulysses*. But the walls of Troy today look like they've been pulverized by a giant hammer. A sailor passing through the Dardanelles would barely glance at this mutilated hillock—an industrial slag-heap, perhaps, or an abandoned Turkish mine?

The frustration is that there has never been just one Troy. Archaeologists have actually found *nine* Troys, each built on the ruins of the last (and just to make things even more confusing, there are forty-seven subdivisions, too). The hill is best thought of as a giant chocolate wafer with layer upon layer of Troys inside. The oldest version of the city, called prosaically enough "Troy I," dates back 5,000 years. The Troy everyone is actually interested in—Heroic Troy, of Homer's heroes fame, which fell around 1260 B.C.—has been identified as Troy VI. The Roman city of Novum Ilium, or New Troy, is the last exposed layer, called Troy IX.

And while there is a glut of Troys on the site, there's not really very much left of *any* of them. The city suffered a second devastation at the end of antiquity. Sacked by Goths from beyond the Black Sea, its port silted, the site was abandoned in the sixth century A.D. Tremors and floods did the rest, burying the remains for 1,500 years. Modern excavations have exposed slivers of one Troy, fragments of another, the rubble of the next.

I wandered about the kaleidoscope of centuries, trying to pry the Troys apart. As it happens, the remains of Troy IX—the lucky, wealthy outpost of Rome's "New Troy"—make the most sense. There are the clear outlines of its two amphitheaters and the definite foundations of the temple of Athena. Of course, just like any ancient tourists, I was compelled to seek out the shreds of Homer's version—Troy VI. Ever-sensitive to foreign interest, Turkish authorities have put up signs pointing out any relic. And there it was—a single exposed corner of the world's most famous fortress wall, angled and steep, just as the poet promised. I stopped, stared, and—pathetic as the fragment was—couldn't help shuddering with amazement.

It was no effort at all to imagine that these stones once echoed with the howls of soldiers.

I could finally taste the sheer anticipation that ancient sightseers felt when standing on this blood-soaked spot. All along their Grand Tour, Romans had been fed a tantalizing diet of Trojan War bric-a-brac. Rhodes had had Helen's personal silver cup, fashioned in the shape of one of her perfect breasts; Sparta, the egg from which she emerged (she was the daughter of Leda, who had been violated by Zeus in the form of a swan; the giant egg was probably an African ostrich's). A temple in southern Italy displayed the carpentry tools that the Greeks had supposedly used to build the Trojan horse; cities in Asia proudly displayed the papyrus letters of war veterans to their loved ones. But nothing could compare to standing on the hallowed turf of Troy itself—or drinking in the famous view of the seashore. By the time of their visits, fourteen centuries of silt had already begun to distort the coastline's shape. But miraculously, everything else about the topography fit the precise descriptions of Homer: the landing cove with its "gaping mouth, enclosed by the jaws of two jutting headlands" (now called Besika Bay); the course of the two rivers, the Simois and the Scamander; the locations of the burbling freshwater springs. On clear days, ancient tourists could make out the distant island mountain peak from which the god Poseidon, swathed in pale sea mist, had watched the battles.

After dinner on their first evening, the visiting tourists would leave their inns and gaze down upon the moonlit scene, perhaps reciting one of the most beloved passages from Homer, when the Trojan soldiers camped before the foray they hoped would shatter the siege:

> The Trojans had great notions that night,
> Sitting on the bridge of war by their watchfires.
>
> Stars: crowds of them in the sky, sharp
> In the moonglow when the wind falls
> And all the cliffs and hills and peaks
> Stand out and the air shears down
> From heaven, and all the stars are visible
> And the watching shepherd smiles.
>
> So the bonfires between the Greek ships
> And the banks of the Xanthus, burning
> On the plain before Ilion.

And I, finally gazing out at the same storied scene, could almost smell the smoke of those fires; once again, the past was lurching to life.

The next morning at dawn, tourists prepared for a sightseeing routine that was by now almost second nature to them. After a perfunctory breakfast of bread dipped in wine, they sallied forth to meet the Ilian guides, accompanied by servants carrying some simple food for lunch—cheese, olives, fruit—a spare cloak in case of rain, and the papyrus guidebook. Many would also have copies of Homer and Virgil—even though educated Romans knew the lines of both by heart. Some had no doubt picked up the pulpy "eye-witness accounts" of Trojan heroes; like war comics, un-poetic, but full of the clash of swordplay and dust of the plains.

And then they set off down the hill to the world's most famous battlefield.

We can reconstruct the standard format of the tour from such disparate sources as the geography of Strabo, the biography of Apollonius, Tacitus' description of prince Germanicus' visit and accounts of Hadrian's trip in A.D. 120. It began with a visit to the beach where the Greeks' thousand black-hulled ships had made the first recorded amphibious landing. The warriors in boar's tusk helmets had forced their way onto Asian soil against stiff Trojan resistance; the armada was soon moored by the "gray churning surf," the tents of troops making a miniature city in the grass. As ever, the "historical" was mixed with the mythological: those ancient Roman tourists clamored to see the actual cave where the Trojan prince Paris judged the beauty contest between Hera, Athena and Aphrodite, starting the goddesses' jealousy that would dog mortals throughout the war, and the exact spot where Zeus, shaped as an eagle, had swept down on the handsome Trojan prince Ganymedes and carried him off to be his wine bearer in Olympus.

Ruins, yes—immortal ruins. Not for 3,000 years has a day passed but some Greek, or Roman, or Byzantine, or modern Occidental has dreamed of Troy, or read of Troy, or gone to Troy. Its fame is imperishable; its romance is inexhaustible. To our own faraway new world its great name has echoed, and I, for one, am proud to have answered its calling, to have lain atop the crumbling battlements in the twilight with the wind whimpering fretfully through the grass-grown ruins, and with the ghosts of Priam and Hecuba, Helen and Andromache drifting beside me, as each night they mount to the Scaean Tower to watch, with hollow anguished eyes, the ghostly horses of the ghostly Achilles dragging Hector's shadowy body before the silent, sleeping, sorrow-laden mound that once was Troy.

—Richard Halliburton,
The Glorious Adventure

As the tour groups proceeded inland, the landmarks allowed them to relive the story.

Here was the site where Achilles, the greatest Greek warrior, had argued with commander King Agamemnon, and in his majestic sulk threatened to abandon the campaign. Over *there* was where Achilles' lover Patroclus was killed by the Trojans, inspiring Achilles with a new lust for blood. *Here* was where Achilles cornered and slew Hector, the greatest of the Trojan warriors (the *Iliad* actually ends after this point; the rest of the Troy tale is recounted in myriad poems and plays). *This* was where the wooden horse was built, *here* it was found by the Trojans. *This* was the spot where the skeptic Laocoon denounced the horse as a trick—and was plucked into the sea by a giant serpent for his pains, with his sons. This divine signal convinced the Trojans that the horse was a genuine gift, convincing them to go on their all-night drunken bender...

The conclusion of the tale hardly needs repeating.

Next stop on the tour was the graves of the war dead—not the common foot soldiers, but Homer's heroes. To keep Roman interest at fever pitch, the Ilians made sure there were helpful visual aids: Each tumulus, or funerary mound, was crowned by a fine statue of the character whose bones and ashes lay inside; Ilian priests kept a small fire burning year-round at his feet.

The hands-down favorite, out on the windy Sigeum promontory, was the tomb of Achilles, the Homeric killing machine—invulnerable except for his famous heel. This was the perfect place for Roman tourists' displays of *pietas*, religious piety. They anointed its weathered stones with oil and perfume, garlanded the statue with fragrant flowers, and burned incense at its base. The more sophomoric ran around the tomb three times naked, mimicking Achilles' chase of Hector around Troy's walls (Alexander the Great had repeated the feat). Two miles east, doused by ocean waves at high tide, lay the cairn of Ajax, the Greeks' second-string warrior. This was the scene of one of ancient tourism's most memorable sensations when, around A.D.120, the burial mound collapsed from erosion and revealed the bones of a powerful giant. Awestruck Ilian priests measured the hero's skeleton at eleven cubits (seventeen feet) high. No less a personage than the Emperor Hadrian himself traveled to New Troy to restore the grave, with all the pomp and ceremony the occasion demanded. He reverently placed the bones into a new marble tomb, kissing and embracing them as he did so.

Again and again, the discovery of "heroes' bones" would prove a tourist boon for Ilium. The most sensational moment came in A.D. 170, when the collapse of a coastal cliff exposed dozens of monstrous skulls and rib cages; sightseers sailed from all over the Aegean to inspect skeletons over thirty feet in length, many purloining them as souvenirs. (In her study, *The First Fossil Hunters*, Adrienne Mayor suggests that they were probably the remains of Mastodons from the Pleistocene Epoch; the skeletons of these giant mammals appear to the untrained eye to be enormous human bones. Ancient scientists like Pliny the Elder studied them closely, and mourned the fact that mortals were obviously becoming punier with the passage of time.)

After Achilles and Ajax came the Trojan tombs—King Priam was buried there, as was Paris, buried with his jilted wife. The local favorite was naturally Hector—the noble, doomed family man, who gave his life to defend Troy, despite his conviction that Helen and Paris' adultery was wrong. It was the perfect site for soulful musings on filial duty: Many a Roman was moved to record his thoughts, such as the prince Germanicus in A.D. 18, who composed an epigram *On the Barrow of Hector*. Unfortunately, the lines are now lost.

In such an emotionally-charged, evocative locale—Troy was more a pagan Jerusalem than an ancient Gettysburg—it's hardly surprising that some Roman tourists had visions.

Specters of the heroes might be encountered by night, illuminated under flashes of lightning; even at noon, the clash of arms could be heard as the pair eternally reenacted their famous duel. The statues astride their burial mounds were credited with supernatural powers by local herdsmen. Achilles' image—a dandyish figure, apparently, wearing a fine cloak and an earring—foretold the future: If it was covered in moisture, floods were coming; a layer of dust meant drought; speckled in blood, plague. Hector's statue was sometimes seen to breathe; during Troy's annual athletic Games, it perspired in sympathy with the competitors. An Assyrian traveler who foolishly insulted Hector's statue was drowned soon afterwards in a raging river; eyewitnesses said that an armored man ordered the waters to rise. And shepherds kept their flocks away from the tomb of Ajax: The Greek hero had gone mad at the end of his life, and started slaughtering sheep, so it was said that the grass around his grave was poisonous.

Christians accepted that Troy was a powerful node of pagan belief, and avoided it on any journey. If forced to travel nearby, they continually crossed themselves—and as they passed Troy's haunted tombs, they hissed between their teeth to ward off evil spirits.

The ghost tales were all fascinating, if a little unnerving, for Roman tourists. But at least one visitor actively sought out the supernatural: Apollonius, the pagan holy man. According to his biography, he took the standard Troy Battlefield Tour in the mid-first century, then at dusk alarmed his followers by announcing that he would spend the night alone at Achilles' tomb.

"Oh Achilles!" Apollonius chants after dark. "Most of mankind declare that you are dead, but I do not agree with them. If I am correct, then show yourself to me…"

Thereupon a minor earthquake shook the area around the tomb, and a man came forth eight foot high, wearing a Thessalian cloak.

Apparently Achilles is far more handsome than his statue suggests, with rippling muscles, long flowing hair, and "the first down of youth" on his cheeks—the contemporary Greek pinup boy. The ghost then grows to twenty feet in height and—in exchange for a promise that Apollonius will travel to his birthplace in Thessaly—allows Apollonius to ask five questions. To modern ears, the queries he chooses are painfully obscure, focusing on the *Iliad's* finer details. (Why does Homer not mention a Greek hero called Palamedes? Was Helen really brought to Troy, or was she hidden in Egypt as some suggest? Is Achilles buried in the way Homer describes? Were there really so many great heroes in the war as Homer says? Yes, answers the ghost—for "at that time excellence flourished all over the earth.")

Achilles then vanishes "with a flash of summer lightning" just as dawn is breaking.

If a modern traveler were put in the same position as Apollonius, the first question would be far more basic: Did the Trojan War ever *really* happen?

Nobody in antiquity ever doubted the historical reality of the Trojan War. The opinion that Homer's epic was a fantasy only emerged in the modern era, when travelers battled their way to the Dardanelles and found no trace at all of the pagan sanctuary—just fields of brushwood crossed by shepherds and camel traders. Romantic visitors grasped at straws. But in the absence of physical evidence, most historians became convinced that the *Iliad* was a beautiful fiction. King Agamemnon, Achilles, Helen, and Hector were fairy tale figures.

Famously, it was the larger-than-life adventurer Heinrich Schliemann who, in the early 1870s, argued that not only did Troy exist, it could be found by using the *Iliad* as a guidebook. He identified key passages which corresponded to physically identifiable locations, and decided that the undistinguished hill of Hisarlik was really the Homeric site. As a fellow excavator later joked, it was as if Schliemann's tiny wiry-rimmed spectacles gave him X-ray vision. The balding, beetle-like German accompanied by his Greek mail-order bride proceeded to dig a series of trenches that revealed an ancient fortress, and then a cache of treasure—weapons, diadems, sixty earrings, and no less than 8,750 small gold ornaments (for dramatic effect, Schliemann combined all the objects he'd found over the course of three years into the one "find"—a rampant case of result-fudging, but the artifacts themselves were authentic). Schliemann proclaimed the cache to be "King Priam's Treasure;" he took photographs of his wife wearing "the Jewels of Helen."

It seemed as if Schliemann really had found Homer's Troy— until it was proven that the artifacts were around 1,000 years too old to correspond to any Bronze Age invasion by Greeks. It was left to another German, Wilhelm Dorpfeld to solve the riddle in 1894. It was he who proved that there were, in fact, nine different Troys. In his excitement, Schliemann had delved down to Troy II—circa 2500 B.C. Dorpfeld did identify the parts of Troy VI we can now see—the imposing, angled bastion that fitted the time frame of Homer's war.

Unfortunately, this in itself did not prove that the Trojan War had ever occurred.

Today, while there is still violent dispute over the historical basis of Homer's war, most archaeologists accept that there is a kernel of truth to the poetic story.

The most thoughtful assessment to date is given by Michael Wood in his book, *In Search of the Trojan War*. Although the finer details can never be entirely proven, evidence for some sort of conflict is now considerable. In 1275-1260 B.C., a Bronze Age Greek force probably *did* mount an amphibious invasion of Troy and lay siege to its imposing walls. Their motive may well have been disappointingly unromantic: seizing the trading routes from the Aegean to the Black Sea. It's certainly not *impossible,* however, that a Spartan woman named Helen was abducted to Troy; the capture of women as prisoners was a common practice in that piratical era. The leader of the Greek alliance may well have been called King Agamemnon and, given the chaotic relations between cities at that time, he certainly would have spent much energy in controlling his unruly gaggle of self-serving warlords from around Greece.

Even the Trojan horse—the least plausible but arguably most beloved part of the tale—may be an imaginative reinvention of a real event. One hypothesis explaining the fall of Troy is that an earth tremor shattered the impregnable fortress (there is some evidence for this at the site). The horse was sacred to Poseidon, god of the sea and earthquakes, and the triumphant Greek warriors—who had clamored to victory over divinely-broken walls—may have left a cult statue of a wooden horse as a thanks-offering when they departed.

Homer himself—if he was only one man, and his works aren't a composite of different poets—didn't visit Troy until around 750

B.C., 500 years after the fact. By then, Greek storytellers had already turned the war into a national epic of Gods and Heroes.

Whatever the original truth, Troy was rebuilt on Greek mythomania.

As the return *dolmus* barreled back through the vegetable patches to Çanakkale, I had to wonder: What was it about the Dardanelles and patriotic myths?

In the Middle Ages, both the British and French royal courts claimed to trace their lineage back to the original Trojan refugees—just as Roman Emperors had looked to Aeneas. Then, in the early twentieth century, two even more remote countries proclaimed that they were 'born' from a defeat on the Dardanelles. Today, their citizens come in droves to pay homage to the war graves, join battlefield tours, lay wreaths and libations—very much like our Roman friends. Their governments fund special commissions to make sure that war graves are kept intact.

Those distant lands—improbably enough—are Australia and New Zealand.

One spring dawn in 1915, the age-old conflict of East versus West was replayed on a grisly industrialized scale when a huge amphibious force stormed ashore on the peninsula opposite Troy, called Gallipoli. The Allies, led by the British and under the command of the young Winston Churchill, planned in one bold stroke to knock the Ottoman Empire out of the First World War; the ANZACs (Australian and New Zealand Army Corps) were chosen as the most expendable shock troops. They were pinned down on the beaches and slaughtered by the thousands before gaining a tenuous finger-hold on the coast; the Turks settled in to brutal trench warfare, with obscene losses on both sides. The stench of rotting corpses filled the air for miles around. (As one observer memorably put it: "the smell of death was tangible...and clammy as the membrane of a bat's wing.") Finally, after nine months of carnage, the Allies withdrew.

As one of the most futile campaigns in the most futile of wars, Gallipoli might have sunk into the black hole of history. But for the Australians particularly, the loss of so many young men in the country's first full-scale war—8,587 killed, nearly 20,000 wounded—was a national trauma, a shocking swathe of casualties torn through the small population. Nationalists hailed Gallipoli as a "baptism of fire." The day of the invasion, April 25th, is still commemorated with undiminished emotion each year in Australia. Every little town has its ANZAC parade. Endless books and newspaper articles annually explore the event. It was the subject of one of Australia's first international hit movies, *Gallipoli*, starring the fresh-faced Mel Gibson.

And thousands of Aussies make the pilgrimage to the battlefield every year—mostly young backpackers who include Gallipoli in their own Grand Tours somewhere between the running of the bulls in Pamplona and Oktoberfest in Munich.

The Turks have certainly buried the hatchet. Dusting the Trojan soil from my boots, I dropped by ANZAC House, the biggest backpacker hostel in Çanakkale and a Middle

---

The curve of the hill startles my eye, delineated by white crosses against a murky landscape of scrappy grass and low-lying shrub. It looks like nothing here could put down a root, find a core. Only rhizomes creeping forward, spreading a lattice of suckers under the sandy earth. We look at our feet amongst the stones and cigarette butts, searching for the detritus of conflict, which apart from the yawning pits capped with marble tribute *In Loving Memory*, is invisible. A pebble draws my eye because it is too round to be a pebble. I pull it out of the dirt and feel remarkable weight. I look at the patina of years since it dropped to the earth and imagine its velocity. I feel no inclination to mourn or celebrate. "Bullet," says the guide, and flicks his cigarette into a pool of water. "We'll find plenty more than that, it has been raining."

—Anna Hedigan,
"Çanakkale," *Meanjin: Fine Writing & Provocative Ideas*

Eastern shrine to suburban Sydney. In the hostel's café were jars of Vegemite stacked up for the breakfast toast. There were towels emblazoned with koalas pinned to the walls, photos of the Opera House and football stars. The Turkish desk clerk grunted "G'day, mate" with a pitch-perfect Paul Hogan twang, while in the back room, a TV showed a scratchy video of *Gallipoli* on a perpetual loop: Mel in army fatigues, the Aussie Achilles preparing to die for eternal glory.

"Ow are yuz?" said another Turkish guy in a Bondi Beach t-shirt (it turned out he'd once run a kebab restaurant in Sydney's Woolloomooloo).

I asked about the battlefield tours they operated every day.

"Too easy, mate. Captain Ali will see you right."

The desk clerk chimed in:

"Captain Ali's tops. Used to be a submarine commander in the Turkish Navy. Knows everything there is to know about military yarns. Just get here at 9 A.M.—*sharp*, eh?"

I paid up with a sinking feeling. Despite the obvious parallel with Roman war buffs visiting Troy, I felt an unexpected resistance to this particular blast from the past.

As it happens, my great-uncle fought in the Gallipoli invasion. He was killed there, at the age of twenty-two. Lesley's own grandfather was wounded there.

Perhaps it was impending paternity again, but it all seemed a little close to home.

At 0900 hours precisely, Captain Ali appeared in the doorway of ANZAC House and cast a disapproving eye around the messy dining room. He was short and intense, without an ounce of fat. His silver hair was trim and slicked down. In his peacoat and creased trousers, with a pillar-box naval cap that emphasized his large ears, he looked like Starbuck from *Moby Dick*.

Methodically, he checked off his clients from a clipboard, then frowned. Two people were missing—apparently they'd gone to the bathroom.

Captain Ali shook his head at the suggestion of waiting. "We have a ferry to catch," he barked. At 0903 hours, he strode pur-posefully out into the street, leaving us racing to catch up.

At 0910, he looked at his wristwatch with a weary, knowing smile. The ferry was late, as it always is in Turkey. The two people who went to the bathroom caught up with panicked looks on their faces. They've learned a valuable lesson. Stragglers will be left behind the lines.

Two hours later, on the opposite shore, Captain Ali was talking about carnage—unimaginable stupidity and waste. He swept his arms dramatically across the stony beach of Anzac Cove, explaining how the Australians landed at this location by a tragic mistake—fol-lowing a light buoy that came adrift in the night—only to be trapped in the surf beneath a steep bluff. It was the First World War's version of Omaha Beach, with corpses clogging the waves.

Captain Ali—nobody ever referred to him by any other name, as if he were born with the title—was unexpectedly eloquent for a submarine commander: In fact, he was the ultimate military guide, the New New Trojan, who spoke with the mixture of envy and compassion peculiar to officers who have never seen action. He orated with a distant expression, as if he was reliving the battle itself. At the most poignant moments, his eyes welled up with tears. Then he paused, embarrassed by his emotion: "Historical fact! Tell it to your children."

The blueprint of Ali's tour might have been taken from the Romans. At a small museum, he carefully pointed out the sacred curiosities—skulls with bullets embedded in them, photos of the battle, bayonets, uniforms. Just as ancient temples would reverently store the papyrus correspondence of Trojan veterans, there was a letter from a young Turkish soldier to his mother, describing the beauty of the cornfields and poppies. He was killed—needless to say—two days later. There was a ritualistic element to the displays, as well as to Ali's anecdotes: Our motifs of war must include tales of sensitive youth untimely plucked. Common soldiers must sur-vive against incredible odds. And there must be unexpected humanity amongst the savagery—assistance of the wounded and informal truces (enemies tossing one another food and drink at festivals, or playing games between the trenches). These are our conventional images of combat, which turn up like some cathartic roster in everything from *All Quiet on the Western Front* to *Full Metal Jacket*, and they all derive from Homer's *Iliad*.

Anzac Cove was the most incongruous place on earth to be talking about slaughter. The day was even more brilliant than when I went to Troy, and we were all lounging about on the downy green grass like this was a picnic scene from Renoir. The golden sun, the lapping waves, the warm sea breeze—it made the idea of Turks killing Aussies more absurd than ever.

Captain Ali turned sternly toward the first cemetery. "Five minutes!" he barked.

After a snack of Vegemite sandwiches, Captain Ali led us into the hills where the most ferocious battles occurred between trenches that were only five yards apart. Whole companies of men were mowed down within seconds of putting their heads above the dirt. For every six feet of soil that each side gained, a thousand lives were lost. The topography of the area seemed to change as bodies were piled into artificial hillsides. Even today, the millions of cartridges and shards of shrapnel turn the soil into a glittering metal conglomerate.

At least the commander of the Turkish forces, Mustafa Kemal—later Atatürk, father of the nation—was frank with his troops: "I order you not simply to attack," he told them cheerily, "but to die. And in the time it takes us to die, other troops will arrive to take our places."

"We call this the Hill of Courage," Captain Ali said. "We Turks respect suicidal valor."

The Australians looked at one another uneasily. We weren't so keen on suicidal valor.

At last, we arrived at Lone Pine Cemetery, a lawn surrounded by cenotaphs engraved with thousands of names of the dead. It's a memorial for those without graves.

———————— ✳ ————————

You, the mothers who sent their sons from far away countries, wipe away your tears. Your sons are now lying in our bosom and are in peace. After having lost their lives on this land, they have become our sons as well.

—Mustafa Kemal Atatürk

"Five minutes, ladies and gentlemen!"

The marble panels were blinding in the afternoon sun. There it was: *B.J. PERROTTET. 1ˢᵗ May, 1915. Age 22.* I ran my finger over the golden letters, amazed that they spelled our name right. He'd lasted only six days here in Gallipoli. I thought of a line from the *Iliad*, about a wounded Trojan soldier:

Gasping out his life, he writhed along the ground
like an earthworm, stretched out in death, blood pooling,
soaking the earth dark red…

At first, Lone Pine seemed poles apart from the war memorials of New Troy, so beloved by the Romans. The ancients glorified their individual superheroes, and sung the praises of Achilles and Hector; the mass graves of Gallipoli convey the slaughter of humble soldiers, many of whose bodies were never identified. The idea of glorious war has taken a serious battering.

But the final effect of both battlefield tours wasn't so different. No Roman tourist would have left the Dardanelles skipping with joy about the human condition.

Coincidentally, nowhere was this clearer than at the ancient site of Gallipoli itself, which Romans would visit on sailing day trips from Ilium. At the tip of the peninsula—a few miles from where Lone Pine Cemetery stands today, they found the most ambiguous of all ancient war shrines—the tomb of the Greek soldier Protesilaus, first casualty of the Trojan War.

As Homer relates, the Gods had decreed that the first Greek soldier to step ashore in Asia would die. In a scene worthy of *Saving Private Ryan*, young Protesilaus decided to sacrifice himself for the cause. He leapt first from the ship—and was immediately speared.

His body was given lavish honors by the Greeks—they certainly also respected "suicidal valor." By the Roman Era, Protesilaus's ashes were still kept in a small temple on the Gallipoli peninsula, surrounded by divinely blessed elm trees: Every time their leaves reached a height where the Asian shore was visible, they miraculously withered—reenacting the warrior's sad fate. And ancient tourists could ponder how Protesilaus's decision had had consequences far from the battlefield. Back home in Thessaly, his wife tore her face in grief, and eventually committed suicide; the house they were building together burned; his father went mad.

It was a place that commemorated the hidden cost of heroism.

For all their bluster about glory, the ancients weren't blind to the downside of war. In Homer, death in battle is never a pretty sight. Wounded warriors scream in agony until seized by "hateful darkness;" the prospect of Hades is cold comfort. Even Achilles, the greatest of the Greeks, meditates around the campfire on the futility of the soldier's life. He reappears in the *Odyssey* as a lonely ghost in the Underworld, confessing that he would rather be alive as the lowliest slave on a peasant's farm than lord of all the hosts of Hades. In fact, much of the poetic force of the *Iliad* comes from its unflagging reference to the domestic lives soldiers have left behind—those distant villages alive with farming, threshing, plowing, goat-herding.

And Homer's broader message in the *Iliad* is rather bleak. Troy, symbol of all great cities, was doomed by its own civilized achievements, which made it vulnerable to the rampaging Greeks; any era of peace, by softening its benefactors, contains the seeds of its own demise. Romans readily believed this idea (as indeed, do many people today, in the midst of our own span of comfort). They loved to scourge themselves for their love of luxury, and predict their own imminent decline. Troy was the perfect place to meditate on the coming holocaust.

But what did all really matter, the *Iliad* finally asks—the end of one life or an entire culture?

> Human generations are like leaves in their season.
> The wind blows them to the ground, but the tree

Sprouts new ones when spring comes again.
Men too. Their generations come and go.

It was getting dark when Ali launched into his last, emotional oration.

"My dear ladies and gentlemen. Have many children. They will be the apple of your own parents' eyes, and make them happy."

The backpackers and I don't know quite how to react, here at this serene slaughter site; we resist the urge to salute, and quietly applaud.

After drifting back to Çanakkale on the ferry in the starry dusk, I pick up some *köfte* for dinner. The smell of spiced lamb is delicious; fresh olives and basil leaves are on the side.

Les is up in our room, reading. She seems to be feeling a little better, but the Urchin has been kicking a lot today. I try to feel him with my hand, usually an absent-minded gesture for me.

I'm surprised how emotionally drained I feel. This is all too profound, this life and death thing. Way too serious for me.

Under a brilliant full moon, the straits are so calm they seem to have stopped flowing.

The whole city is still under that bright night sky. Even Hector and Achilles must be asleep tonight, dreaming of their distant hearths.

Tony Perrottet is a travel writer and editor with numerous Insight Guide *titles to his credit. This story was excerpted from his book,* Route 66 A.D.: On the Trail of Ancient Roman Tourists.

THOMAS GOLTZ

The Barefaced Pleasure

Getting a shave teaches a cultural
lesson that lasts a lifetime.

IT TAKES A CERTAIN AMOUNT OF FAITH TO LET A PERFECT stranger singe your ears, stick scissors up your nose, and run a straight razor around your throat.

But it is all part of a visit to a Turkish barbershop, a hallowed institution that, I hope, will remain unchanged: Men with three-day stubble themselves lather you up twice or thrice, scrape away at your chin with a piece of steel that could slice a sheet of paper in half the thin way, and then wipe your shorn whiskers on the thumb of the hand that was just pushing back your nose to align with your right ear—chatting with another honored client in waiting all the while.

Yes, the Turkish barber—*"berber"* in Turkish, not to be confused with *"barbar,"* a Greek word that filtered into Turkish during Ottoman times that means barbarian, not the individual you are seeking in the City of the Sultans.

After some fifteen years of visiting or living in Turkey, I've got a tip for all newcomers: get thee to the nearest barber straightaway. It is always my first stop in Istanbul. Not only is it a fine way to immediately get over jet lag, but, if one can speak Turkish, also a far better way to take the political pulse of the nation than, say, the traditional method of chatting with cabdrivers. I'm fluent now, due in large part to the time I have spent in the barber chair over the past two decades, I am sure.

I had my first shave in Turkey in 1976. Then a bearded young hippie traveling to Africa from Europe via the Middle East, I found myself in a central Anatolian bus station with a lot of time on my hands and a ferocious itch beneath the handsome whiskers adorning my cheeks and chin. I was sure it was lice, and getting rid of the itchy critters was going to require a radical move. But having no razor handy—I had not shaved for several years—I was obliged to take an even more radical step: to enter the tiny, dingy cubical in the bus station for a shave.

"Hoshgeldiniz!" exclaimed a ferocious-looking barber, addressing my reflection in the cracked mirror. I spoke no Turkish at the time, and had no idea what he was saying as he was running his blade over the throat of his current client. The customer was so still that, had it not been for his bobbing Adam's apple, I might have taken him for a corpse.

With growing trepidation, I felt a dim memory play through my brain of Ottoman Turkish barbers doubling as executioners, and I was tempted to flee before I became a headline in a local newspaper: BEARDED HIPPIE INFIDEL BITES THE DUST IN BUS STATION SLAUGHTERHOUSE!

But it was too late. A young man bearing a tray with small tulip-shaped glasses filled with tea had blocked the door, and the ferocious-looking barber was growling something at me, indicating that it was my turn to mount the swivel chair. The previous customer was on his feet; at least he was still alive.

In retrospect, it was a turning point in my life.

First, I was shorn like a sheep, my beard falling away in curls to mix with the sawdust on the floor. Next came the first lather and rough shaving of the remaining stubble. Not content with this, the barber then proceeded with yet another lathering, and, with a new blade, scraped away a second time—only now against the grain of the remaining stubble.

"Bak," he barked, laying aside his mini-scythe and directing my eyes to the cracked mirror to admire his handiwork.

＊

Indeed. Aside from the unsightly blotches on my alabaster white chin that had not seen the sun for an age, there was not a nick or a scratch. I looked about thirteen years younger, too.

"*Atesh?*" asked the barber. I presumed he was fishing for a compliment, and nodded approval.

"O.K.!" I said, adding the internationally recognizable thumbs-up signal for good measure.

I regretted my ignorance of his language bitterly a moment later. As amusement turned to amazement and then horror, I watched as the barber spiked a large nail through a ball of cotton, dipped it into some sort of lighter fluid, struck a match to ignite the torch—and then began bouncing the burning swab on my cheekbones with one hand while flicking away the ash of incinerated hair with the other.

The process did not cause any pain. Nonetheless, I tried to move my arms to defend myself. But the effort was in

Turkey is home to some unique and ancient forms of grooming and hygiene. Visitors to a spa named Balikli Kaplica (*balik* means fish) undergo a very particular form of treatment: skin removal. Or maybe I should say repair. As bathers stand or sit in the water, fish calmly swarm around them, attaching themselves to the bathers' limbs and torsos, nibbling away at any body part afflicted with a rash or skin condition such as eczema or psoriasis.

—JV

vain. The towels and bib pinned them down for the two seconds needed to singe away not only the little white hairs on the upper cheek, but also the little white hairs that grow, unnoticed by most, on the top and back sides of the ear.

"*Atesh,*" repeated the pyromaniac barber, this time not as an interrogator, but in a slightly hurt tone of voice. There was nothing else to do but let him do the other side of my face, too. Clearly, I had offended him in some manner. I assumed as much because as soon as the burning swab had been doused, the barber grabbed me by the nape of the neck and wrenched me forward. But rather than finding myself thrown down among the dead hair and sawdust on the floor, I was staring at the bottom of a shallow sink. Before I could protest, a torrent of water was pouring over my head while the barber dug his soapy fingers into my ears and even up my nose.

Then, with another lurch, I was thrown back into the chair, and the world suddenly grew dark, hot—and delicious. A heated towel had been wrapped around my head. It smelled of eucalyptus, but it was probably opium, because all I could think of doing was remaining exactly where I was, allowing the lovely fumes to permeate every pore. Meanwhile, the barber was working his fingertips into my skull in a rough yet gentle massage whose rhythm went straight to my brain.

An age passed that was probably only two minutes, and I awoke to a melodious jingle, a tiny spoon stirring sugar in a tulip-shaped glass of tea. I sipped and smoked a Turkish oval cigarette and dreamed, only marginally conscious of the fact that the barber was now working small drops of cream into my parched and flayed skin, and then delicately snipping away at the inner nose hairs with a scissors after having straightened out what remained of my mustache.

"Saatlar olsun!" he said, removing the towels and bib with a final flourish before dousing me with lemon cologne.

The process appeared to be over. I rose, reached into my pocket, and stuck out a wad of money. The barber shyly plucked a few bills. The charge was less than a dollar, including a tip for the assistant who was busy brushing off my jeans with a whisk broom.

I have never looked back.

Indeed, not only is the barber now my first stop whenever I arrive in Turkey, it is usually my last task before sallying forth to even more exotic places like Azerbaijan or Chechnya, where, I have discovered, it is next to impossible to get a decent shave.

And now, more than twenty years after that first experience, I make him work for his keep. Advocating the radical solution to a much-receded hairline, I demand the crown-to-chin treatment. Not a hair is left on my head when I leave—and it still only costs around four bucks.

Thomas Goltz is the author of Azerbaijan Diary: A Rogue Reporter's Adventures in an Oil-rich War-torn Post-Soviet Republic *(M.E. Sharpe). He is currently working on a book on Chenchnya, when he is not organizing three-wheeled motorcycle tours through the Caucasus. He is also Tim Cahill's traveling companion, the inventor of Tommy-Talk, in the Part Three story "Anybody Seen a Tiger Around Here?"*

JAMES VILLERS JR.

The Best View of Istanbul

An apartment provides the window
for making the city his own.

FOR ONE BITTERSWEET YEAR, I LIVED IN AN APARTMENT WITH a balcony overlooking what my friends described as the best view in all of Istanbul. It was maybe the only view that could irrefutably prove I was not dreaming, that I was, in actual fact, living in old Constantinople. From my balcony, I could see the peninsula of Sultanahmet thrusting into where the waters of the Bosporus and the Golden Horn converge and flow into the Sea of Marmara, the lesser-known cousin of the Aegean and Mediterranean.

Though I paid more than a handful of visits to the peninsula's famous monuments, I was more often content to sit and watch the spires and walls of Topkapi Palace and the domes and minarets of the Blue Mosque and Hagia Sophia change color and hue with the passing of the sun and the seasons. The sun rose from the left and set to the right, rolling along the sky, arcing above the shining waters. In the summer, fireworks lifted from the waterfront below Topkapi, flowering the night. The sky and water embraced me or smacked me across the face, depending on my mood, my company, or the number of drinks I'd had. The call to prayer drifted on the breeze with the seagulls. It was quite a show. Ever changing, never familiar, no matter how many times I looked at it.

Every single person who visited me in this apartment would tell me that I, as temporary owner of this view, was perhaps the luckiest person he or she knew. I would hear them say this, and I knew they were right. I knew the view was beautiful, knew that it was a once-in-a-lifetime view for me. But I still couldn't shake the feeling that something wasn't sitting right. That, in spite of the eternal play of light and air currents, in spite of the undeniable panorama of history there for the gazing, the view really didn't belong to me. Or maybe I felt that I didn't belong to it.

In large part, I feel the same way about the city itself. I never felt completely at ease in Istanbul. Maybe that's just because of our conflicting temperaments. Istanbul is

---

⁂

Few have captured the ancient city as Jan Morris did in *Destinations*: "Istanbul does possess, as you can feel from the deck of your ship, the arrogance of the very old; like the rudeness of an aged actor whose prime was long ago, whose powers have failed him, but who struts about still in cloak and carnationed buttonhole, snubbing his inferiors…. It is only when you get closer that you realize the illusion of it, just as you observe, if he leans too close to you on the sofa, the creases of despair around the actor's mouth."

—JV

---

one of the world's oldest and most storied metropolises, full of smoke and flowers, shadow and light. Me? As much as I strive to stretch beyond my origins, I'm a California suburbanite, born and bred, and had never before lived in a big city. But that handicap certainly didn't stop me from getting around; nor did it stop me from finding aspects of the place that do, as it turns out, belong to me. And included in those aspects is an internal view of my own, one of memory, that I'd put up against my old apartment's view any day.

Istanbul is made up of numerous neighborhoods, each with a distinctive feel, as if dozens of separate villages were plopped down willy-nilly along both shores of the Bosporus. Cihangir

(Jee-han-geer), where I lived, is a chaotic maze, home to a large part of the foreign community. Two members of my rugby team, both French, lived four doors down from me, and none of us knew it for close to three months. According to a Turkish acquaintance of mine, foreigners somehow lend an upper-class feel to a neighborhood known, in the past, for its drug dealers and prostitutes. I wasn't astute enough to sense any such aftertaste, but I loved the mishmash of nationalities, the contrast of wealth and squalor. From the booming and humming downtown of Taksim Square and Beyoglu (New City), Cihangir trundles down sloping streets and crumbling stairs to the scimitar cut of the Golden Horn, across which Sultanahmet shines in silent glory, somehow untouched by the blasting of cruise ship horns and the buzzing of fishermen's boats.

I visited the shadow-dappled neighborhood of Sultanahmet more than once during my stay, but my first visit was in the company of a small and particular tourist group, little brother to the massive groups that consistently descend on this historic neighborhood. We—myself and the other newly arrived teachers of our school—were led around the area by John Freely, history professor at Bosporus University, writer of several acclaimed books on Turkey's past, and the father of our primary school principal. He knew everything, it seemed, the significance of each rock we walked past in Gülhane Park, the date every tree was planted and by which sultan. I wished that I could see the bygone days of horse races around the Hippodrome.

We walked from the bright sunshine of outdoors into the coolness of Hagia Sophia, shoulder to shoulder with tourists whom I pitied, because they were just passing through while I was staying for at least two years. John Freely knew people in the museum, and we were allowed to peer at as-of-yet unveiled mosaic restorations. From Sophia, we walked across the street and went underground, visitors to the ancient cisterns. The pillars stood tall and many, roughly ankle deep in the water (if pillars had ankles), and they made me wish I was a boy giant with this place as my playground, so that I could splash among the pillars, playing hide-and-seek in the shadows.

The Grand Bazaar, a short tram ride away from the history-packed Sultanahmet, almost feels as if it's subterranean as well. Housed within a huge and ancient building, the bazaar is corridor after corridor of shop after shop, filled with all kinds of goods, from fine leather to silk rugs to hand-painted pottery to gold jewelry, as well as the skilled craftsmen who make the goods and the touts and salesmen who rope you in. In a strange and inviting way, the bazaar feels like a small city. My friend Marissa, a teacher at another school who also spoke Turkish, showed me around. She had already done what I wanted to do: the Christmas visit back to family in California, arms laden with little bits of Turkey, charms against the evil eye, decorated wooden boxes, tiny pots and saucers painted in vibrant blues and greens.

Back across the Golden Horn, and shining with a much younger and more hectic light than Sultanahmet, Taksim is ringed with hotels and office skyscrapers of glass and steel, screaming with life. "Today, today, today!" it shrieks, threaded with the din of countless yellow taxis, native Turks, and hungry tourists. Women in headscarves and raincoats walk near those with cropped tops and bellybutton rings. And two other extremes, neither of which I'm ever likely to know: black and shiny Mercedes crawling past dirty street boys in men's blazers and hard-soled loafers, rags soaked in glue clenched in fists held to their noses. Once, walking a rarely deserted downtown street—5 A.M., and I was headed to the airport—I passed two such boys huddled in a doorway; the glue aroma was so strong, so pungent, even from three feet away, that I almost vomited.

Istiklal Caddesi, or Independence Avenue, stretches from the sandwich vendors of Taksim through Beyoglu to Tünel, another of the quirky neighborhoods, home of music shops beyond counting. Istiklal is a pedestrian thoroughfare, the length of which old trolleys run. The glue boys fearlessly jump aboard the backs of these trolleys, while the inside overflows with all other manner of folks—tourists, both delighted and agape; covered women from the provinces, seasoned enough to eschew the long walk down Istiklal's crowded cobblestones; dark-browed men clicking prayer beads in what looks like absent-minded communion with Allah.

Sometimes you can hear the trolley bells, and sometimes you can't: Istiklal is *the* main shopping avenue of Istanbul, and music is a popular item of merchandise. The latest and hottest pop musician—be it Madonna or Tarkan—thumps or whines, jangles or pounds out of these stores' loudspeakers. At times, it seemed that the avenue was little more than an eccentric shopping mall. At others, just a walk down its chaotic length was the equivalent of a joyful outdoor festival, to which people from all corners of the earth had been invited.

When I was happy with my life as a temporary urban dweller, my favorite thing about the city were its bars and restaurants; they run the spectrum of cost and cuisine. Most of my preferred places, though, I didn't discover right away; Istanbul streets can be so narrow, crammed full of cars and pedestrians, and doorways can appear so uninviting that, until friends showed me what I was missing, I usually raced down the streets, never stopping until I reached wherever it was that I was going.

So many of these dark and unassuming doorways, however, hide eye-candy interiors, warm and well-lit, excellent to hang out in. And the best part is the open-air courtyards, with tables and chairs placed among lush greenery, the sky above, and often an unexpected view of the water. Once I'd discovered a place like this, it was tough to stay away; I always felt like going there and sitting, ordering beer after cold beer, staring at the ancient waterside and the beautiful women, to hell with any work I had to complete.

When work did ease, Istiklal was normally the place my friends and I would head, wandering the side streets until we'd found a place with the music and ambiance we wanted. And we invariably found what we'd been searching for. Downtown is always jumping, and it jumps to the beat of any taste—unbelievable dinners at a tasty place called Changa that my friend Anthony introduced me to, where they serve stuffed nasturtium appetizers, and where I heard (after the fact, or I'd have run down for a spontaneous drink) that Cameron Diaz visited; tiny beer halls, where a cold one cost next to nothing, and where men stand or sit, shoulder to shoulder, quietly sipping; Hayal Kahvesi, glowing darkly just off Istiklal, packed with the more cosmopolitan, more approachable of Istanbul's women, who you could see but not hear because of the volume of the usually excellent cover band. Traditional restaurants abound, too, complete with belly dance shows, though I never did get around to seeing one.

The playgrounds of the rich—Etiler, Bebek, Ortaköy, and the like—lie north of Taksim, up the coast road that meanders along the Bosporus, a short distance but a long ride away, due to the perpetually horrendous traffic (the city is not at all planned to house the millions who live there already, nor the thousands more who arrive each day). Dirty buses, taxis, and *dolmus* jockey for position against gleaming Mercedes and BMWs. I was one of the bus riders, packed in with other mere mortals; but I was never that bitter, because I couldn't help noticing that a crawling pace serves as a great leveler. Ancient homes, some from the times of the sultans, line the shores. The smell of money permeates everything in this area, despite the poor children diving into the Bosporus, their fathers and uncles and grandfathers with lines cast out nearby for the incredibly small fish that swim the filthy water. Istanbul's more privileged youths hang out in the tree-shaded park near the Etiler McDonald's in the daytime, then dance away the night in posh clubs on the waterfront, the music pumping and the lights flashing on the dancers, and on the underside of one of the great suspension bridges that connect Europe to Asia.

Twice, when spring rolled over and threw off winter, my good friends Alan and Joanna invited me on a cruise up the Bosporus to the mouth of the Black Sea. The waters are cleaner there, and we felt safe enough to swim. We set out from Etiler in the late morning sunshine, the boat laden with food and drink, guitars and African drums, and glided along the storied waterway, admiring the stately wooden villas along the shore, waving at fisherman and other pleasure cruisers, eating and drinking too much, singing along with Alan's strumming. Late afternoon, the sun softening as it set, we headed back to the city, to finish the day floating lazily past the mosque and outdoor cafés of Ortaköy, still full of people enjoying the newly arrived warm weather. If we'd cruised just a short bit further, we'd have been able to pick out my apartment building among the many that ascend the hillside. We'd have been tiny water bugs skating across the vision of anyone standing on my balcony.

Home now, in California, the view from my living room is of an apartment courtyard. It's pathetic, really, even with the little pool. I miss the view I had in Istanbul, which is strange, because I rarely miss the noisy city itself. Fortunately, though, I have an answer for such unexpected nostalgia, and that is to fling open a different sort of window. One that exists in my memory.

When I open that window, these moments are some of the things wafting in: the friends I made in Istanbul, the sights and sounds and smells of its crowded streets, of its many waterfronts. These sensations comprise the new view I've discovered, the one that, finally and undeniably, belongs to me. And the view from my old apartment, the one in Cihangir, now has stiff competition for the title of "best view of Istanbul."

James Villers Jr. is the editor of this book.

ROBERT D. KAPLAN

Who Are the Turks?

They are defined by their history,
ancient and recent.

WHO ARE THE TURKS? THERE MAY BE FEW MORE IMPORTANT
questions for the early twenty-first century.

The word *Turk* first makes its appearance in the sixth century
A.D., in the Chinese form *Tu-Kiu*, to denote a nomadic group that
founded an empire stretching from Mongolia to the Black Sea.
These nomads spoke an agglutinative tongue, which, like
Mongolian, Hungarian, and Finnish—languages spoken by peoples
vaguely related to the Turks—belongs to the Ural-Altaic group
and stems from the region between the Ural Mountains in eastern
Russia and the Altai range in Mongolia. It was the Chinese, a mortal enemy of the Turks, who gave definition to this nomadic organism that spread like water over the bleak tabletop of inner Asia.
The Great Wall of China, begun in the third century B.C., may
have been built to keep these Turkic tribesmen at bay.

The succeeding centuries witnessed a series of Turkic migra-
tions over the Central Asian steppe that involved such obscure
horsemen as the Uighurs, the Oghuz, and the Khazars. Empires
briefly coalesced, leaving little residue as they compounded with
yet another Turkic onslaught. "On the black earth he pitched his
white pavilion; his many-colored tents reared up to the face of the

sky. In a thousand places silken rugs were spread." So goes *The Book of Dede Korkut*, a collection of stories set in the heroic age of the Oghuz Turks: a wine-consuming horde—whose women were expert riders, archers, and wrestlers—that succumbed to Islam simply as a religion, not as a complete social system. This latent paganism, common to all Turkic groups, would help the leader Mustafa Kemal Atatürk secularize Turkey in the 1920s and 1930s.

These footloose Turkic tribesmen pressed against the walls of China, as well as northward and westward against Russia. It was the Russians, another historical enemy, who invented the term *Tatar* as a catchall for Genghis Khan's Mongols and their Ural-Altaic cousins—the Turkic tribes. The Mongol Golden Horde subjugated Russia in the thirteenth and fourteenth centuries, shielding it from the Renaissance. The Tatars were, by and large, responsible for Orientalizing Russia. Ever since the days of Ivan the Terrible in the sixteenth century, the Russians, burdened with feelings of cultural privation and a thirst for revenge, have been on the offensive against the Turkic peoples. Stalin's assault on Turkic unity in Central Asia and his imposition of the Cyrillic alphabet on his Turkic subjects—in order both to Slavicize them and to cut them off from fellow ethnics in Afghanistan, northern Iran, and Turkey—were examples of this hatred. So was the Russian war against the Muslim Chechens in 1995.

In the ninth and tenth centuries, the Finns and the Magyars became the first Ural-Altaic peoples to arrive in Europe. The cultural genius of these horsemen of the steppe was apparent: within a century or so they had adopted European manners and customs. In the second half of the eleventh century, eastern Anatolia saw its first Turkic nomads, the Seljuks (named after their founding chieftain), who annihilated a Byzantine army in 1071 at the Battle of Manzikert. The Byzantine Greeks held out at Constantinople until 1453, when another Turkic tribe, the Ottomans, having vanquished and absorbed the Seljuks, conquered the city and later called it Istanbul.

The Ottoman Turks were to establish a polyglot empire stretching from the gates of Vienna in the north to Yemen in the south, and from the border of Morocco in the west to Mesopotamia in the east. The Ottoman threat soon made the word *Turk* a European synonym for savagery. Martin Luther, in the sixteenth century, prayed for deliverance from "the world, the flesh, the Turk, and the Devil." Yet the romance of the Ottoman court in Istanbul's Topkapi Seraglio fashioned another, more benevolent stereotype: that of the "Grand Turk," with evocations of harem girls, tulip festivals, love poetry, brocaded silks and rich carpets, trays of sherbet and other sweets, and pencil-thin minarets reflecting in marble pools—the most sensuous of indulgent Islamic civilizations.

Topkapi was, originally, a nomadic court, its turrets reminiscent of tents of the Kara Kum Desert in central Asia, its military campaigns each year in Europe reflecting seasonal wanderings on the steppe. By the dawn of the twentieth century, however, Topkapi was a calcified theocracy, much as Greek Byzantium had been prior to the Ottoman conquest four and a half centuries earlier, and like some of the Arabian Gulf sheikdoms at the dawn of the twenty-first century.

Modern Turkey, which arose from the death throes of the multinational Ottoman Empire after World War I, was the dream of one man, Mustafa Kemal Atatürk (Father Turk). Kemal Atatürk was an authentic revolutionary—one of history's handful—because he changed a people's value system. He divined that the European powers had defeated the Ottoman sultanate not on account of their greater armies, but on account of their greater civilization. Turkey would henceforth be Western, he said. Not coincidentally, no Muslim enjoys so high a historical reputation in the West as Atatürk. In the 1920s and 1930s, Atatürk abolished the Muslim religious courts. To wrench Turks away from their traditional Islamic past, he forbade men to wear the fez and discouraged women from wearing the veil. He moved the capital from Istanbul—the symbol of the backward Islamic empire—to Ankara, rooted in pagan Anatolian Turkism, where the bull god reigned over the crescent. By replacing the Arabic script with the Latin one, he oriented Turkish culture to the West. Even Atatürks's definition of nationality was startlingly modern. "Atatürk declared

M uch of what distinguished Atatürk was the thoroughness with which he sought to Westernize Turkish society. "Perhaps this is the only historical case in which a country decided through political will to have a shift of civilization." Göle laughs slightly. She is tall and thin, tense, with a taste for Western fashion. "I interpret the reforms of Atatürk as an effort to define the civilized man as a Western man. This has had such important repercussions, consequences in our lives that we are still unaware of them.

"This change of civilization was mostly important in terms of women. Because women—I think that, in all these Muslim countries that were involved in this process of modernization, women's status was not a marginal issue. It's directly related with this question of civilization. It is the touchstone of modernization. Because the way we proved our belonging to the Western world was through the visibility of women. The participation in public life of women was the cornerstone of these reforms."

—Scott L. Malcomson,
Borderlands: Nation and Empire

that whoever says he is a Turk, speaks Turkish, and lives in Turkey is a Turk," I was told by Altemur Kiliç, an Istanbul newspaper columnist whose family roots go back to Georgia, Abkhazia, Uzbekistan, and Aegean Rhodes. Atatürks's emphasis on language as the arbiter of nationality made Turkey not only a melting pot of Balkan, Caucasian, and Central Asian Muslims, but also a hospitable place for Turkish-speaking Jews. Atatürk made Turkey not a blood republic but a modern one.

"Kemalism is a desire to be identified with the West, a way of life showing contempt for the Arab world," said Nilüfer Göle, an Istanbul sociologist and feminist. "Kemalism celebrates paganism over Islam, it provides Turks with an emotional, nation-building myth that is completely secular and therefore has no equivalent in other Muslim societies, where all the powerful myths are religious." In other words, Kemalism enables secular Turks to fight just as strongly for their beliefs as the newly religious Turks in the *gecekondus* fight for theirs. [*Gecekondus* are slum houses or shantytowns; the term literally means "built in the night."]

Atatürk's mausoleum in Ankara, the Anitkabir (Great Tomb), is an assertion in marble and stone of this secular *will*—which aims to utilize, and to subsume, the dynamism of the *gecekondus* within the grand vision of Atatürk's "Republican Turkey." A gigantic Hellenistic temple, the Great Tomb is architecturally pagan, with sculptured torches by the walls, wolf tracks carved into the floor, and relief etchings of soldiers embracing mother goddesses. It is a ferocious place. As I walked around this temple precinct, guarded by white-helmeted troops, I felt that had Adolf Hitler died a natural death, this is the kind of tomb he would have had.

But there is another tomb in Turkey: not in Ankara, but in Istanbul—the city of magnificent mosques, of Islam, the Ottoman capital that Atatürk spurned that came back onto the strategic map after the fall of communism. This is not a "great tomb." The view from its humble precincts is of a modern highway; the sound you hear is that of automobile acceleration. But they come, *they come*, the slippered men and kerchiefed women of the *gecekondus*, to pray at this *türbe* (tomb of a Muslim holy man). Here lies Turgut Özal, the prime minister and later president of Turkey, who died in office in 1993—the second great Turkish revolutionary of the twentieth century.

While Kemal Atatürk was an aloof general, a ladies' man with a well-cultivated taste for Scotch whisky, Turgut Özal was a short, fat, scruffy peasant whose neck disappeared within his shoulders; who talked while he chewed his food; who never learned properly how to use a knife and fork; and who was not ashamed of his faith:

"Though Turkey is a secular state, I, the president, am not a secular man."

And if Özal could be a Kemalist while still being a religious Muslim, why couldn't the people in the *gecekondus*? Why should there necessarily be a contradiction? Secularism, as Özal redefined it, meant just that—not atheism. Not that these people in the shantytowns knew, or cared, what "Kemalism" was. They just knew that, under Özal, they were part of the system. Özal, who loved the

American notion of social mobility, who traveled with both a Koran and a laptop computer, deeply intuited the dreams of his people: They merely wanted a better life without spurning their religious traditions. The supreme monument to Özalism is the Kocatepe Mosque in Ankara, one of the largest religious shrines in the world—built with a supermarket complex beneath it.

Özal softened Atatürk's fierce, Western-oriented secularism. Whereas Atatürk ignored the Turkic east in the Caucasus and Central Asia in order to turn his people westward, Özal saw the East as a new market for Turkish goods. Whereas Atatürk looked westward for a cultural standard, Özal lifted Turkey out of its self-imposed isolation by trying to assert a Turkish Muslim power block in the Balkans. But Özal's most important contribution was his rediscovery of the multinational past, rectifying the tragic flaw in Atatürk's vision.

Robert D. Kaplan is a contributing editor of The Atlantic Monthly *and the author of several books on travel and foreign affairs, including* Balkan Ghosts: A Journey Through History, The Arabists, *and* The Ends of the Earth: From Togo to Turkmenistan, from Iran to Cambodia: A Journey to the Frontiers of Anarchy, *from which this story was excerpted. He has traveled in nearly seventy countries and now lives outside Washington, D.C.*

JEREMY SEAL

A Visit to Soapmakers

*The author travels deep into rural Turkey
to explore the tensions between Turkish history,
urban life, and ancestral homes.*

THERE WAS NO SIGN OF AHMET THAT JANUARY MORNING, A
morning so cold that any sign of him and the warmth of his car
would have been welcome. What light there was reflected weakly
off gray potholes of crushed ice. Refrigerated wind blew in pulses
off the street as if timed to signal the arrival every half-minute or
so of another overnight bus from Trabzon, Konya, and Amasya,
distant cities of the Turkish interior and the Black Sea coast.
Glimpsed faces at the windows stared out at the blear dawn, and
what they saw was concrete, skittering litter, and unfamiliarity at
the beginning of a new life.

They clambered from the buses, these families, gathered their
shapeless coats around them, and started to unload their belongings. There were old cardboard boxes bound by string that once
held cartons of soap powder. There were blankets and rolled-up
mattresses. There were suitcases straining with necessity. There was
an ironing board and a small table and an empty birdcage, and piles
of pots with bottoms seared by cooking.

A thousand people were moving to Istanbul today, just as a thousand people had done so every day for the last ten years, turning the
city's outlying villages into sprawling suburbs housing hundreds of

thousands. Not long before, I guessed, the day had come when these families had finally realized that there was nothing to do but leave, the cruel, indifferent processes of economics and history turning the screw tight until it could no longer be borne. Such was their situation that the things that mattered—their friends, perhaps a tree, a courtyard, or a scrubby hillside, views from a window that they and their grandparents had known as long as they could remember—had become sentimental luxuries that they could no longer afford. Today, economic necessity had defeated a thousand more Anatolians, and the old life became the past as they shouldered their ironing boards and empty birdcages and took the only chance remaining at the jostling margins of the big city.

Ahmet's parents, newly married, came this same way and took such a chance in 1946. They left their village and their families for the city, a common story of the twentieth century. They were lucky. Ahmet's father did well, making cakes and pastries from honey, walnuts, and pistachios. He sold them to sweet tooths across the city, became rich while dentists prospered on the teeth he had ruined, and then he grew old. Now Ahmet was running the family business.

A group of migrants were arguing over the price of a cart.

"We could get a truck for that!" a man exclaimed disgustedly at the price mentioned.

"Where are you from, brother?" replied the carter, hugging himself repeatedly to keep warm. "Trabzon? Ordu? You might get a truck for that price in Ordu. Here, you get this." And he pointed to a broken horse standing patiently between the withers. Carter and migrants stood around making comments about Ordu and the horse, respectively, of a desultory, unflattering kind that hardly seemed designed to lubricate the negotiations. One of the younger women stood back from the group. Dressed in a head scarf, she looked over her shoulder at the departing buses and perhaps only now realized what it had meant, that last glimpsed view of the village on a winter afternoon before it disappeared among tucks in the hills.

A car drew up and hooted. When I reached Ahmet, he was watching the negotiations intently but from the warm cocoon of a car all his own while he listened to Turkish pop. He wore an expensive tweed jacket. On the back seat lay a newly savaged carton of 200 Marlboros. I asked him how he was, and Ahmet tugged ruefully on a cigarette. Last night's hangover, it transpired, came courtesy of Chivas Regal. Twenty-eight-year-old Ahmet lived a European life on the fringes of geographical Europe. Except that his car, jacket, and taste in whiskey were more expensive, he was very like me.

"Sandwiches," said Ahmet, thrusting a bag toward me. "Rose-petal jam." Only in Ahmet's sandwiches, it seemed, did traces of his past linger. Grimy concrete buildings disappeared in low cloud around the second floor. Gray figures milled along the pavement, skirted around tarpaulins where salesmen had spread their wares—bundles of sheeny-gray socks piled like catches of fresh fish, a neat stack of paper tissues, a pile of worry beads shiny like viscera—and spilled across the road in breaks between

They approach the conversation formally, discussing answers between themselves and often responding as "we," which sometimes means the representative *we*, "women like us." "We were always Muslims. We did not discover Islam." They're both from provincial families that came to Istanbul. Few people on campus, they say, are religiously in-between, and few of the secular or wealthy students have converted," though they hope more will. Relations with other students are usually fine, though tensions do arise. "For example," the more serious one says, "club activities and sports. We must follow the *harem* rules, which makes it difficult. But we can make up the credits by taking private classes. I'm taking private tae kwon do classes.

—Scott L. Malcomson,
Borderlands: Nation and Empire

the traffic. "Life is hard," said Ahmet sententiously. I nodded, thinking that but for a brave decision by his parents in their youth, Ahmet might now be a new arrival in Istanbul standing in the cold arguing the price of a horse and cart. Or he might be persevering with life in the same Anatolian village where his grandparents and several uncles' families still lived—six hours away if we drove fast. As the migrants poured in from Anatolia, Ahmet was taking me back to the world they had forsaken. Sentiment and memory were luxuries that Ahmet could now afford.

As we crossed the Bosporus Bridge, coal smoke rose from countless houses beneath us to be lost in the haze above a litter of roofs, brown and broken. Minarets gleamed in the morning, a broken bed of nails above the city. Then the bridge was behind us and we were in Asian Turkey, in Anatolia.

Beneath the cigarettes and the music, Ahmet seemed preoccupied. "My family, you understand," he eventually explained, "are very poor people. Very simple." There was instinctive pride in this, but a stronger, tragically learned element of apology. "Poor!" As if he feared me to exclaim, "I didn't come here to see poor people, even if they are your family. Haven't you got any rich friends I can sponge off, sleep with?" Ahmet looked relieved when I said something trite about the privilege of meeting them, and my apparent lack of concern encouraged him to emphasize the point. "I mean, really poor," he insisted.

We climbed gently onto the high Anatolian Plateau, flat and interminable, a kind of underfunded Holland on stilts where the trucks were always breaking down. Engine guts and various tools lay scattered around stricken vehicles while their defeated drivers warmed themselves by roadside fires and wondered how miracles worked. Low horizons appeared on all sides with occasional dun hills streaked with old snow. There were broken fence lines and unnaturally precise stands of poplars protecting more featureless dun hills from the wind. Unfinished buildings regularly appeared, as illogically situated as the poplars.

"What are the buildings for?" I asked.

"Maybe for watching the poplars." Ahmet was clearly feeling better.

Poplar progress observation posts, we agreed, abandoned when it was recognized that poplars do the growing themselves. Unlike buildings. And so brick or concrete-block constructions that would never finish their growing stood beside piles of bricks or concrete blocks topped in snow. Steel rods protruded from each roof, buildings condemned to know nothing but neglect, the wind, and the memory of confused builders' voices.

At the small town of Düzce, our road became unfinished, and we left it for a minor one leading into the mountains. Ahmet was now smoking at a ferocious rate; something else was worrying him. "One more thing," he eventually said. "My family. They do not use toilet paper."

"Toilet paper?" I replied dismissively. "Toilet paper's for sissies." But although we laughed together, you could tell whose was the laughter that did not ring hollow.

"When in Rome" is all right up to a point, and that point is generally accepted to be well passed when it comes to, say, head-hunting with the natives of Papua New Guinea. Nor, in my view, does the point extend to smearing one's fresh droppings over the left hand. Nothing had been more firmly impressed upon me in my journey through life than the signs along the way saying "Do not touch the kaka," and on this at least I had been a quick learner. I hid my discomfort with the thought so successfully, however, that Ahmet's mood was transformed, and he changed gears with extravagantly dramatic flourishes that left his arm hanging in the air with open hand long after the new gear had been found. I kept thinking he was releasing doves into the confined space of a small car going fast.

Early that afternoon we reached Karabük, where a great iron foundry stood against the mountains in dystopian grandeur.

"What does *karabük* mean?" I asked, leafing through the possibilities in my mind. Anvil? Blacksmith? Forge? Fritz Lang?

"Blackberry," replied Ahmet.

One of Ahmet's uncles had come to live in Blackberry ten years ago. Less intrepid than his brother, he had chosen to compromise at a dusty little house on a hill an hour and a half from the village that would always be home. He had found work as a security guard at the foundry and was not at home. But his aunt was there, along with a selection of Ahmet's cousins. Among the younger girls was

Emine. She greeted Ahmet—with his car, his wealth, and the sheen of the big city—by touching his outstretched hand first with her lips and then her forehead before rising to kiss his proffered cheeks. Emine, who was fourteen, had lost her father six months earlier when he shot himself to escape gambling debts.

We sat wreathed in smoke, drinking tea and discussing cousin Mustafa's appendix. He had complained of stomach pains on Tuesday night, been admitted to Blackberry General the next day, and was operated on the same night. Light snow was falling on Blackberry and coal smoke from the foundry turned the night sky mocha at the window. Dogs fell silent as the muezzin started singing from a nearby minaret.

For much of the evening, a black-and-white television chirruping away in the background was affectionately ignored like a senile senior of the family. But everyone came to attention with the main news item. One of Turkey's most highly regarded journalists, known for his democratic and secular views, had been blown into a hundred pieces by a car bomb in Ankara, 150 miles to the south. An organization called Islamic Jihad was first to claim responsibility. Emine turned away from the television and the reminders of loss that it served, hoping that her retreat into sorrow would not be noticed.

Before we left the next morning, Ahmet distributed money on the instructions of his father. Distance had not undone the family bonds, bonds otherwise expressed in the manner that the family referred to the village where they all had their origins. They spoke of it not by name but in the possessive, referring to "our village" long after they had moved away. It was a kind of yearning constantly expressed in spite of the townie haughtiness they had consciously adopted in its place; people have been taught that big-city life confers a respectability, but village rhythms are not easily unlearned.

Ahmet's evident excitement grew as we drove through a bright and cloudless morning. I could detect it in the way he hummed indistinct tunes and changed gears in that elaborate manner of his. Orchestral conductors could have learned something from Ahmet.

"Where the Bee Lands," he said, announcing the name of a village where the metaled road gave way to track, and broken ribs of ice straddled the deep tire tracks. We climbed steadily through hazel and pine woods and slalomed our way up north-facing slopes where ice and snow lay unbroken among the shadows. That morning, I had noticed Ahmet sling two shotguns on the back seat.

"So what are we hunting?" I asked him.

"Kurds," he replied.

I knew something of Turkish–Kurdish enmities and of the persisting troubles in the southeast of the country. But I did not know that young men from Istanbul had them in their sights when they packed their shotguns for a weekend's sport in the northwest.

"You often shoot Kurds, do you?"

"Oh yes. There are many about in the winter. They take our chickens."

Taking chickens struck me as an arcane separatist gesture.

"And you're allowed to shoot them for taking your chickens?"

"Oh yes. Deer are rare so we don't shoot them."

"But you shoot Kurds."

"Yes."

"Why?"

"I told you!" Ahmet exclaimed in exasperation. "The chickens!" And as we followed the rutted track around a corner, the village finally came into view. But since it was not my village, I refer to it by its proper name of Sabuncular, or Soapmakers.

Soap has not been made in Soapmakers for as long as the villagers can remember. So to suggest that Soapmakers has remained unaltered for 500 years is not entirely accurate. Equally, change hardly encapsulates the prevailing mood in late twentieth-century Soapmakers. While the rest of the world is being transformed, change meanders into Soapmakers, makes the vaguest of gestures at the future, and then goes away again. Seasons pass much as they always do; it gets hot, it gets cold, but the village spring continues to run.

Something did happen in 1962 when the village mosque was restored by Ahmet's father, flush with new cash when his cakes went down a storm in distant Istanbul. But since there were no shops, no school, no police station, just a room in the mosque building where the village elders gathered to make their decisions, the restoration of the mosque served only to reinforce the influence of the past.

We drew up in a small yard before the mosque. Below us, tracks threaded their way between a cluster of some fifteen houses where smoke rose in orderly plumes. Chickens pecked between rafts of ice and dogs skulked against stone walls larded with old snow.

Ahmet's grandparents lived opposite the mosque. We pushed our way through an old wooden door and found a man bent double by age, tending to his two donkeys in the stable on the ground floor. Grandfather was known as Haci Baba and wore a beard in recognition of the fact that he had made the hajj to Mecca. He wore a brimless woolen cap and puzzled over my interest in his donkeys.

"Donkeys," he said simply, frowning as I scratched their ears. Perhaps, I reflected, I would have been equally puzzled by his disproportionate interest in my electric lawn mower.

The living quarters were upstairs. Grandmother was tending to the stove in the middle of the kitchen. On my appearance, she hugged, kissed, and patted me more like a lover—and not so long lost—than a friend of her grandson's.

"It's your blue eyes," Ahmet told me. Eighty-eight-year-old Grandmother had not seen many blue eyes.

She was as hunched as her husband. In fact, one could have inserted extra floors on every level and neither resident would have been in the least danger of bumping heads. Like Haci Baba, Grandmother's face was gnarled, knotted, and lined, the color of old wood, and their eyes were similarly bright. It was as if, in the course of their long lives together, the differences between them had been gradually eroded. The brightness of their eyes was important, for without those spots of light I would have struggled to locate their faces against the ancient woodwork of the paneling around them. Whenever I met their eyes, hers were always smiling, and his expressed something that I took to be a vague fear for the welfare of his donkeys.

They gave us lunch at ten o'clock in the morning, soup, bread, and a salad of fresh onions and eggs, wheeling out a wooden table that stood six inches from the floor and making space for us around it.

"So who is this man?" Haci Baba asked his grandson.

"He's my friend from England, Haci Baba."

The old man nodded vigorously. "England, where's that?"

"Europe, Haci Baba."

"What does he want?" Haci Baba could be a trifle suspicious.

"Nothing. He's here as a guest."

"Oh, that's good." Haci Baba thought a moment. "Does he need any chickens?"

Haci Baba had once run a farm of 600 sheep. But as his sons moved away or found more easeful ways of making money, the old man sold his land and sheep until all that remained were his chickens. In the summer, he would take the donkeys to the higher ground and gather wood for the winter. In his old age, he had more time for his God, had been to Mecca three times, and was often to be found reading his battered copy of the Koran in the light of the window as the snowmelt dripped off the roof. Haci Baba was the aga, the head of the village. He was in his eighties now. And for a few short years, I calculated, he would have been a fez-wearing Ottoman.

When the muezzin started, Haci Baba, bemoaning the latest village priest's inability to sing straight, hunched off to find his boots. Ahmet grabbed the shotguns and took me hunting. I was uncomfortable about this but was enough of a shot to know I could always make sure I missed any chicken-stealing Kurd we happened upon.

We walked among young Turkish oaks and pines, trunks surrounded by scraps of snow. The ground at our feet was a wet mulch of red-brown earth and pine needles warmed by a weak sun. The crisscross patterns of animal tracks in the remnant snow indicated dogs, wild pigs, small deer, and rabbit. There were also bears in these mountains, although Ahmet had never seen one. At one point he stopped suddenly and gestured me over. "Kurd," he said with authority. But he was pointing at a large paw mark, and no Kurd has paws. But a *kurt*, the Turkish word for wolf, does. In fact, we did not encounter so much as a rabbit. Ahmet unleashed his frustrations by letting off the two rounds of his shotgun. The echoes resounded around the hills, returning to us with the distant noise of alerted dogs and alarmed cattle.

By the time we got back to Soapmakers, night was falling. In the mosque, the men were finishing prayers. The door was eventually opened by a small boy with a plastic machine gun who sprayed Ahmet, me, and a couple of nearby dogs with imaginary lead. I wondered what he'd been learning for the last ten minutes. Happily, he took a tumble on the ice in his attempt to finish us off.

"You just shot yourself in your manhood," Ahmet told the boy, helping him to his feet as the congregation emerged.

They were seven elderly men and a much younger, gangly man who turned out to be the tuneless village priest, or *hoca*. They mostly wore woolen caps in the style of Haci Baba. One wore a turban in the wild style once favored by British washerwomen. Later, Ahmet told me that its wearer felt safe from those who might disapprove but would be unlikely to wear it on a visit to Blackberry. There was not a fez in sight, but nor was there a brim. The men of Soapmakers wore hats designed for prayer. Only the *hoca* was bareheaded. As an employee of the secular government, he was not expected to wear anything other than Western hats.

"I prefer," the *hoca* would tell me theatrically, "to wear nothing."

In the manner of Emine, Ahmet touched his lips and forehead to a number of wrinkled hands. Familiar with villager statuses, he chose the major players and left me to follow his lead. In the confusion, I ended up bowing and scraping to a short man with a round face and trouser legs that hardly reached his shins. A hand on my shoulder alerted me.

"You are honoring the village idiot," said Ahmet.

The village idiot, who had never known anything more than affection, was now receiving a foreigner's respect. In the shine of his eyes, I could see that he would not forget me.

The approaching lights of the lurching village *dolmus* jabbed crazily through the darkness, illuminating stroboscopic sections of wall, earth, and sky. *Dolmus* derives from the word "to stuff," most vividly expressive in its frequent use to describe peppers or vine leaves stuffed with rice. But as I looked in at faces, limbs, vegetable sacks, and livestock squashed against the glass in jumbled proximity, I was reminded of nothing so much as bottled preserves.

As the minibus came to a halt and the contents piled from the doors, the natural order in Soapmakers was rapidly restored. Women, who moments before had been crushed out of necessity against all manner of male anatomy, slipped away into the night, dragging their vegetables behind them and reinstating the demarcation lines between the genders that should properly exist in Soapmakers. Meanwhile, the men joined us to stand in the cold and smoke cigarettes. When we had finished, Mehmet, another of Ahmet's uncles, led us back to his house.

A stove dominated the front room. The floor was covered by pieces of random carpet and linoleum. A cuckoo clock was stopped at two fifteen; the cuckoo had slumped forward, lifeless between its little open shutters amidst a spill of visceral mechanisms, as if the victim of an irritable sniper. In the corner stood a small table covered in plastic red-check gingham on which a solitary plastic salt-cellar stood. A postcard from Istanbul featuring the Bosporus Bridge was wedged between the wall and the electricity cabling. As men filed into the room—the *dolmus* driver, the *hoca*, a baker from a neighboring village, and a number of farmers—Mehmet lit a pinecone with his lighter, opened the stove door, and tossed it in.

As young boys ferried back and forth from the kitchen with bowls of chicken stew, rice, and meat pastries, the villagers started to talk.

"We got electricity twelve years ago."

"No, it was fifteen."

"It was two years before Ali got the telephone."

"But six months ago, we got direct lines. Now, we've got six telephones in the village."

"And televisions."

"And in England," asked Mehmet, apropos of little, "what yield do fields give?"

"I'm afraid I'm not a farmer," I replied.

But even tourists know about yields, the expression of a man too polite to say so protested before telling me about theirs. "Ours give between seven and ten times depending on the weather."

"Good," I replied lamely.

"I once met some tourists in Istanbul," said Mehmet. He had worked there for two summers in the seventies. He opened a cupboard, removed an object with great care, and handed it to me.

It was a calendar dated 1976 and featuring pastoral scenes from Bavaria, complete with statutory lederhosen and foaming pints of beer in lidded pewter tankards. There were neat stacks of firewood and light filtering through the linden trees. Everybody crowded around for a glimpse of this otherworld.

"It is England?"

"If only," I replied. "It's Germany."

"It looks like the village," said somebody else.

"Except for the mugs," came another voice.

"And the silly trousers."

"And the beautiful women." And everybody laughed. Then the man in the calpac walked in.

I noticed his hat before I noticed him, and not only because I was becoming increasingly hat-obsessive. I had seen such a hat before, a kind of astrakhan associated with the Turkish military in the early years of the twentieth century, in a portrait of Atatürk that was often featured on the walls of Turkish shops and homes. In it, the great man leans forward as if into a merciless headwind, intent on direction. The picture portrays Atatürk in action during his famous victories at Gallipoli in 1915 and the independence war four years later. But there is perhaps more to the picture than martial glorification, for it struck me that these victories were characterized not so much by going forward in the manner suggested by Atatürk's posture but by crucially holding the line. Modern Turkey's emergence, in military terms anyway, was founded on heroic defense. So I read the picture's meaning as figurative, a heroic representation of his political charge against the forces of reaction, a grim determination to advance, whatever the cost. In the picture,

Atatürk is in mud-brown military fatigues, and he too is wearing a calpac.

The calpac reminded me of fading daguerreotypes of the Young Turk officers who had opposed the sultan in 1908 and forced him to concede significant constitutional reforms. Historians have called the actions of these officers a revolution, but in truth they were little more than a modification, for all these young men in calpacs had wanted to do was tinker with a system that they largely accepted. They could not accept that the confederation of anarchies that composed the late nineteenth-century Ottoman Empire was unsustainable. The Young Turk position on hats was similarly indecisive. In shape at least, the calpac was no more than a tinkering with the sultan's hat, the fez. For although the calpac was made of black lamb's wool, although it did not sport a tassel and widened to the top rather than the bottom, it was nevertheless conical and, most importantly, brimless, identifying the Young Turks with those who put prayer before practicality.

Mustafa Kemal had been a young officer at the time of the Young Turk modification and quickly took to wearing a calpac. He was sympathetic to the aims of the Young Turks but only insofar as they went. Fifteen years later, he would embark on a radical transformation of Turkish society that mocked the Young Turks' notions of revolution and outlawed their hat along with the fez. In the meantime, the calpac provided him with a stepping-stone, another sartorial caravansary, an initial means of breaking free from adherence to the Ottoman orthodoxies symbolized by the fez. Use of the calpac expressed disenchantment with the old system, but moderate disenchantment, and for a young officer looking for preferment, the appearance of moderation was all.

The man in the calpac was called Ali Bey. He had round mournful eyes, a great stomach for ballast, and a mustache that continually drooped despite the repeated efforts of his fingers to twist it into horizontal obedience. A young child was soon clambering all over him and reaching for something in the area of Ali's pocket.

"Ali Bey is my uncle," Ahmet explained, "and will be aga when my grandfather dies." Clearly, Haci Baba had sired many sons. The child eventually emerged from the folds of Ali Bey's jacket brandishing a pistol. Then he aimed it at me. Ali Bey slapped him down and apologized. I asked him why he carried the gun.

He shrugged as if the answer were obvious. "There are no police for miles and we don't know what trouble might come our way. Besides, there are wolves in the winter. You'll hear them tonight. Leave the gun alone, child. Where's your water pistol?" The child backed off to gaze enviously at Ali Bey's holster.

The gun-toting, calpac-wearing village lieutenant turned to me. He was fondling a medal that hung from his left lapel in so manifest a way that my next question was prompted. He sat back, trying to appear surprised when I asked him about it.

"It's my war of independence medal," he replied. "Atatürk's war against the Greeks."

"But Ali Bey, you look much too young," I said admiringly, and since he was referring to a seventy-year-old war, I wasn't simply being polite. Ali Bey, it transpired, was indeed much too young. The medal had actually been awarded to his wife's grandfather. But in this village, medals won in distant wars filtered down through the generations like the ownership of fields.

The fact that the medal was borrowed did not seem to trouble the villagers, who gathered reverently for one more look before Ali Bey insisted on slipping it into his top pocket, as if he'd been obliged to boast against his modest will. Nor did it matter to me, for Ali Bey looked every inch one of Atatürk's brave irregulars. He told me that he wore his calpac as he was wearing it now, along the head so that it fanned out at the top when he stood in profile, in the course of his ordinary working life. On special occasions such as *bayrams*, or holidays, he would wear it across his head like a bishop's miter. Then he would buff up his medal and revel in the glory of 1919 to 1923, when Atatürk and his soldiers carved a Turkish motherland out of their heroics, even if only because he had happened to marry a valiant bandolier's granddaughter.

"I am Atatürk's greatest admirer," Ali Bey told me.

But Ali Bey also told me that, unlike Atatürk, he was not a rim wearer. Nor, in this alcohol-free village, did he drink alcohol; Atatürk had drunk raki, the local Pernod with muscles, to distraction if not to death. Like most of the men in the village, Ali Bey supported Refah, the Islamic Welfare Party, and its call for the restitution of the *seriat*, or code of Islamic law. He would not brook the notion of the women of the village voting or even holding political views even though they had been granted the vote in 1934—by Atatürk. Ali Bey seemed to revere Atatürk, in spite of himself.

But that was the elastic appeal of the Turkish icon.

"Of course he is revered," Vedat proclaimed about the great reformer who expelled the invading Greeks, re-energized a broken nation, replaced Arabic script with the Latin alphabet, secularized the schools, and abolished polygamy, all in the twenties. "Quite simply," Vedat declared, lifting his chin, "without Atatürk we would be Iran."
—Hatsy Shields, "Inside Anatolia," *The Atlantic Monthly*

Multiple distinct incarnations of the man seem to exist in the Turkish mind, the product perhaps of numerous Atatürk images not only in the portraits and pictures gracing walls throughout the land but also in the thousands of statues in town squares from the border with Greece in the west to those with Iraq and Iran in the east. Atatürk has fractured and multiplied until every aspect of his character and achievement stands alone and distinct. He has become the pick 'n' mix icon, everything from the doughty fighter, the national father, the great educator, to champion of women, of panama hats, and of western coattails. As such, every Turkish constituency can find something in the man of which they approve. It may be imagined that further manifestations of his personality and achievements will be manufactured so that new constituencies, as they emerge, can tailor make their own images of Atatürk if existing versions do not fit their worldview. Atatürk in the calpac was the one that appealed to Ali Bey, no matter that Atatürk's calpac period was merely a piece of politicking, a transitional period on the way to a hatless future free of calpacs.

Another image, conspicuously popular in government offices and in Westernized parts of Turkey, depicts Atatürk hatless, in tails and wing collar. In this picture, which unsurprisingly I did not see in Soapmakers, he has considerable poise and looks like a cross between the Duke of Edinburgh and Fred Astaire. Of the images in widespread use in Turkey, this is probably closest to the true spirit of the man. But for Ali Bey and many of the villagers of Soapmakers, it was Atatürk at his most unrecognizable. From his reading of the Koran, Haci Baba had doubtlessly warned the villagers about the dangers of bare heads: "The wicked man will be dragged down to hell by his exposed, lying, sinful forelock."

I wondered then how versatile the Atatürk icon could be. Was the elastic beginning to perish? Ali Bey, who, with the help of his grandfather-in-law's medal, had fallen for the image of the brave Gazi forging a nation by force of arms, could soon look no closer at Atatürk for fear of the complications that might arise to undermine a simple, stirring image.

Ahmet lit a cigarette and leaned across. "Refah," he said dismissively. "My uncle is crazy. Uncle," he shouted, "our visitor wants to know why you vote Refah."

Ali Bey paused to consider a moment. "Because Refah will make our village rich," he replied. "Refah will pay for tractors and farm machinery and new buildings."

"Dreams, dreams," murmured Ahmet. "You know, Uncle, politicians aren't like that."

"Tractors," Ali Bey insisted.

"Tractors," Ahmet mocked him quietly.

"And they'll tidy things up—stop the fucking on the streets of Istanbul," Ali Bey added, warming to his theme.

"Do they really do that?" asked the village idiot, appearing at the back of the room behind ranks of villagers. "Can I go sometime?"

But for once, the Turkish sense of humor was not tickled. Uncle and nephew stared at each other with a mutual lack of comprehension. They clearly felt too much love for each other to be truly at variance, but the differences between their lifestyles and beliefs were all too apparent. Uncle believed himself to be Turkish and thus Islamic; Ahmet believed himself to be Turkish and thus European. Families have divided over less. A Turkish journalist called Ugur Mumcu had died in a car bomb in Ankara the previous day for championing the essentials of Ahmet's instinctive convictions.

Refah has existed in various guises through the turmoils of Turkish political life, but at no time has it enjoyed its present levels of support. Nor has it ever been so effectively organized. The party receives significant funding from Saudi Arabia, which it ploughs into communities at grassroots levels to fund the construction of new schools and hospitals. The Islamic Welfare Party can afford to live up to its name and deliver promises that other parties can only hope will be conveniently forgotten.

As the evening grew late, the conversation was steered into safer waters. The villagers wanted to know where I was next headed, and hearing my destination was two hours to the east, imagined me entering another world where none of them had ever been. The *dolmus* driver wanted to know about prices in England.

"Well," I said, short of conversation and noticing a pile of discarded husks in a corner of the room. "Pistachios are very expensive in England." A whispered command woke a young boy and sent him scurrying from the room. The foreigner who could not afford pistachios would take a large bag of them from Soapmakers the next morning.

Ahmet and I skirted the village dogs, which stirred malevolently at our presence, slipped into Haci Baba's house, and threw mattresses down as waves of heat blurred off the stove.

"Refah," murmured Ahmet dozily. "Bah!"

There was moonlight at the window and, as I fell asleep, the distant howling of wolves.

I awoke early to a similar sound; Haci Baba was right about the new *hoca's* singing. After breakfast, I washed and then went with misgivings into the lavatory. I looked through the hole in the floor, looked at my left hand, and promptly left.

Haci Baba found me examining the old farming gear in his shed. Strange how little the foreigner knew; only this morning, Mehmet Bey had told Haci Baba that the Englishman did not know what yields his fields gave. "A *döven*," he explained patiently. "A horse drags it across cut wheat to separate the ears from the chaff."

It was a large wooden sled, similar to the one I'd seen on the wall of Halil Bey's hotel in Pomegranate. But this one was covered in winter cobwebs, not coated in shiny display varnish. It would be some time before the *dövens* of Soapmakers slipped from the present to serve as a nostalgic reminder of the past.

When the time came to leave, Haci Baba received my kisses and handed me a plastic bag. Inside was a chicken rough plucked. I thanked him as convincingly as I could.

"He always does that," muttered Ahmet as we drove away. "What's a man supposed to do with a chicken in this day and age?" He glanced at me, irritated. "Your hair," he exclaimed. It was damp from a cursory wash that morning. "You should have borrowed my hair dryer."

"It's wonderful, your village," I told Ahmet in an attempt to placate him as we bumped along the track.

"Your village too," he replied, "now that you've been here."

After a few hundred yards we drew up opposite the village cemetery. Ranks of simple stones topped with snow abutted a ploughed field.

"A fine place to be buried," I mused.

"Yes," replied Ahmet. "I'm almost looking forward to it."

"But you live in Istanbul."

"And this is my village. Refah or no Refah."

I tried to picture how they would one day bring Ahmet here and lay him down alongside his forebears to return to the earth where his heart—in spite of his absence—had always been. But vague recollections of a recipe that somehow incorporated both chicken and pistachios to spectacular culinary effect kept nagging at me, and Ahmet's final scene eluded me.

Jeremy Seal speaks Turkish fluently, worked as an English teacher in Ankara, and wrote A Fez of the Heart: Travels Around Turkey in Search of a Hat, *from which this story was excerpted. He has also written* The Snakebite Survivors' Club *and* Treachery at Sharpnose Point. *He lives with his wife and daughter in Bath, England.*

PART TWO

SOME THINGS TO DO

Ye Pipes, Play On

Time seems to slow in the
smoking salons of Turkey.

ON ONE OF MY FIRST VISITS TO A NARGHILE SALON, WHERE
Turks gather to smoke water pipes, I met a seventy-one-year-old
pensioner named Ismet Ertep. He and the men who gather every
afternoon at this salon beside the Bosporus, along with the few
women who join them, are heirs to a centuries-old tradition.
Their worlds revolve around the soft sound of bubbling water; the
sensation of drawing filtered tobacco smoke through long curled
tubes, and the love of contemplation and understated camaraderie.

"Smoking a narghile is nothing like smoking a cigarette," my
new friend told me when I asked him to explain the attraction of
this vice. "Cigarettes are for nervous people, competitive people,
people on the run. When you smoke a narghile you have time to
think. It teaches you patience and tolerance, and gives you an ap-
preciation of good company. Narghile smokers have a much more
balanced approach to life than cigarette smokers."

My travels in Turkey confirm these observations. Every time I
arrive in a new town, I seek out the narghile salon. It is the ideal
place, even better than the barbershop, to discover what is hap-
pening and what local people are thinking. The pace in these salons is slow, and time is plentiful. Usually there is not much noise.

Conversation is only occasional, always soft and punctuated by long pauses. The sound of dominoes being played or backgammon tokens being moved is often all that competes with the pipes' gurgling. Some patrons work absently on crossword puzzles and others seem lost in reverie. No alcohol is served, only tea and sometimes coffee. Open windows keep the air fresh.

After a while I realized that I enjoy narghile salons not just because they are good places to take the local pulse but because the sensation of smoking a water pipe is so seductive and satisfying. It starts when the elaborate hookah is placed before you, its bowl cleaned with a soft cloth and then filled with damp tobacco. Some patrons choose strong Turkish tobacco grown on plantations near the Syrian border, but I prefer aromatic apple or cherry blends imported from Egypt and Bahrain. After an attendant fills your pipe with the weed of your choice, he comes by carrying a copper tray piled with burning coals. He picks up a couple of them with a pair of metal pincers and sets them atop the tobacco plug. With a few puffs, you are under way.

It takes at least half an hour to smoke a pipeful of fruit tobacco, even longer for the more potent stuff. The smoke is noticeably cooler than cigarette smoke, and lightly intoxicating. Before long the water begins to turn brown; smokers say it is filtering out many of the harmful substances they would normally be inhaling.

Perhaps no habit is associated more closely with Turks than smoking tobacco. Herman Melville reported walking along Istanbul streets lined with cafés where "Turks sit smoking like conjurers." By the nineteenth century, when he visited, narghiles had become an important sign of trust, and withholding it could be taken as a serious insult. In 1841 a diplomatic crisis broke out with France when the French ambassador demanded a formal apology for not having been offered a chance to smoke with the sultan during a visit to the royal palace.

Today smoking is not only acceptable but almost mandatory in Turkey, especially for men. "A 'manly man' is one who is brave, loud, virile, does not hesitate to fight for what he believes in, does not show his emotions or cry, and knows no fear," the social historian Arin Bayraktaroglu wrote in a treatise on the Turkish psyche. "He usually has a mustache, and drinks and smokes a lot."

Narghiles were first used in India, but they were primitive ones made from coconut shells. From India the custom spread to Iran and then to Turkey, where it flowered. A separate guild of craftsmen was established to make each of the narghile's pieces. The mouthpiece is traditionally made of amber, the tube of fine leather dyed in different colors, and the sphere that holds the water of glass, crystal, or silver, sometimes decorated with floral motifs or other designs. In olden days the water itself used to be scented with perfume or herbs, but that custom has faded.

Turks took to smoking narghiles almost immediately after the first tobacco leaves arrived from America in 1601. Smoking quickly became a craze. People indulged at home, at work, and in cafés. "Puffing in each other's faces, they made the streets and markets stink," wrote the contemporary historian Ibrahim Pecevi.

The authorities were not pleased by this development. At narghile cafés, then as now, people do not just smoke. They talk. In a society where the sultan's political power was supposed to be absolute and submission to it unquestioning, the specter of leisurely social gatherings where the topics of the day would inevitably be discussed and debated was unsettling. Ottoman rulers did not like being unsettled, and in 1633 Sultan Murad IV issued a decree that banned smoking on pain of death. An underground immediately took shape. Those afraid of being traced by smoke resorted to inhaling the aroma of chopped leaves. After fourteen years the ban was finally lifted. Tobacco soon became one of the empire's main exports, and Pecevi concluded that it had joined coffee, wine, and opium as one of the four "cushions of the sofa of pleasure."

No one believes the narghile will ever regain its supremacy in the tobacco world. Indeed, logic suggests that the narghile salon should be a dying tradition in Turkey. The atmosphere inside is distinctly Oriental, the pace leisurely to the point of torpor. With Turks now turning ever more decisively toward Europe and modernity, they might be expected to shun such places. But although the number of salons is slowly declining, the tradition will not die. Every year brings a new crop of pensioners who have the time and often the desire to spend hours in quiet reflection. On some evenings I even see college students and other young people sitting and puffing. They embrace an experience that is at once solitary and convivial, that evokes nostalgia but also inculcates the values of peace, dialogue, and tolerance that today's Turks must absorb if their nation is to fulfill its destiny.

In days gone by, some smokers used to fill their narghiles with illicit drugs. Some still do. I know a small hotel in Istanbul where there is a secret back room that the owner opens for friends and special customers. There they don rich Ottoman costumes, sit on embroidered velvet cushions and smoke a blend of fruit tobacco and hashish. The pleasure of such an interlude approaches that enjoyed by the sultans, who smoked a special mixture of opium, incense, and crushed pearls.

"The important thing is not what you put in the pipe but who's with you when you're smoking," a sailor I met in one salon told me. "It's a complete experience. In a café like this one you find the good people, the old people, the interesting people. As long as there's a need of company and friendship, as long as people want to stop and think, there will be narghile cafés."

Stephen Kinzer also contributed "A Dazzling Kaleidoscope" in Part One. This story was excerpted from his book, Crescent and Star: Turkey Between Two Worlds.

LAURIE UDESKY

Clash of the Camels

A Western rodeo, it's not.

BELLS CLANK IN THE DISTANCE, AND A RHYTHMIC CHIMING gets closer as men with berets, stout guts, and weathered skin like leather lead their camels into the ring. The sound of Zeybek music—a squeak reminiscent of a kazoo, made by a wooden flute-type instrument and a drum—is carried on the growing wind. Locals say it's the music that makes the camels dance.

The clouds are turning dark, threatening rain. Yet thousands of people, some in makeshift bleachers, others sitting in beds of trucks surrounding the ring, have flocked from villages on the outskirts of Nazili, about 170 miles southwest of the Turkish port city of Izmir, and from other parts of Turkey's western Aegean to see this winter spectacle.

Under a rainbow of umbrellas, they munch treats from their picnic stashes and sip raki, the Turkish national alcohol, a licorice-flavored aperitif that turns billowy white when mixed with water and incites its imbibers to kick up their heels in sweeping folk dances.

In contrast to their owners, the camels are dressed in their finest: elaborately woven, beautifully colored tapestries; bright reds, blues, greens, pinks, and oranges that cover their two humps, shifting

93

slightly as the camels' front legs move elegantly forward, as if they are dancing through water. Their bums carry a banner announcing their name and *Masallah*—the Turkish idiom that means, "May Allah protect you from the evil eye."

"Their get-ups cost about $3,000," notes Ali Onal, who had introduced his camel, also named Onal, to me the day before. As Ali talks, Onal the camel gives him a sloppy, frothy kiss. Thousands of dollars may seem a high price to pay for one suit of camel clothes, but it's on par with the worth of the beasts. The camels, which are bred in Iran, cost about $25,000 apiece.

The announcer barks two contestants' names over the scratchy sound system: "Gözluklu (Spectacles) from Soke will wrestle Faruk from Antalya."

Through the air rings a high-pitched *"Kuhhh, kuhhh, kuhhh"*— like a nail across a blackboard. This is the sound of camels grinding their teeth, which are covered before they challenge their opponents so that no blood will spill.

The camels are released into the ring and the match begins. The two animals lean into one another, using the might of their back legs and their weight to try to force the opponent to its knees. Then each uses its weight and long neck to pin the opponent's head down. Whether or not Gözluklu is nearsighted, in short order he has pinned Faruk's head on the ground between his front legs. In this position, the camels are locked together like Siamese twins, making it hard to decipher where one ends and the other begins.

The spectators in the stands leap to their feet, chanting "Gözluklu, Gözluklu." One boy, overwhelmed with excitement, sweeps a rolled-up poster in his hand toward the action. "Come on, son! Come on!" he yells.

Great deep groans issue from somewhere in the wrestling hold, and white froth, like the head of a badly poured beer, flies from the camels' mouths. This hovers in the air like soap bubbles or arcs onto the ground; soon splotches of it cover the muddy ring. The announcer, squatting with his cordless microphone just inches away from the beasts, flails his free arm up and down. "It's down, it's down, it's down! Yes, Gözluklu is the champ!"

Then a primordial tug of war ensues between beast and man: It takes twenty men to pull the camels apart. Ten men stand in a line behind each camel. The leaders expertly lasso one of each of the camel's front legs. On cue, with all hands grasping the length of the rope, they heave each 2,000-pound beast away from its opponent.

These men spend a good part of the day running in circles around the wrestling camels, always keeping vigil with their ropes, lest two clashing camels tumble into the crowd. At one point there is a close call, but a wave of spectators undulates out of the way in the nick of time.

One hundred forty camels are wrestling today, one match at a time lasting up to eight minutes, with the next two sets of contestants galloping around the periphery of the ring. No one is really a loser here. The victors win the equivalent of $140 plus a carpet; the losers win $85. But because camel owners represent an elite class of villagers in Turkey, all the money, including the revenue from ticket sales, goes to schools or hospitals. "Camel wrestling isn't a job," says Ali Onal proudly. "It's a tradition from my father and my grandfather, so I give all the money away."

To prepare for the matches, the owners have the camels on a walking regime for two months prior to the beginning of wrestling season in November. They walk them about eight miles a day the first month, working up to twelve miles. Their food intake in winter is minimal: four and a half pounds of veggies and half a gallon of water per day.

In the off-season, on the other hand, the camels are pampered pets. They consume enormous quantities of vegetables and about thirteen gallons of water. During their thirty-year life span, they will wrestle from the age of seven until they're twenty.

According to local legend, Turkish camel-wrestling dates back 150 years to a time when two agas, or wealthy landowners, turned the male camels' winter mating ritual into sport. By nature, or more precisely, by the male hormonal drive, camels wrestle each other over the nearest female in heat.

At least one camel owner today is deferring to his camel's natural instincts. He's brought along a female friend, who walks next to her male counterpart as he readies for the match, frothing happily at the mouth.

Camel owners insist that their beasts are extremely intelligent, never forget, and are fiercely loyal to those they like. "When one of our camel owner friends died, his camel cried," maintains Alkan Demirtas, who hails from nearby Mugla. "Camels are like angels," he continues lovingly.

"India has its sacred cow. For us, it's the camel. The prophet Mohammed rode one from Medina to Mecca," adds camel owner Tayfun Bayir.

Camel loyalty apparently extends to other animal species. One camel is accompanied by a compact little donkey, its cheerleader of sorts, which is led in the camel's view while it wrestles. "He's the camel's buddy. When the camel sees its donkey friend, he feels more courage and confidence," explains one camel-wrestling fan.

Friendships aside, camel owners say their two-humped animals have dramatically affected the quality of their lives. "My life changed. I've met a lot of people and friends, and it gives me good luck," says Demirtas.

"It's our tradition, it's from our ancestors," says a fan who travels up and down the Aegean coast during winter weekends to catch the matches in different towns. "Americans have eagles, Russians have bears, the Turkish nation has camels," adds another fan as he sips his raki. "Being Turkish," he says, pausing for effect, "is being a camel!"

While not every Turk may agree, the villagers in the Aegean region of Turkey eagerly look forward to the matches as an oasis from the wet winter monotony.

Laurie Udesky is a writer whose work has appeared in The Nation, *the* Turkish Daily News, *and* Salon.com. *She is currently living in Turkey.*

LAURENCE MITCHELL

The Road to Urfa

A meeting with pilgrims at Abraham's pool
creates a feeling of common humanity.

WE ARRIVED IN URFA IN THE EARLY HOURS OF THE MORNING,
greatly relieved to get there in one piece after an extended demonstration of Turkish driving skills. I had had enough: we had been
on the road for ten hours since Adana. I was tired and my nerves
were on edge. Only a handful of us got off the bus; most of the
others were traveling on to Cizre, at least another six hours away.
I wished them all luck.

Urfa was enjoying a warm balmy night with a slight breeze,
blowing north from the Syrian Desert, to relieve the humidity. The
stars were shining like beacons in the moonless sky.

The city was asleep and most of the hotels seemed to be locked
up for the night, but we found one that still had a light on. We
were hailed by a man who was sitting outside the hotel entrance
making the most of the night air. The man was called Ali Baba,
and he was quite used to jokes about his forty thieves.

Ali Baba was an English teacher and self-styled guide to the region. He was also an enthusiastic Muslim, not uncommon in this
holy city even for young men. More surprisingly perhaps, he was
a nonsmoker, which really was quite unorthodox for a Turkish
man of his age.

97

Over the next couple of days, whenever we met up, Ali would pleasantly harangue us with a lot of well-rehearsed arguments endorsing his Islamic beliefs. It was that typical East-meets-West scenario where, in having a foot in both camps—a traditionalist with a modern education—he was keen to rationalize his religious convictions. We were told of the scientific validity of the Koran, and how there was no need for a belief in the infallibility of Mohammed's word when all the claims of the Koran could be proved by modern scientific method anyway.

It was a well-rehearsed lecture, but he lost me after a while. He did get a bit fanciful, too, I thought, in his claim that in a nearby village there was the perfectly preserved body of a three and a half-meter giant, frozen in the prayer position. This, he claimed, was a miracle bearing witness to the power of Islam: a living statue made by Allah demonstrating the way men should prostrate themselves to Him. Every religion needs its miracles, I suppose, but the idea of a supplicating giant with permanent rigor mortis was a bit hard to swallow.

It seemed to be the sort of place where miracles might be possible. Urfa—or Sanliurfa, "glorious" Urfa as it had just been renamed—seemed to be much more like the Middle East than any other Turkish city I had visited. There was something of the Arabian Nights about it, even without Ali Baba's presence.

There were few cars, but a multitude of donkey carts thronged the dirt streets. Porters carried huge items of furniture on their shoulders, and the covered bazaar echoed with metallic chimes, as craftsmen fashioned household utensils out of raw metal. In the vegetable markets, gold-toothed women chattered behind enormous mounds of watermelons, and the glottal stops of Arabic and silken vowels of Kurdish greeted the ears as much as did Turkish.

Urfa is a city that generally sees few tourists and, consequently, everyone was welcoming to a fault. The hospitality was boundless, even by Turkey's high standards. It was friendly curiosity for the most part. People would stop and talk and show you pictures of their families, and tulip-shaped glasses of *çay* (strong black tea) would be procured out of nowhere, delivered by little boys with tin trays.

Wandering the city streets, I was frequently invited to take photographs of people; by cobblers and tinsmiths in the market, by workmen loading salt onto a truck, by a group of shoeshine boys. In the male-only tea shops, waiters would greet you like long-lost friends and refuse to charge. Even gruff old men with baggy-arsed trousers and gray stubble would stop and have a word. Inevitably it was, *"Merhaba! Alman?"* "Welcome! Are you German?"

"Hayir Ingiliz." "No, I'm English."

"Ah! Ingiliz, çok iyi." "English, very good."

As everywhere else in Turkey, the most well-known foreign country was Germany, simply because so many Turks worked as migrant laborers there. But they had mostly heard of Ingiltera too, especially the infamous "Missus Tacha, The Iron Lady." They loved strong, hard leaders in Turkey—even if they were women—and the right-wing, quasi-militaristic leadership of our erstwhile prime minister was the sort of thing that the obedient Turks tended to admire. I did not hold it against them but joined in the mutual congratulations.

"Kemal Atatürk, çok iyi." "Atatürk's very good too."

In our few days in the city we made numerous friends, and our visit became a round of meeting up with people to drink tea at various hours of the day and night. Not wishing to cause offense, it was a struggle to keep up with the many instant friendships that we had made, but I did not mind too much. In fact, I loved it. I loved Turkey. I loved its people. But I was still a bit confused about the country's true nature.

In Istanbul and Ankara, I had found myself asking the same questions. Where did Turkey really belong? Was it European or Asian, secular or Islamic? I could only say that it was all of these things: a frontier region where east meets west, where religious fatalism meets scientific empiricism. It was the best (or worst?) of both worlds, and that, I suppose, was really its appeal. But here in

Urfa, there was no such quandary; this was undoubtedly the east, as Asian as Damascus or Karachi.

A lot of the pilgrim buses that we had seen on the road here had stopped for the night. Urfa bears a particular significance for pilgrims to Mecca, and not just as a staging post on the way south to Mohammed's holy city. Urfa is the city where Abraham is said to have been born, and Old Testament prophets like Abraham are as important to Islam as they are to Christianity. People come from all over Turkey to view his birthplace and many of the hajjis were taking in a visit to Abraham's cave on their way south.

These were the same pilgrims that we had seen cheerfully drinking *çay* at service stations on the way here. They had seemed light-hearted and gregarious as they wandered around in groups, stretching their legs before being shepherded back onto the buses by their adrenaline-crazed drivers. Now they were seeing the sights of Urfa before continuing to Mecca. It must have taken years to save the necessary funds to finance a hajj, but they seemed to be making the most of the trip and were investing their once-in-a-lifetime journey with an infectious, joyful enthusiasm.

There were large groups of pilgrims all over the city, billowing like dust clouds through the streets, a seething mass of loose white cotton. Everyone was dressed for the pilgrimage: the women embalmed head-to-toe in cream and white, the men in skullcaps with little Turkish flags sewn onto their jackets.

We came across a pilgrim group gathered on the citadel above the old town. The leader was carrying a large Turkish flag to identify himself. The view from the top suggested that Syria and the desert were not so far away, with the dun-colored mud dwellings of the city's outskirts fading into parched low hills that defied shade. With the hajjis all grouped together in their pilgrims' attire and the brown biblical hills beyond, there was nothing to belie the effect that we were looking at a spectacle that had not changed much for centuries. It could well have been a scene from the golden years of the Ottoman Empire. That is, if you managed to ignore the Mercedes buses waiting for the pilgrims below.

We climbed down from the citadel's fine vantage point and went to visit the nineteenth-century mosque dedicated to Abraham. Nearby, more pilgrims were quietly queuing to visit the cave that was the prophet's supposed birthplace, the same cave where he was said to have spent the first ten years of his life, hiding from the paranoid Assyrian tyrant, Nemrut, who in a fit of pique had decreed that all newborn children be killed without mercy.

The crowd was respectful of the holiness of the place but the stereotype of dour, unsmiling Muslims disdainfully looking down on foreign infidels was not at all apparent. In fact they went out of their way to be amiable.

A middle-aged woman from Malatya tried out a little German on us. She and her husband were going to Mecca, but, despite the more mundane reasons for our journey, she did not seem to make any judgment about the relative merits of our respective trips. There was no overt piety. We were accepted with good grace, as fellow holiday-makers sharing a good time.

The whole crowd was like her and the common courtesy that was shown to each other, the consideration, the politeness, the camaraderie—the love even—was a joy to behold. This was not a throng of intolerant fundamentalists, but a group of quite ordinary middle-aged, working-class people who were having the time of their lives. They were so open and congenial that I believe they would have smuggled us onto the bus and onwards to Mecca if they could have. Part of me would have wanted to go with them.

Near the mosque stood a pool containing a large number of carp, said to be sacred because of the legend which tells how Abraham was saved from a fiery death by an act of God.

After coming out of hiding, Abraham became a stalwart opponent of the Assyrians' megalomaniac leader, Nemrut. Abraham attempted to destroy all the idols of the Assyrian temple and, naturally enough, this angered Nemrut no end. The despot decided to have Abraham put to death by plunging him off the citadel battlements into a fire below. Fortunately, the prophet was saved by the command of God who made the flames turn into water and the firewood turn into carp. Legend has it, of course, that these were the very same fish that you see in the pond today. This would make them about 2,500 years old.

It is strictly forbidden to catch the fish, and to do so would probably result in the same sort of fate that a curious non-Muslim would suffer if he sneaked into Mecca: sudden death by divine intervention.

These oversized goldfish had grown fat on the countless offerings pilgrims had made over the past two millennia, but still they had not lost their appetite. I bought a bag of hemp seeds to feed the fish.

The water boiled in an orange whirlpool of feeding frenzy as I threw my seeds to the waiting carp. The pilgrims at my side smiled and remarked on the prodigious appetite of the fish. I smiled back and gave some seed to a little boy so he could throw it into the pool. We all beamed contentedly at the thrashing forms in the water.

We were starting to become that same creature, the pilgrims and I—tourists with a spiritual bent, for want of a better description. Our aspirations were not so radically different, really. Our different religious and cultural worlds were starting to lose their focus as self-imposed boundaries began to break down. I could not go to Mecca, nor could I ever be a Turk, and my natural skepticism probably prevented me from ever becoming a Muslim, too. But none of this really seemed to matter that much.

For a few brief minutes, I was another pilgrim participating in a small, enjoyable ritual that was part of life's journey. They would go on to travel to Mecca, I would return to England. For the time being, however, we were equals in spirit.

Laurence Mitchell has traveled widely on five continents. He has worked at various jobs but these days concentrates his energies on travel writing and photography. He finds that the condition affectionately known as "wanderlust" does not improve with age, but, rather, becomes more acute, like rheumatism or hair loss. Despite a love of mountains, he lives in a flat part of England: life is rarely perfect. He is currently working on a book about Egypt and Sudan.

LAURA BILLINGS

How to Buy a Turkish Rug

True shopping is a bonding experience.

NOT LONG AGO, A FRIEND CALLED TO INVITE ME ON A CHEAP, off-season tour of Turkey. She promised that I would see the ruins of Ephesus and the fairy chimneys of Cappadocia, that I would wake each morning to the sound of the Muslim call to prayer and go to bed each night with a belly full of aubergine. Yeah, whatever, I said, just as long as I get to buy a rug. The truth was that ever since I bought my first car and was introduced to the delirious back-and-forth of negotiating, I had dreamed of going toe-to-toe with the guys who invented the dealer showroom. Since flying carpets were our first automatic conveyance—and if you've read *The Arabian Nights* or seen *Aladdin* you know this is true—rug merchants were actually the world's first automobile salesmen.

And they're outstanding salesmen, living as they do in the busy confluence between Europe and Asia, a ripe spot for studying humanity and perfecting the first salesman credo: Tell the customers what they want to hear. On my first day in Istanbul, I nearly fell prey to a green-eyed charmer who accosted me in the Kapali Çarsi, the famous covered bazaar that holds more than 4,000 shops. (Take that, Mall of America!) "You are a great beauty," he said so wolfishly that it was clear the antiseptic threat of harassment charges hadn't drifted into this pungent corner of the world. "You must be Italian," he added for extra measure. Actually, I'm a poster girl for the corn-fed Midwestern look, and was so pleased to be deemed Continental that I was opening my wallet when my Turkish tour guide dragged me away.

After another half-hour in Istanbul, I discovered that merchants' flattery flew almost as quickly as the prices they quoted, but it was the numbers I had to pay attention to. At the time I visited, each U.S. dollar was worth about 35,500 lire, a complicated ratio, but one that gave me the heady thrill of announcing, "A million? No prob!" I spent the week learning, but it wasn't until I passed the souvenir stands outside the ruins of Ephesus that I felt I had hardened myself to the Turkish marketing come-on. There, a young man bearing an armful of dolls and a striking resemblance to Johnny Depp deliberately bumped into me. "Excuse me, madame," he said, his voice as warm and rich as ripe olives in sunshine, "You dropped something."

I looked to the ground and then to him. "What did I drop?"

He paused for a moment, searching my face soulfully. "It was my heart," he oozed, but I kept walking. I was finally ready to buy a rug.

So we went to Oba, a veritable rug ranch of low-slung buildings and grassy courtyards, just down the road from the House of the Virgin Mary. A hawk-browed Turkish man in a double-breasted suit greeted us and gave a lesson about rug craftsmanship designed to dispel any notions we may have had that a good rug could be purchased on the cheap. He showed us baskets of tobacco leaves, onion skins, and indigo used for dying fibers. He showed us the silkworms boiled alive for our textural pleasure—a sacrifice that Doublebreasted assured us the worms were only too glad to make. Same went for the young girls in the weaving room whose hands shuttled and knotted wool with the fluttering speed of hummingbirds. Doublebreasted promised that the girls got full health coverage, nutritious meals, and a good wage, and that they didn't complain when the small-motor demands of rug weaving forced them to leave the work by their late teens. "It is a privilege and an honor to make something so beautiful," he said, but I couldn't stop the piteous look that swept across my face as I watched a young girl squatting and squinting before an intricate Persian pattern. An equally sympathetic look crossed her face as she saw us herded into the carpet showroom, lambs to the slaughter.

We were led through a series of rooms where vibrant rugs and kilims were layered like sheets, rolled into columns, and tacked to the walls—each room duplicating and expanding upon the previous room's treasures. At the end of the procession was a ballroom-sized showroom where we were offered Turkish apple tea, soda, beer, and wine (American car dealers should reconsider the popcorn and Coke routine, I thought). While we were served by a long-lashed girl in harem pants, her counterpart—a sulky John Malkovich look-alike in Western clothes—quietly shut the heavy wood door that was our only escape route.

Like a Turkish caravansary floor show in which a slim-hipped belly dancer preps the crowd for the heftier model and finally for the cartilaginous creature who shakes her extra-wide-load hips to tambourines and thunderous applause, the rug show started slowly. Malkovich and Harempants lifted each rug by the ends, walked to the center of the room, and let gravity unfurl it, the bright colors of Anatolia, Kars, and Kayseri washing over us. As the pacing built, the rugs started to cover the shining wooden floor, then overlapped one another. Soon we had left our perches on the wooden bench that lined the wall and begun crawling around on the rugs, examining their fine weaves and lustrous textures. The climactic crescendo arrived with the unfurling of a massive silk Persian of geranium reds and robin's-egg blues. Though we were already breathless, Doublebreasted clapped his hands and Malkovich and Harempants, moving like choreographed game-show models, picked up either end of the carpet and turned it by 180 degrees, shifting the rug's palette to crimson and cobalt. Amazing! we cried. Astonishing! we clapped.

At that, a cluster of salesmen who had been gathering in the room suddenly converged on us and pulled us to separate corners. Three men whisked me into another room. Their leader was a raven-haired fellow with cheap shoes and a wistful expression. His name, Ogün, means "That Day" in Turkish, a fact that was the source of huge laughs for his two squat henchmen who clearly understood my English, but spoke only in Turkish with Ogün. I started to say that I was in the market for a five-by-seven kilim with a lot of red in it, but Ogün shot me a pained look that suggested such a request was as déclassé as demanding that an Old Master painting match my sofa. Instead, he ordered the henchmen to unroll a series of rugs at my feet. When I shook my head at the choices, the henchmen tossed their arms up in disgust, but Ogün had a more courtly approach. With each selection I dismissed, he nodded appreciatively and moved closer to me, as if irresistibly drawn to my aesthetic.

Soon he began dismissing rugs for me—"Can't you see she won't like that? She wants real beauty," he would scold the henchmen. He asked if my husband would like my choice of rug, and I said I didn't have a husband. He shouted in Turkish to the henchmen, who eyed me up and down, and again tossed their hands up in disgust. "They think this is a tragedy," Ogün said, and then sighed toward his cheap shoes, "and so do I." At this point he asked if I had a credit card with me. I said yes. The haggling began.

The rug I selected, or that Ogün had selected for me, was a jewel-toned affair of blacks, pomegranate reds, jade greens, and deep blues. Ogün explained that normally he would start the bidding around $1,000, but since this was the end of the season, and since I had no husband, he would start at $500. I shook my head at the price, and though my blood was racing, I couldn't coax out a counteroffer. Ogün strode away from my side with his hands thrust deep into his pockets, his shoulders hunched. He nodded his head and Henchman No. 1 scurried to the other room. Ogün smiled, puffed out one side of his cheek, and slowly blew out a low whistle of air. A few minutes later, the henchman returned and whispered in Ogün's ear. Ogün told me that Doublebreasted had insisted that I leave with a rug today—how did $260 sound? Well, it sounded pretty good to me, now that my lust for bargaining had flagged. Ogün wasn't a shrewd creep, I thought, he was a fellow connoisseur. Just then, my friend walked in and saw me handing off my credit card.

"What are you doing?" she demanded, and I explained the situation. "No way," she said to Ogün. "Two of 'em for $260!"

Quickly, my friend's bad-cop display made me realize I had allowed myself to be swept along too easily. Ogün looked to me. "Two for $260?" he asked, and I nodded. He held his hand to his heart. He walked to the corner of the room and sighed. "We are friends, Laura?" he said, coaxing a small tear to the corner of his eye. "Why do you hurt me like this?" Finally, I understood the theatrics required here.

"Ogün," I said, so forcefully I convinced myself I was truly affronted. "I don't think you're being honest with me..." and I snatched back my Visa card.

At that there was a very pregnant pause in which Ogün and the henchmen bored their Turkish eyes at me. They huddled and Henchman No. 2 threw his hands up in the air and pointed at me. Henchman No. 1 made a spitting noise. Ogün looked over his shoulder. "So you want two rugs?"

"If the price is right," I said. Henchman No. 2 sniffed and gestured again. Ogün came back to my side and put his arm around me, hand to his collarbone in a gesture of sincerity.

"My friend, you know that I must make a living?" I clenched my fist around my plastic. He let out a heavy sigh. "My friend, you may have two for $400. No lower please."

"Three hundred," I said.

"Three sixty," he said.

"Three hundred," I said.

"Three twenty-five," he said.

"Sold," I said, and at that there were cheers from the henchmen and from the small crowd from my tour bus that had gathered for the final negotiation. As I handed off my Visa, Ogün took my hand and wrapped it under and over his forearm as though we had been wedded by this exchange of currency. He lovingly folded and packed my rugs in brown paper and then in a nylon case he promised would fit nicely under my plane seat. It did.

Now I come across my two rugs, one in my living room, the other in my bedroom, and I feel a wave of pleasure at my purchases. But the souvenir that pleases me most is a photograph I have of Ogün and me. We are standing in the courtyard of the rug ranch—I have my hands clasped and my head tossed back in laughter; he gazes at the camera with the smallest trace of a smile. We both look so satisfied—like we each ripped off the other just a little bit.

Laura Billings is a columnist for the St. Paul (Minnestota) Pioneer Press.

JOHN FLINN

* * *

The Blue Voyage

These wine-dark seas yield luxurious bounty.

RESPONDING TO NEEDS UNVOICED, CAPTAIN MAVIS APPEARS
on the deck of his yacht *Surgun'd* with an armful of frosty-cold Efes
Pilsen beers, just as the setting sun transforms the Mediterranean
into a sea of gold.

He hands me a bottle and I raise it in a silent toast...not just to
Mavis and his gorgeous boat, but to the trio of frisky dolphins that
escorted us across the bay this morning; to the ruins of vanished
civilizations clinging to the hillside behind us; to Cleopatra, whose
alleged bath we splashed around in this afternoon; to Gür the
cook, down in the galley whipping up a lobster feast; and most of
all to Cevat Sakir Kabaagaç.

In the years after World War II, Kabaagaç was part of a group of
Turkish writers, artists, and intellectuals who set out on coastal
voyages to rediscover their nation's rich trove of history and natural wonders. They hired local fishermen and their boats, called
gulets—wooden fishing caiques that have been working Turkey's
rocky coastline for time immemorial. Kabaagaç wrote a book
about these journeys called *Mavi Yolculuk—Blue Voyages*—and a
new form of tourism was born.

Today a small fleet of these *gulets*, outfitted specifically for pleasure cruising, plies Turkey's Aegean and Mediterranean coasts, from Ephesus to Antalya, from spring through fall.

If you can get together a group of like-minded friends, hiring a *gulet* and crew for a week is almost ridiculously inexpensive. This past spring six of us spent eight days and seven nights sailing Turkey's Mediterranean coast aboard the 80-foot *Surgun'd*, and the bill, including three enormous meals a day, came to only about $1,000 a person.

Built of polished teak and mahogany, the two-masted *Surgun'd* has five cabins, each with a double bed and its own bathroom. There's a downstairs lounge with a TV and VCR, a shaded aft deck for dining and napping, and cushions for sunbathing on the foredeck. It can easily accommodate ten passengers. With just six...and a crew of four to attend to our every need...it felt like something out of *Lifestyles of the Rich and Famous.*

As we stepped aboard in the port town of Marmaris, Mavis handed each of us a glass of sparkling Turkish wine. His real name is Muharrem Baykuslar, but the thirty-year-old David Hasselhoff look-alike prefers to go by "Mavis," a Turkish nickname meaning "blue eyes." Lined up to greet us was the shy first mate, Ceyhan Kirli; the fun-loving cabin boy, Hakan Hacioglu; and the brooding, taciturn cook, Gür Arpat.

We motored out of the docks, past a castle built by Sultan Süleyman the Magnificent for the siege of nearby Rhodes, and through a protected harbor where Admiral Nelson once hid his fleet from Napoleon.

Precipitous, craggy, pine-covered mountains jutted straight out of the turquoise sea. This stretch of Turkey's Mediterranean shore is called the Lycian Coast, after an ancient civilization whose isolation and reputation for fierceness kept it out of the mainstream of history. The Lycians show up as bit players in Homer's *Iliad* and Herodotus's histories, but their main legacy is the magnificent rock tombs they carved into the sides of the cliffs around Dalyan and Fethiye.

The Greeks, Romans, and Byzantines also flourished along this coast, leaving behind ruins almost too numerous to count. We grew used to seeing the outlines of sunken Roman villages in the vodka-clear water beneath us, and we encountered Byzantine homes that were fully intact and still inhabited.

One afternoon Mavis anchored the *Surgun'd* in a little jewel of a cove and we went for a hike on a trail that climbed past untended olive groves and ramshackle shepherds' huts. Near the crest of the hill I paused to have a sip of water and noticed that the rock I'd sat down on felt odd: It was part of a beveled stone column, with Latin inscriptions chiseled into its top. A little further we rounded a corner and found ourselves staring, slack-jawed, at the acropolis of a long-forgotten Roman town.

There were more toppled columns and ornately carved blocks of stone, and the square-cut walls and arches of a temple, its floor littered with the shards of terra cotta urns. We peered into a dark hole beneath the temple and could see vaulted catacombs.

And here's the thing: It didn't appear as if archaeologists had ever excavated this site. There were no signs, no fences. Turkey's coastline is so densely packed with antiquities...it was far more heavily populated in ancient times than it is now...that researchers have had to focus their efforts on the bigger, more important ruins.

In a little valley on the far side of the hill stood the rest of the Roman town, with the outline of a neat grid of streets and bits of crumbling walls. I heard the metallic tinkle of goat bells, and through binoculars could see shepherds sharing a meal in the shade of an ancient cistern. Down the valley stood a new stone house, with a chunk of wall looking suspiciously like the chunk missing from one of the old Roman houses.

We saw bigger and better ruins throughout the week, but these were my favorite. We felt as if we'd discovered them; they belonged to us. I could find no mention of the town in books about the Lycian coast, but one map did identify it as Lydae. (And while archaeologists may have ignored them, the ruins are well-known to *gulet* captains; on our way down we met the passengers of another boat, coming up.)

Our days aboard the *Surgun'd* quickly took on an idyllic sameness: We'd roll out of bed and plunge into the Mediterranean, which was just bracing enough to wake us up, but not jarringly so. Hakan would be waiting on the deck with steaming cups of strong Turkish coffee. As we toweled off, he'd cover the table with baskets of crusty bread; tubs of yogurt, butter, and pine-scented honey; plates of feta cheese; three kinds of olives; slices of sweet melons and rich, sun-ripened tomatoes; sliced cucumbers; and enormous, juicy strawberries. Just as we finished gorging ourselves he'd return with the main course: heaping platters of omelets or French toast.

We'd motor east along the Big Sur-like coast for two or three hours, slicing though the glassy blue water of various bays and gulfs. One morning I was standing on the fore deck, lost in a little Homeric reverie, when Mavis came rushing out of the wheelhouse and vaulted over the railing. Startled, I looked over the side to see him balancing barefoot on a steel bow cable, just above the water, reaching down to stroke the backs of three dolphins playing in the bow wake.

Around noon Mavis would anchor his *gulet* in a rocky cove and we'd leap off the deck again to paddle and splash in the sea while Hakan laid out platters of spicy lamb meatballs called *köftes*; stuffed eggplant; *börek*—cheese wrapped in phyllo pastry; a green bean and tomato salad, an onion and cucumber salad, yogurt, and Kalamata olives.

Sultry afternoons presented vexing choices: Nap or swim? Read a novel or poke around ruins? Backgammon or gin rummy? Sunny foredeck or shady aft? White wine or red? "It's a dog's life," somebody said. "All we do every day is sleep, eat, and get taken for walks."

In late afternoon, Mavis and the crew would hoist anchor and we'd scud across another gulf. Once, when the wind was good, they hoisted the *Surgun'd's* sails; but mostly we traveled by motor, like other *gulets*.

As the evening sky turned pink Mavis would personally supervise the sundowners, pulling the cork on a bottle of crisp, dry Turkish white wine called Villa DeLuca—pretty darn good, we all agreed—or dispensing chilled bottles of Efes Pilsen.

In the last light of day he'd anchor in another protected cove, and out from Gür's little galley would come yet another feast: octopus with cheese and mushrooms, fried calamari, boiled prawns, fried lamb, fish, a lobster salad with lemon and garlic—accompanied by several bottles of Villa DeLuca or the California Chardonnay we'd brought from home. (Please understand that I'm not describing dinner variations throughout the week: this was the menu for a single meal.)

We'd wake up the next morning and, with minor variations, do it all over again. If eight days of this sounds monotonous, trust me: it wasn't. At the end, all six of us would have gladly signed on for another eight days.

One day we hired a little motorboat, which looked like the *African Queen*, to sail us up the reed-filled Dalyan River to view the coast's best Lycian rock temples, explore the overgrown ruins of the large Greco-Roman city of Kaunas, and splash around in an outdoor mud bath (which, my Lonely Planet guidebook later informed me, is "mildly radioactive"). Another day we poked around in the remains of an ancient, half-sunken Turkish bath that, according to local legend, had been built for Cleopatra. (Historians scoff at this, but it's not entirely out of the question: the Egyptian queen cruised along this coast with Marc Antony.)

One evening, Mavis anchored the *Surgun'd* alongside a pretty little pine-covered

In the garden of the church there is a modern statue that shows Saint Nicholas with a sack slung over his back, flanked by three small children. This evokes the most famous Santa legend of all, when in order to save three poor girls from prostitution, he dropped a bag of gold down their chimney.
Conveniently for the young ladies, and for future mythmakers, the coins fell into the row of stockings which were hanging up to dry.

—Theresa O'Shea,
"Desperately Seeking Santa"

island called Gemiler Adasi. In the water beneath us I could make out the walls and columns of an old Byzantine port, submerged by a series of powerful earthquakes. Hakan swam ashore and tied our stern line to one of the ancient shops and storehouses clinging to the side of the hill.

Mavis led us up a rocky pathway that wound through stone arches and past cisterns, with bits of mosaics scattered on the ground, to a series of churches built in the fifth century to honor Saint Nicholas, the former bishop of the area. The son of a wealthy landowner, Nicholas had a habit of tossing sacks of gold down the chimneys of impoverished neighbors. Along these sweltering Mediterranean shores, and not at the North Pole, is where the real-life Santa Claus lived.

The trail climbed past olive trees and old stone tombs and bits of shattered domes to the very top of the island, which was crowned with a sixth-century Byzantine church. We sat down amid the ruins to drink in the sweeping vista of the sparkling sea and the islands, coves and rocky mountains stretching down the coastline.

As the setting sun once again painted the Mediterranean gold, Mavis reached into his backpack and produced two bottles of chilled Villa DeLuca. Far, far below us, in a little turquoise cove, I could see the last light of the day striking the *Surgun'd*, where Gür the cook was no doubt hard at work in his galley, preparing yet another feast.

John Flinn was the travel editor for the San Francisco Chronicle *for seven years and now is the staff travel writer.*

In the Hands of Kismet

Local road rules turn this visitor
into a philosopher.

I WISHED I HADN'T LOOKED OVER THE DRIVER'S LEFT shoulder. But I was in the back seat, leaning against the window on that side, and I couldn't help it. And having looked, I couldn't turn away.

We were doing at least 100 miles an hour, maybe even 110. I couldn't see the whole speedometer.

"How fast are we going?" I asked Jim, who was sitting on the other side of the back seat.

"You don't want to know," he said.

"Tell me!"

He demurred and fell asleep. (It was out of our control, he explained later.)

Riveted awake, I envied him. I'd been warned about situations like this—by the U.S. State Department, no less—in the same near-desperate tone that worried parents use on wild teens.

First mistake: It was dusk. "Dusk is a particularly dangerous time," the State Department cautioned, "because most drivers delay turning their headlights on until well after dark."

Second mistake: Our driver, whom we'd hired for safety's sake, had been at the wheel for eight hours and needed rest. "In Turkey," the State Department said, "drivers should be hyper-vigilant."

Third mistake: We were speeding. Oh, heck, make that the first mistake.

At 100 mph, survival depends on everything staying the same: no driver sneezes, no lug nut loosens, nobody hits a sheep. But you can't count on that. The result was like a nightmare with us in a Blue Angels formation, flying wingtip to wingtip, without rehearsals.

By this point in our trip around Turkey, we'd been tailgated by semi-trailer trucks at 100 mph. We'd been passed in heavy traffic by vehicles doing 100 mph with oncoming traffic in their lane. And we'd watched in shocked awe as cars and trucks passed us on blind curves, at 100 mph, changed their minds, and squeezed back into line with only a foot between their bumpers and ours.

I am not exaggerating. Neither was the State Department's "Driver Safety Briefing for Turkey." Some of its warnings were predictable: Always wear seat belts, carry jumper cables, drive defensively. Some were wise all over the Third World: Watch out for "herds of sheep, goats, and other animals on the

The TEM, Turkey's auto-bahn, is the main thoroughfare from the border of Greece east to Ankara, Turkey's capital. On this road, there are speed limits posted; but the only reason I can think of for this is that it's an E.U. compliance effort.

The only place that the disrespected police can catch you is at one of the few tollbooths along the motorway. Their vehicles, generally four-door Fiat sedans with varying degrees of serious neglect, are the equivalent in size and power to a 1984 Ford Escort. That makes it impossible to chase down, or even pull out in front of, a BMW or Mercedes, which are the ubiquitous choices of Turkey's financial champions.

—Dean Eliason,
"TEM-tation Highway"

roads" and for "pedestrians seemingly completely oblivious to oncoming traffic."

But some advice was disturbingly new: "Turkey has completely
inattentive drivers" who "drive in the middle of the road and yield
to no one" or, my favorite, "vehicles backing up—in reverse—on
exit ramps."

And for nowhere else had I ever been advised to carry a piece
of chalk in the car. "To mark accident scenes," the State Department said. It was the chalk that got me.

I've read warnings on war zones that weren't this scary. This one
read as if it had been written from a hospital bed.

The warning concluded with a list of handy terms and road
signs in Turkish.

I figured we could master *dur* (stop) and even *tek yön* (one way),
but I wasn't sure about *araç çikabilir* (vehicles exiting), *yaya geçis*
(pedestrian crossing), *yol çalisma* (road work), *tirmanma sagdan* (slower
vehicles use right lane), or *tehlikeli madde* (dangerous materials).

But could we read any of them at highway speeds, let alone
react in time?

The last terms on the list sounded the most dire but also the
most useful: kismet (fate) and *Allah korusun* (may God protect me),
said to be a sign often seen on trucks.

I e-mailed a copy of all this to Jim, and on the eve of the trip,
we both chickened out and decided to hire a driver. A travel agent
put us in touch with an agent she knew in Istanbul, who found us
Erkan, an energetic, friendly guy with lightning reflexes.

He didn't speak English, but the agency's director wrote down
a few common driving terms in Turkish. We couldn't pronounce
them, and the paper became a bookmark.

Hiring Erkan cost about $600 for the eleven-day trip, but it
added immeasurably to our peace of mind. Except here we were,
Jim asleep and me fretting, going 110 mph across the Anatolian
Plain. When I couldn't stand the tension anymore, I leaned forward
and touched Erkan gently on the shoulder, intending to have him
slow down.

He wasn't expecting it. I startled him so badly that he jerked the wheel, the car swerved, and my heart nearly stopped. When we were both calm again, I made what I thought would be a universal gesture. Palm forward, I patted the air. "Slow down," I mouthed in English.

Erkan smiled, nodded, and sped up. I had, apparently, given the Turkish signal for "You're doing a nice job, keep it up."

That's when I gave up and decided to follow the State Department advice, leaving it all to kismet.

Catherine Watson is senior travel editor for the Minneapolis Star Tribune. *Her work has won many national awards, including the two most coveted in travel journalism: Photojournalist of the Year from the Society of American Travel Writers and Travel Journalist of the Year from the Lowell Thomas Travel Journalism Competition, both awarded in 1990. She has taught at several universities, most recently in the Split Rock Arts Program of the University of Minnesota. Her current passion is the 130-year-old farmhouse she restored in the National Register Historic District of Galena, Illinois (the town from which U. S. Grant left for the Civil War).*

STEPHEN KINZER

Turkish Wrestlemania

*At a 640-year-old tournament, competitors are slathered
with olive oil and the winners bathe in public acclaim.*

THERE IS ONLY ONE WRESTLING TOURNAMENT IN THE WORLD
at which contestants use tons of olive oil. It is held each year in
western Turkey, and its tradition reaches far back into history.

Rules for the matches have changed only slightly over the years.
In olden times, some bouts went on for hours or even days, since
the only way to win was to pin one's opponent to the ground.
Some contestants expended so much energy that they died on the
field. Now it is also possible to win on points, and matches are
stopped after forty-five minutes.

But in most other ways, the one-on-one combats staged every
summer closely resemble the first ones held nearly 700 years ago.
Wrestlers are stripped to the waist, wear specially designed leather
trousers, and enjoy the boundless respect of their countrymen.
Most important, they begin fighting only after being drenched
with olive oil from head to toe. Three tons are consumed this way
at each year's tournament.

Oil wrestling tournaments have been held in Turkey every year
since the first ones were staged as tests of strength for Ottoman soldiers and amusements for their rulers. Now the three-day event is
not simply a sporting test but a festival that attracts a colorful cross

section of Turkey, from gypsy families who camp near the stadium to appliance manufacturers who display their newest refrigerators and microwave ovens. It reveals an aspect of this multifaceted country that many visitors miss.

Although Turkey is in many ways a modern nation that embraces its European heritage, it still revels in its ancient Turkish history. Many of the same Turks who cheer for soccer or basketball teams also love the three traditional sports that reflect the Central Asian origin of Turkish peoples. One is camel fighting, another is the fast-moving horsemanship and javelin-throwing competition called *cirit*, and the third and perhaps most evocative is oil wrestling.

The Ottoman Empire is often thought to have been established in 1453, when Sultan Mehmet II crushed Christian Byzantium by conquering its capital, Constantinople (now Istanbul), and establishing a Muslim dynasty in its place. But in fact the Ottoman house was founded by Sultan Osman more than a century and a half earlier, and it was during his reign that the first oil wrestling tournaments were organized. They were held, as they are today, on the outskirts of Edirne, the Thracian city formerly known as Adrianople.

Edirne is near Turkey's border with Greece, two hours west of Istanbul by car, and the rented minivan in which I made the trip with a few friends passed through the plains where Osman and other early Ottoman sultans marshaled their troops for expeditions that would ultimately propel them to world leadership. Today the city of around 150,000 is out of the mainstream and not visited by many tourists. That is unfortunate because it boasts some fine architectural treasures, including a grand mosque built by the sixteenth-century architect Sinan that some connoisseurs consider the finest in Turkey. But at the beginning of each summer, Edirne attracts thousands of people who watch some of the country's most admired athletes test their skills.

After parking our van, my friends and I walked toward the concrete stadium. A veritable carnival had sprung up on the adjacent grounds. It was centered around an entire circus, complete with scary rides for kids. Bypassing the circus, I spent an hour walking past scores of booths that sold an extraordinary combination of wonderful crafts like hand-painted ceramic plates and intricately carved chess and backgammon sets, juxtaposed with great amounts of kitsch-like plastic kites decorated with skull-and-crossbones motifs and heart-shaped red pillows embroidered with "I Love You" in English.

As is common when large numbers of people gather in Turkey, some of the picnics spread out by women for their families looked overwhelmingly appealing, better than what one could find in any restaurant. But I knew from experience that it is dangerous to stop and admire these homemade banquets, because one will inevitably be invited to sit and join in. Then one is a prisoner for hours, eating marvelously but unable to say goodbye.

So we walked slowly past, eating only what vendors were selling. I bought a sandwich made of lamb meatballs, onions, sliced tomatoes, and spicy peppers, while one of my friends wolfed down a chicken kebab.

In the background we could hear rhythmic drumming from the stadium. We stopped to see two exhibits of photos of oil wrestlers that were certainly not intended to be homoerotic, but seemed so nonetheless; the sport is said to have developed a gay following in recent years.

We had bought tickets in advance, and found our gate by one of the photo shows. An usher showed us to our seats and brusquely refused to take my proffered tip. This was the third and final day of the tournament and we had come to see its climax.

The wrestlers were powerfully built, but looked nothing like the intricately toned men who display their physiques in body-building magazines. At one side of the quadrangular grassy field, a corps of volunteers doused each contestant's naked chest, back, and shoulders with oil, which is supposed to make the competition more difficult than ordinary wrestling, a sport in which many of these fighters also compete. Once oiled, the combatants skip across the field in lines, about half a dozen at a time, slapping their knees and jumping as they move forward. Each man faces off against his designated opponent.

Several matches take place at once, each with its own referee. Points are won by turning a rival upside down, pinning one of his shoulders to the ground, or executing other maneuvers.

Because the matches last so long, they seem more like stylized dances than quick-paced contests. Thankfully, it is not necessary to understand the rules to appreciate the surges of activity and seemingly calm lulls, which the fighters use to gain subtle tactical and psychological advantage.

Matches go on for most of the day, and spectators watch respectfully. Many take this tournament very seriously, occasionally breaking into cries of encouragement, triumph, or anguish, but otherwise remarkably focused.

Besides the drumming, the matches are accompanied by recitals of traditional poetry. Announcers sing the praises of "Ye, oh great wrestlers" and recite verses with lines like these:

Every woman can give birth,
But not every boy can be a wrestler.

The undisputed king of modern oil wrestling is a former factory worker named Ahmet Tasci. Considered a superman because he continues to win even though his is well over forty, he is an eight-time champion in the heavyweight division. The only man to have defeated him in the last decade is a whippersnapper in his mid-thirties named Cengiz Elbiye. Ideally, the two should face off in the final match; the tournament I saw featured what the man sitting next to me called "an early final" as the two drew each other as rivals in the quarterfinals.

More than 700 contestants participate in the oil wrestling tournament, most of them in the free-weight category but also youngsters, some not yet into their teens, who are classed by age. The eyes of every aficionado, however, were on these two as they faced each other. It was the classic confrontation of an aging champion with a rising challenger.

The match had been underway for more than half an hour when suddenly, so fast I am not sure I actually saw it, the veteran Tasci smashed his younger opponent to the ground, pinned his shoulders, and was pronounced the winner yet again. He had effectively won his ninth title. Elbiye, his defeated rival, remained on his knees with his face pressed to the ground for several minutes. I couldn't tell if his face was wet from tears or oil. That is certainly how he wanted it.

Stephen Kinzer also contributed "A Dazzling Kaleidoscope" in Part One and "Ye Pipes, Play On" in Part Two.

RICHARD HALLIBURTON

Swimming the Hellespont

The author crosses the famous straits,
swimming in the wake of legends.

WE ALL HAVE OUR DREAMS. OTHERWISE WHAT A DARK AND stagnant world this would be. Most of us dream of getting rich; many of us of getting married; and some of us of getting unmarried. I've met people whose great dream it was to visit Jerusalem, or Carcassonne, or to look upon the seven hills of Rome. I'll confess to a sentimental lifelong dream of my own—not of riches, or weddings, or Jerusalem, however—something far less reasonable than that. I've dreamed of swimming the most dramatic river in the world—the Hellespont. Lord Byron once wrote that he would rather have swum the Hellespont than written all his poetry. So would I!

Sometimes, once in a long, long while, sentimental dreams come true. Mine did, and it was as colorful and satisfying as all my flights of fancy had imagined it would be. To me, the Hellespont was not just a narrow strait of cold blue water, discharging the Black Sea and the Sea of Marmara into the Aegean. Far more than that: it was a tremendous symbol—a symbol of audacity, of challenge, of epic poetry, and heroic adventure.

The nature of the Hellespont's first records seem to have set an example for all the historic events that have clustered about it. Its very naming is a dramatic story. The name of "Hellespont" ("Dardanelles" on the modern maps) goes back to legendary ages, receiving its title from "Helle," the King of Thessaly's daughter who fell into the channel from the winged ram with the golden fleece, on whose back she was fleeing from her enemies.

Through this same Hellespont, Jason, in his immortal ship, the *Argo,* sailed in quest of this same fleece. For ten years, from 1194 to 1184 B.C., the fleets of the Greeks were beached at its entrance, while their armies, led by Agamemnon, Achilles, and Ulysses, thundered at the lofty walls of Troy. It was across this stream that Leander nightly swam to keep his clandestine trysts with Hero. In the very wake of Leander, in one of the most spectacular military exploits in history, King Xerxes of Persia, the mightiest ruler of his time, crossed from Asia to Europe with a colossal army for the invasion of Greece. Here, in the following century, Alexander the Great ferried his Macedonians from Europe to Asia to begin his conquest of the world. Back once more in the fourteenth century rolled the tide of invasion from east to west: this time the Turkish conquests that were to turn the Hellespont from that day to this into Saracenic property. Through this strait the piratical Turkish cruisers moved for generations, making all of the eastern Mediterranean a Turkish lake. Since 1600 Russia has fought periodic wars for the possession of this storied channel. And now the shores of this same Hellespont are dotted with the wrecks of sunken Allied battle fleets and strewn with the graves of a hundred thousand French and English soldiers, whose blood was squandered in rivers in the desperate attempt in 1915 to plant the Allied flags over the rocks where Hero joined her drowned romantic lover in dim antiquity. Indeed one's spirits surge to read the amazing record of this fateful stream and realize how repeatedly it has shaped the destiny of the world.

This, then, is the Hellespont, and the scene where my dream came true.

Nature was most capricious when she created this eccentric corner of the earth. She drives the enormous volume of the Black Sea past Constantinople through a narrow channel called the

Bosporus—and then again by more reluctant, prolonged, tortuous degrees, through a winding canal-like gash in the mountains, forty miles long, and from one to five miles broad. Down this insufficient Hellespont, with Europe on her right side and Asia on her left, the Black Sea, unleashed at last, rushes at top speed, foaming with indignation at her long imprisonment. For ten thousand years she has poured herself into the greater ocean, season in and season out. Tides she scorns. South—south—south, her waters always swirl so that one may well call the strait a river since, but for its briny nature, it qualifies in every respect to this term.

Few watercourses can boast of having seen the rise and fall of as many stately cities on its banks as can the Hellespont. Of these the two most familiar to us (though they have long since crumbled into dust) are Sestos and Abydos: the former on the European side of the narrowest part of the Hellespont; the latter almost opposite on the Asian, some three miles away. And why are these two cities, from among the scores of their contemporaries, alone favored with immortality? Is it because of their great military conquests, or their celebrated soldiers, or their marble temples? No, none of these. They are immortal because a youth—an undistinguished, undescribed youth of Abydos, named Leander—tragically loved an equally undistinguished maid of Sestos named Hero: the legends of love refuse to die.

One loved fiercely in legendary Greece. Hero, priestess of a temple though she was and consequently sentenced to a loveless life, was no less human than her lay sisters. She craved love as they, and when on the occasion of the popular Sestos Temple festival, her eyes caught the concentrated glance of a graceful and sturdy youth, she did not run away. The moment he guardedly spoke to Hero, her vows, her veil, quite properly, lost their power. She learned that his name was Leander and that he had sailed across the straits in his boat from his home in Abydos to attend the festival. They must not be seen together, since she was a priestess, prohibited by the gods from the society of man—*by day*. But that night, might he come in the moonlight, to the temple garden? Find me the girl of ancient Greece, or modern Greece, or any other land, who would have said no.

And so they met in secret, high on the Sestos cliffs, and looked out over the glittering ripples of the Hellespont that swirled ceaselessly past. And the next night again, and the next. All went well until one of the temple orderlies saw the lovers together and betrayed them to his superiors.

In a rage the head priest seized the unfortunate girl. He dragged her down the cliff-path to the very edge of the Hellespont, and then up to the top of a tower where the wretched maiden was left in solitary imprisonment, safe from the approach of any more sacrilegious lovers.

From his homeward-bound boat Leander, in the moonlight, had witnessed the figures entering the tower-prison that rose above the wave-lapped rocks, and in his heart he rejoiced. They were casting her into his very arms—for he was the strongest swimmer in Abydos.

Impatiently from his Asiatic shore he watched the sun go down beyond the cliffs of Sestos, across the swirling Hellespont. While they were only three miles away, it was necessary to take horse and servant and ride upstream along the Abydos side until he reached a point well above Sestos. Sestos lay sharply upstream, and the tideless current, squeezing through the narrowing channel, raced past at such a rate that no swimmer, save a god, could have swum against it. From above, though it would require four miles or more of furious swimming to reach Hero's tower and not be carried past, he might hope to succeed.

Strange and desperate things are done in the name of love. Shortly after nightfall, Leander, ready to face any obstacles for one caress of his mistress, plunged into the Hellespont. He had hoped Hero would guide him by means of a light from her tower window—nor was he disappointed. A spark from her small oil lamp cast a faint path across the water. Thus directed he steered his course to Sestos, and drew himself up on the rocks beneath the tower. Hero was half expecting him to come, and watching.

Tearing the cover of her couch into strips she made a rope by which, on the hidden offshore side, he could pull himself up to her apartment. And then, what an eager reunion!

Partir, c'est toujours mourir un peu. Yet part they must, while darkness hid them.

The journey back, though difficult and cold and unrewarded, was not so long as the first crossing, for the Abydos point extended deep into the stream and assisted the swimmer to reach the Asian shore.

Did I not say that love drives us to desperate ends? Again the next night, undiscouraged, unsubdued by the sinister river's power, Leander swam his way back to Hero's arms—and many nights that followed.

But high on Olympus the fates were spinning to an end the immortal lovers' thread of destiny. They saw the storms and the winds that were churning the Hellespont as winter seized the land; they saw the madness for Hero that burned increasingly in Leander's heart, driving him recklessly into the face of any danger. Indeed, whom the gods would destroy, they first make mad.

And it was madness for the youth to defy the furies on such a night as this, and attempt as usual to swim across to his mistress's tower. Heaven and earth warned him back. But Hero's eyes beckoned, and to them he surrendered. Plunging through the surf he met the oncoming rollers. He looked anxiously for the little lighthouse. Nowhere was it to be seen, for the storm had obliterated the faithful lamp.

The usual hour of Leander's arrival had come and long since gone; and dawn, shrill and ominous and glowering, found Hero still at her heart-breaking vigil. And then she saw that Leander had come at last. There on the seething rocks below her window, the strong white body of her lover lay, tossed at her feet by some pitying water god. A flame swept through Hero's heart. In despair she cried out Leander's name, and plunged from her window into the swirling waters.

And so today, because a man died for a maid and a maid for a man, Sestos and Abydos are not forgotten as were their great contemporaries. Time annihilates all things but romance. In every land, in every generation it is romance that the human heart perpetuates. I do not doubt that in some distant time, when our modern world is dust, the story of Hero and Leander will stir mankind far more than all the futile foolishness of our own unheroic age.

Three thousand years later, Lord Byron was so gripped by the sapphire beauty of the Hellespont, and by the drama of its storied shores, that he ceased his restless wanderings and for an entire year rested in a charming little house at the very edge of the water near the site of Abydos. Like every true romanticist, Byron was deeply moved by the story of Leander, and decided, being a swimming enthusiast, to try to swim the Hellespont himself.

Early in April, 1818, accompanied by a friend, he undertook the crossing from Sestos to Abydos. Finding the water of an icy chilliness, the two swimmers postponed their venture until the following month. It was the third of May when the attempt was made again, and although, as Byron wrote in one of his notebooks, "the water was still extremely cold

Byron most likely became a "swimming enthusiast" because he was born with a clubfoot, a painful disability and disfigurement that embarrassed him, pushing him to excel at sports.

—JV

from the melting of the mountain snows, we swam from Sestos to Abydos." This was slightly incorrect because, as the poet added, he began the swim high above Sestos to make sure of gaining the sand point at Abydos. "The whole distance," he continues, "from the place where we started to our landing on the other side, including the length we were carried by the current, was computed roughly by our companions at upward of four English miles, though the actual breadth is less than two. The rapidity of the current is such that no boat can row directly across. Its rate of flow may be estimated by the fact that the whole distance was accomplished in one hour and ten minutes. The English consul at Dardanelles could not remember the straits ever having been swum before, and tried to dissuade me from the attempt. The only thing that surprised me was that, as doubt had been entertained of the truth of Leander's story, no traveler had heretofore endeavored to ascertain its practicality."

The poet, on landing safely at Abydos, in one of his typically facetious moods, celebrated his swim in the following familiar verses:

> If in the month of dark December,
> Leander, who was nightly wont
> (What maid will not the tale remember?)
> To cross thy stream, broad Hellespont!
>
> If, when the wintry tempest roar'd
> He sped to Hero, nothing loth,
> And thus of old thy current pour'd,
> Fair Venus! How I pity both!
>
> For *me*, degenerate modern wretch,
> Though in the genial month of May,
> My dripping limbs I faintly stretch,
> And think I've done a feat to-day.
>
> But since he cross'd the rapid tide,
> According to the doubtful story,
> To woo—and—Lord knows what beside,
> And swam for Love, as I for Glory;
>
> 'Twere hard to say who fared the best:
> Sad mortals! Thus the gods still plague you;
> He lost his labor, I my jest;
> For he was drowned and I've the ague.

It was not many years after this that Byron followed Leander to Hades. However, the house in which the poet lived at Abydos on the edge of the Hellespont continues to stand intact to the present day, for Roderic and I occupied it.

In the actual wake of Ulysses at last, we had left Skyros behind, and, like Ulysses, returned to the mainland of Greece—he (proudly escorting Achilles) to reunite with his fleet, we to find a ship that would take us to Troy at the entrance to the Hellespont.

We found such a ship, but not being on the warpath for the recovery of anybody's wife, as was Ulysses, and having all the time we wanted to indulge in side excursions, we did not disembark at once on the long sandy shore of the Trojan plain where the 1,186 Greek ships were drawn for ten long years. Instead we passed by for the moment, a stone's throw from it, and twenty miles on upstream to Abydos, to investigate the Hellespont swim.

We found any "investigation" unnecessary. The sites of Sestos and Abydos were conspicuously, unmistakably, there. At the former place the acropolis ruins establish its exact location. The Mound of Xerxes, up the slopes of which Abydos climbed, and the sand peninsula, which is a spur of the mound, establish Abydos with equal certainty. The only way to "investigate" my ability to swim the intervening distance was to dive in and swim. As previous endurance tests I had swum the Nile and the Mississippi, but either of these was mere paddling compared with the Hellespont.

The first problem was to reach Sestos, the starting point, in a boat big enough to buck the savage current, and yet small enough to escort and safeguard me on my return journey. The Turkish officials (suspecting we were British spies) made this exasperatingly difficult. In order to move at all against the relentless flow of the water and constant south wind, it was necessary to push off at four A.M., at which time the elements were comparatively calm. Each morning for a week the police delayed our departure till almost noon by which time all the oars and sails we could muster were utterly futile to combat the onslaught of the current.

Each day with renewed determination we tried to beat and tack our way upstream with every device in our power. Back and forth, back and forth, sailing endless miles in the blistering sun, trying to gain a yard. Then by sunset, utterly exhausted, we would look back toward the Asiatic shore to find we were still just off the Byron house, *exactly* where we'd been that noon.

On the eighth day, in desperation, we managed to sail straight across to the European shore, and, though we were almost as far

from Sestos as ever, we were at least free of the obnoxious and suspicious Asiatic officials.

That night we spent in one of the Gallipoli battlefield graveyards, with thousands of wooden markers of thousands of British
soldiers spreading grimly across the hillsides. We slept on the
ground, using a grave for a pillow. Next morning long before day-
break, when the wind was stilled, Roderic and the two boatmen
and I each took an oar, and heading our sailboat straight upstream,
bent to the task. One moment's relaxation, and we would lose
ground. For five hours we fought our way toward Sestos—and attained it. But this was not enough. Being by no means a swimmer
of Leander's caliber I thought it wise to take the precaution Byron
had taken, and continue on upstream some two miles more above
Sestos in order to give myself more time to get across before the
current swept me past Abydos Point.

Finding a semi-sheltered cove, we anchored our craft and
waded ashore for a rest. From the top of the bluff we could see
Abydos dimly visible through the summer haze—about five miles
away. Up to this moment we had been much too busy to think
about a meal. Now with our first objective attained we turned rav-
enously to our provision basket. It was absolutely empty. During
the night the two Turkish boatmen had consumed every vestige of
our food. Not so much as a crumb of bread was left. No, not quite
as bad as that—a small can of Norwegian sardines they had been
unable to open. It was this or nothing. Roderic, realizing I had to
make the swim, magnanimously insisted I consume the entire
available supply of fuel; so I did.

Then at two o'clock I removed my clothing, and, my heart
pounding with excitement, stood at the water's edge, praying to
the water gods to deliver me safely on the other side. The summer sunshine blazed from a cloudless sky upon the sinister, sapphire stream that lapped invitingly at my feet. With nerves keyed
up to the highest pitch, I yet held back in fear lest I fail. Despite
the fact that Xerxes had scourged the Hellespont with chains in
punishment for having destroyed his bridge of boats, I knew its
beautiful, villainous waters had not been humbled. Here was my

Siren Dream, beckoning to me. This was the Great Hour. I recalled a similar moment, in Japan, when on a zero January morning I faced the iceberg of Fujiyama at the timber line, ready to plunge up the glassy slopes to the blizzard-swept summit. Again, and stronger, came the spiritual exultation, the sudden strange pulse of power that makes cold chills of courage race through one's blood. My body whispered: "You cannot possibly swim five miles in such a current," but Inspiration shouted: "This is the *Hellespont*—what matter if it's fifty!"

I plunged.

The Asiatic shore across the channel rose hazily. I struck out straight for it, with Roderic and the boat hovering close beside.

Before I had gone half a mile, whatever "form" I may have begun with soon vanished, and I thought only of covering the greatest possible distance with the least possible exertion: backstroke, sidestroke, dog paddle, idle floating, any old thing to keep going. A big Greek steamer bore upon us, rushing furiously downstream. It was our place to get out of the way. The officers of the bridge, not seeing me in the water, made frantic gestures. To protect me, our sailboat stood its ground in the very path of the oncoming ship, and the steamer had to take a violent veer to one side to keep from colliding with our craft. As she passed by, not forty feet away, the officers hurled upon our heads every unprintable name in their broad vocabulary—but it was all Greek to us.

By half past two I looked back toward Europe to find, to my alarm, that I was already abeam the Sestos bluffs. It made me realize how relentlessly I was being swept downstream. And Xerxes' Throne, the conspicuous last-chance goal above Abydos, where the Persian king sat to watch his army cross the Hellespont on a bridge of boats over the very channel I was swimming, seemed to have moved laterally miles up the coast, though not toward me.

Before three o'clock I was in midstream. The wind had constantly increased, and was now churning the water with white caps. Every few minutes I was half-drowned when the resentful waves broke unexpectedly over my head. It seemed to me I swallowed half the Black Sea. Nausea seized me so painfully that several times I was ready to give up. But the increasing cold was the worst thing of all. The water flows so rapidly, even the surface has no opportunity to be warmed by the sun. After the first hour I began to grow uncomfortably numb.

However, the Throne of Xerxes was not far off now. All along, this had been a guide-point. And yet, as I drew near to it, I realized the ricocheting current was sweeping me parallel to the shore about ten times as fast as I was approaching it. The trees and rocks began to gallop past. From midstream I had calculated that I would land half a mile above the tip of Abydos Point, but the mile soon became a quarter, a sixth, a tenth. After two hours in the water, within 300 feet of shore I was being swept past the "last chance" of solid ground, just as, and where, Leander had been swept 2,500 years before...and should I fail to reach the beach by ever so little, the current would drag me across the Hellespont, back to the European shore whence I had started.

Never have I felt such utter despair: a five-mile swim—my Hellespont—to miss achievement by 100 yards! Never have I struggled so desperately. My eyes became blurred, seeing only the land not far from me. I ceased to know where I was, or what I was doing, here in this cold, tormenting, boundless ocean. Mechanically I thrashed the water with my weary arms and legs.

Then—bump!—my *knees* struck bottom. I was swimming hysterically in less than 3 feet of water, for the shore sloped so gradually that, even at 300 feet out, the water was not waist deep. With not one second to lose, I stood upright and staggered ashore, with Rod, who had jumped into the surf, right beside me, and flopped on the last foot of ground at the point.

And so the Hellespont, that treacherous and briny river, was swum once more. Though I am but one of several to have battled successfully with its evil current, I have a distinction no one else can claim. Leander swam to look into a lady's eyes; Lord Byron, that he might write another poem; but I can boast of being the only person, dead or alive, who ever swam the Hellespont on a can of sardines!

Richard Halliburton was a writer, lecturer, and world traveler. He published numerous books in his short lifetime, including The Royal Road to Romance, The Complete Book of Marvels, *and* The Glorious Adventure, *from which this story was excerpted. Halliburton is known for having paid the lowest toll to cross the Panama Canal, which he swam in 1928, paying thirty-six cents. Born in Tennessee in 1900, Halliburton died in 1939 as he and his crew attempted to sail a Chinese junk, the* Sea Dragon, *from Hong Kong to San Francisco as a publicity stunt.*

MARY LEE SETTLE

In Cappadocia

*Central Turkey hides treasures
in its mountains and caves.*

LOOMING OVER KAYSERI, PROTECTING IT, AND ALWAYS THERE
to destroy it, is the main reason for its choice as a capital city, not
only of the Seljuks but of the Hittites, the Romans, the Phrygians,
the Byzantines. Erciyas Dagi is one of the highest mountains in
Turkey, an extinct volcano where in late August we could see snow
on its peak. Its fantastic explosion millennia ago formed the
strange landscape of Cappadocia.

There are none of the famous carved pinnacles in the city, but
there is, underground, said to be another city of rooms and tunnels, hollowed out of soft volcanic rock, where the people hid until
whatever swirl of trouble, natural or man-made destruction, was
over and they could come up again.

Erciyas Dagi and its sister mountain, Melendiz Dagi, dominate
the flat land west of Kayseri. Eons ago, they spewed out the new
world of tufa and granite rocks for hundreds of miles around them.
Gradually, through time, the slow sculptor, water, carved out river
valleys, hills, caves in the soft rock. Much of Cappadocia looks like
a desert tossed by the wind. It is some of the richest agricultural
land in the country.

The mountain seemed to follow us as we drove for miles west from Kayseri along the central plain. After a while it was as if the car weren't moving, a sensation like being on a ship at sea, motionless, going nowhere. The land moved past around us. The plains were flat to the horizon, so far away we seemed to see the earth's curve, blanketed in August with huge fields of sunflowers all turning toward the east. In Turkey they are called moon flowers; like the moon dependent on the sun's reflection for their color and light.

From time to time we saw cars and the ever-present tractors with carts behind them parked beside the road by green fields. We stopped, too. People from the villages were bent over the low vines, picking grapes. Yusuf went into the field and brought back large bunches of fat white grapes, but he would not let me eat them until they had been washed. He said they had medicine on them.

Beyond the fields, stone sheepcotes were scattered over the low hills that were the first glimpse of a changing land. They looked so like ancient houses that the locals say that once people did live in them. They were built on solid stone plateaus with such thin topsoil that the stone showed through, and runnels that might have been old drainage ditches or ditches made by snow melt. The protective cotes foretold winters of deep snow when the sheep, part of the lifeblood of the central plains, have to be sheltered from the winds that blow all the way from Asia, and from the deep snow that in the spring melts and pours down into the hidden valleys and makes the land so lush.

Cappadocia was once the name for a great plate dominated by the two mountains, where, during the second millennium B.C., the Hittite Empire covered a huge area of central Turkey, from Ankara southeast to Malatya, and from the Black Sea in the north to the Taurus Mountains in the south. Now Cappadocia is the unofficial name for a much smaller area, pitted with deep valleys, roughly between Nigde in the west and Kayseri in the east.

Ahead of us, a high hill was pierced with caves as small as windows in the honey-colored rock. We dipped down below the plain, on a steep Ottoman road finely paved with square black stones so that I had a sense of hands, thousands of hands, carefully placing them there. The road curved around the first of the tufa hills, and there they were, the buildings of the troglodytes, carved into the rock, the first sight of the villages, the churches, the dovecotes where, for centuries before what we think of as historic time (which seems to be pushed back every year as we find out and learn to read the signs), people have lived, protected themselves, and carved perfect retreats for religious anchorites.

Think of a huge cave without a top, where the stalagmites, some of them as high as ten-story buildings, are exposed to the sun and the deep blue sky. Think of them as blush pink. It is as if suddenly the moon landscape, which we are now familiar with in its desolate beautiful skeletal forms, were to become a Garden of Eden, for they are surrounded and permeated with vineyards, with fields of bright vegetables and fruit, with lush river valleys and lines of formal cypress trees growing along their banks, green below the brown and fawn level of the high plains of central Anatolia.

Xenophon and his hoplites got drunk in one of Cappadocia's underground cities. Early Christian saints carved monasteries in its hills. There are Byzantine cave churches. More than a hundred underground cities, like the one rumored to be under Kayseri, have been found there, and more are being discovered all the time.

Once it was thought that djinns carved the cities. Medieval travelers said that the strangely shaped cones were huge religious statues. To Muslims, the cave churches were haunted by figures with the "evil eye" that they found in frescoes painted on the walls, so that the eyes of many of the figures have been carefully scratched out. But the natural carving of the soft rock is more fantastic than fantasy, more eerie than ghost stories.

Cappadocia was lost to the Western world for centuries until the early twentieth century, when Père Guillaume de Jerphanion, a French Jesuit priest, riding on horseback through central Anatolia, happened on "valleys in the searingly brilliant light, running through the most fantastic of all landscapes."

We drove down from Avanos into the steep gully that hid the monasteries of Göreme from an alien world for so long. Göreme, now deserted of people, has been made into the most famous of the outdoor museums of Cappadocia. Even filled, as it was the day we saw it, with tourists from all over the world, there is still the strange atmosphere of secrecy that it depended on when it was a Christian monastic retreat. Most of the churches are hidden behind the camouflage of small windows that make them look from outside as if they were houses or storerooms. They hide, like a vast beehive, up ladders, in caves, through labyrinthine entrances, around the steep walks of Göreme—here a church with tenth-century frescoes, there an earlier one, probably second century. But once within, their wall paintings are vivid. Some of them have columns like theatrical sets, since they are formed within the soft rock and need no such supports.

Some are primitive, some like more sophisticated Byzantine churches. The earlier ones are decorated with the red ochre that has been used in sacred

---

If Fred Flintstone took drugs, he'd probably hallucinate about living in a place like Cappadocia. Its geologically bizarre hills have been the site for some of the most eccentric settlements in human history. Soft, red rock is topped with harder, darker layers, allowing for a process called differential erosion. So what? So...people down the centuries have been able to gouge living spaces from the soft underbelly, while the hard outer shell preserved—and continues to preserve—those same living spaces intact. The Hittites were the first to dig in. Then, from the sixth to the thirteenth centuries, came Christians on the run from marauding Arabs. Speaking of marauding, these days it's the turn of the hordes of backpackers...except, of course, if you break with convention and come in the winter.

—David Cox,
"Cappadocia in January"

places since prehistory, with drawings of animals and saints, hiero-
glyphic signs, secret symbols.

I followed Yusuf up rickety ladders, through tunnels, around the
steep sand-colored paths. In one, we stepped over shallow, empty
graves carved into rock, some small enough for children. In another we found life-size frescoes of the fourth-century Emperor
Constantine and his mother, Saint Helena, holding between them
the True Cross, which she is said to have discovered on a pilgrimage to Jerusalem.

A fresco of a strange hermaphroditic figure with a woman's
body and a man's face is life-size too, an image once sacred to the
Mother Goddess, the most powerful deity in Asia Minor long before the foundation of the coastal Greek cities. She was served by
priests who were *castrati*, and one of her incarnations was as a
bearded figure dressed as a woman. Here, the figure has been
turned by legend into a Christian saint. She was a beautiful
woman, they say, so pursued by men that she prayed for protection
for her chastity, and her prayer was answered with some extremity.
She was given the face of a bearded old man.

The most elaborate church at Göreme is called the Church of
the Buckle, after a carving in the inner dome. Inside, it is a pure
Byzantine church—the carved columns, the story of the Virgin
Mary around the walls, the intimate side chapels. Sunlight streams
in from the barrel entry and turns the underground vault into
gold. Beyond it, deeper within the small, elaborate main body of
the church, concealed lights re-create the illusion of candlelight.
The place commanded such quiet that I forgot that I was under a
high hill, surrounded by tourists. The whole place is a carved and
painted version of a prehistoric sacred cave.

It would take weeks to see all of the churches of Cappadocia. It
is estimated that there are more than 400 of them in the area, and
there are more to be discovered.

For centuries, Göreme was a training ground for priests; tradition
has it that it was visited by Saint Paul, who saw it as a perfect place
for teaching missionaries to go into a still-shamanistic country.

The colors in all of them are rich. Why they have not long since faded is a mystery. But at first an even greater mystery is why these rock formations have provided homes and hiding places since pre-Hittite times. Coming from the east, the pathway of Hittite, Persian, Greek, imperial Roman, and Byzantine Roman, Turkish marauders for so many centuries, you can sense why.

In a wonderfully fertile land, these were sanctuaries for people, their animals, and their goods, out of sight of the great sweeps of armies and of nomads that passed by on the high steppes of central Anatolia, above their hidden valleys.

Many of them have been occupied ever since. Up until about thirty years ago, the village of Zelve was a fully populated, working town. It is carved into the rocks around a natural amphitheater, with two deep ravines opening into it. There is still the rock-carved mosque at the entrance to the Muslim ravine, and churches, hard to reach, in the Christian ravine.

I climbed up into the Christian ravine, and there was a mill with the mill wheel still on its cave floor, and a church with stalagmite columns. There were storerooms, houses, some of them out-of-bounds because they were dangerous.

Christians and Muslims seem to have lived amicably side by side for centuries. With the fine farming around them, the cave mills, the hidden stores, they were self-sufficient people.

But after all the years, the village reached its capacity. The walls between the cave rooms were too thin. There were rock falls. The rooms were becoming overcrowded and dangerous. So the people have been moved to the new village, Yenizelve (New Zelve). We passed them, the women still veiled, riding donkeys to their fields. Now Zelve is deserted, except for the thousands of tourists who come to see a ghostly and silent village of stone.

But for centuries, people lived there and carved homes out of the tufa hills and the volcanic pinnacles. They were so easy to carve that a family simply whittled out another room for each child born. The rock is so soft that it cuts like soap, but it hardens as soon as it is exposed to the air. After centuries of exposure to air and wind and water, the curved surfaces seem to have gone back to being organic shapes.

Nowhere is this more true, and eerier, than in the underground "cities," carved deeper and deeper into the earth, which shows the depth of the volcanic tufa. The largest known one—only rediscovered in 1965—is at Derinkuyu. Eight levels have been opened to visitors. Stone tools and graffiti have been found that prove that it has been in use since pre-Hittite times, at least 5,000 years ago and probably more.

The carving of the low corridors is like a living intestinal organism. I became a troglodyte, head down, following the single file of tourists deeper and deeper into the labyrinthine rooms, past the mills, the churches, the baptisteries, the empty graves. There were round sculpted stones that were used as doors to close off whole sections in case of discovery or attack.

It was cool. The temperature never changes and the air, all the way down the eight levels that have been opened to visitors, is as fresh as the surface. I looked down a deep air well. It seemed bottomless—there are at least twenty more stories, not yet fully explored, below.

When I went, there must have been hundreds of people moving slowly along the dimly lit corridors, following the arrows that pointed the way. Otherwise, it is easy to get lost in a wrong turning, deep underground. What had been protection for the people who made these places through the centuries is a modern nightmare. Sound is muffled. The cave-like "city" demands silence. The silence of wonder and not a little controlled fear.

About three stories down, there was a large central room with five or six exits. We found a French girl, crying. She had lapsed into blind claustrophobic panic, and she was frozen against the wall, afraid to move. Yusuf offered to take her back to the surface, after making me promise, which he didn't need to do, that I would not move until he came back. In one of those lacunae of emptiness that can happen, even when there are so many people, I found myself completely alone there. I could feel the panic rise like a temperature, but curiosity outweighed fear, and when he came back I went on with him, down to the pit bottom, where the corridors were little more than waist-high and the rooms dead.

To go from life underground to the town of Ürgüp, as old and as new as all the rest, is to witness the birth of cities, from cave to mansion, still going on today. When I walked along a street of Ürgüp, I could hear truck engines revving in a garage inside the mountain. When I went to one of the small hotels, the rooms at the back were carved out of the high hill behind it. The exterior stone trim on the doors, the balconies, the dentils of houses in Ürgüp reflect a history of kingdoms. There are beautiful Seljuk-Turkish facades, Greek columns, a half-fallen Roman temple façade to a tomb, an Ottoman-Turkish gateway, all sculpted of honey-colored stone that gleams in the sun.

Ürgüp is a green city, a city of flowers. I sat in the section of the park reserved for women and families and had tea, surrounded by a garden and huge funeral urns, like the urns Ali Baba hid in, that had been found underground. I could glimpse, as I passed, the flower-decked columned courtyard of a restaurant that was once a *medrese*, or perhaps a palace, for this has been a kingdom, lost for centuries to the outside world.

But the people who have lived there since their ancestors, and in some cases their own parents, came out of the caves, go on, un-aware of being lost and found and lost again, from the time of the Hittites or Xenophon or the Byzantines or the Turkish tribes. They have made the best wine in Turkey in the mineral-laden vol-canic soil, raised fruits and vegetables, and hidden their beasts and their food and their families down below the ground when they had to.

There is level after level, ancient and modern, of Cappadocia, from the underground cities to the latest tourist hotel perched above a honey-combed hill, to the fortress of Uçhisar. The fortress is one of the highest points in Cappadocia. It is carved out of a great pinnacle of tufa, corridor after corridor, room above room.

We climbed outside steps in the wind, going up and up until we came to shallow graves at the pinnacle, hollowed out of the rock like the graves at Göreme.

It is a natural skyscraper above the surrounding country. We looked, as Hittite, Greek, Roman, Seljuk, Ottoman soldiers on watch had done, over the tangled, deceptively desolate valleys, their towers and castles and statues and chimneys formed not by men but by time and water. We could see all the way to the horizon of tableland above them, and to the mountain, Erciyas Dagi, that began it all with its ancient eruption, said to be one of the greatest ever on earth.

Mary Lee Settle also contributed "Above the Ruins of Ephesus" in Part One. This story was excerpted from her book, Turkish Reflections: A Biography of a Place.

PART THREE

GOING YOUR OWN WAY

BRUCE S. FEILER

Looking for Noah

Is the ark still there, nestled in
the snows of Mount Ararat?

THE CALL TO PRAYER SOUNDED JUST AFTER THREE O'CLOCK
P.M. It came from a minaret, echoed off the storefronts, and stopped
me, briefly, in the middle of the street. All around, people halted
their hurrying and turned their attention, momentarily, to God. A
few old men pulled cloaks around their shoulders and slipped into
the back of a shop. Two boys rushed across the road and disappeared behind a stone wall. A woman picked up her basket of
radishes and tiptoed out of sight. Part of me felt odd to be starting
a journey into the roots of the Bible in a place so spiritually removed from my own. But continuing toward the center of town,
I realized my unease might be a reminder of a truth tucked away
in the early verses of Genesis: Abraham was not originally the man
he became. He was not an Israelite, he was not a Jew. He was not
even a believer in God—at least initially. He was a traveler, called
by some voice not entirely clear that said: Go, head to this land,
walk along this route, and trust what you will find.

Within minutes, the afternoon prayers were complete and people returned to the streets. Dogubeyazit, in extreme eastern Turkey,
was thuddingly bleak, with two asphalt roads intersecting in a neglected town of 30,000. Just outside of town, hundreds of empty

oil tankers were parked in a double-file line waiting to cross the border into Iran. The trucks, the town, as well as most of the surrounding countryside, were completely overshadowed by a looming triangular peak with a pristine cap of snow.

Mount Ararat is a perfect volcanic pyramid 16,984 feet high, with a junior volcano, Little Ararat, attached to its hip. The highest peak in the Middle East (and the second highest in Europe), Big Ararat is holy to everyone around it. The Turks call it Agri Dagi, the Mountain of Pain. The Kurds call it the Mountain of Fire. Armenians also worship the mountain, which was in their homeland until a brutal war in 1915. I later met an Armenian in Jerusalem who took me into his home, where he had at least 150 representations of the mountain, including rugs, cups, coats of arms, bottles of cognac, and stained-glass windows. Mount Ararat is the first thing he thinks of every morning, he said, and the first thing his children drew when they were young.

I had come for a different reason. Genesis, chapter 8, says that Noah's ark, after seven months on the floodwaters, came to rest on "the mountains of Ararat." Mount Ararat is the first place mentioned in the Bible that can be located with any degree of certainty, and it seemed like a fitting place to begin my effort to reacquaint myself with the biblical stories by retracing the first five books through the desert. The topography of this part of Turkey, which includes the headwaters of the Tigris and Euphrates, permeates the early chapters of Genesis. Chaos, Creation, Eden, and Eve are all drawn from the fertile union of Mesopotamia, "the land between the rivers" and the birthplace of the Bible.

In recent years, however, this region has been one of the most volatile—and bloody—in the Middle East. Over 40,000 people have died in a largely overlooked war in which indigenous Kurds have tried to gain autonomy from Iraq, Syria, and Turkey. In every travel book I read about the region the author was at least briefly detained. The *Rough Guide* I brought actually superimposed a blank area over the region, saying it was too unsafe for its correspondent. "In our opinion, travel is emphatically not recommended." In some cases, it said, security forces respond to the rebellion by "placing local towns under formal curfew or even shooting up the main streets at random."

Though Dogubeyazit was calm today, the underlying tension was still apparent. Approaching the center of town, I had barely made it past a string of cheap jewelry stores when a man approached me, eagerly.

"Hello," he said, in English. We shook hands. "You just drove into town in that brown car, didn't you? You're staying in the hotel, in room 104."

The secret police are working overtime, I thought.

"What are you doing here?" he asked.

"Um, I'm here to find out about Noah's ark," I said.

"Noah's ark!" he repeated. "Well, if you want to learn about the ark you have to go to the green building at the end of this street. Go inside and up the stairs until you get to a dark room. Inside there's another set of stairs. Go up those and you'll find another dark room. In there you'll find the man who knows everything about Noah's ark."

At first I thought he was joking, or laying a trap. I thanked him and continued strolling. I had heard enough horror stories—and seen enough tanks on the road into town—to ignore directions like these. I walked around for a few minutes, bought some plums in the market, and was heading back to the hotel when I stopped myself: Why exactly had I come here anyway?

Inside the green building I found the sagging staircase and proceeded to the second floor. The room was dark and smelled of discarded cigarettes. I hesitated for a minute, took a step forward, then reconsidered. I was just turning back when I heard a noise from above, then steps. Seconds later a figure appeared. It was a man in his early forties, lean, with black hair and an enormous bushy mustache that cascaded over his lips. His eyes were concealed by the gloom. He appraised me for a second, before saying, in perfect Oxonian English, "May I help you?"

"I was told you know about Noah's ark," I said.

He considered my answer. "But you were supposed to go up the second set of stairs."

I agreed.

"Maybe you don't really want to know."

He retreated as quietly as he had appeared and left me standing in the dark. This time I didn't hesitate.

Upstairs, the man was just settling onto a low chair covered with carpets. He gestured for me to sit next to him. Between us was a table covered with books and a handful of photographs. He poured me a glass of tea and we exchanged niceties. He was a native of Dogubeyazit, a Kurd. Ten years ago he had served time in prison for his role as an insurgent. He refused to talk about the war and when I asked his name, he gestured toward his mustache: "Everyone calls me Parachute." He was wearing a blue and white horizontal-striped t-shirt that, along with his dark hair, made him look like a Venetian gondolier. After a while I asked if it was possible to climb the mountain.

"It is forbidden," he said. "Since 1991, nobody has been to the top."

"Is there anything to see?"

"If you believe something, you can see. If you don't believe, you cannot see."

"What do you believe?"

"We believe. When we are children, we hear things. They tell us that this is Noah's countryside. Even today, when something happens, the people say that it's the luck of Noah."

"Do you have the luck of Noah?" I asked.

"We know that something is there. We find something there."

"I'm confused. You're saying that you know something that everybody else does not know?"

"Yes." His eyes were big, with deep bags under them. He didn't move at all when he spoke. "I know it's there. I find something there."

"What is it that you found?"

"Ah."

"You won't tell me."

"Hmm."

"When will we hear?"

"One day you'll hear."

"And you'll be famous around the world?"

He crossed his arms in front of his chest in a sly-satisfied way.

As Parachute well knew, almost since the Bible first appeared, stories of sightings of Noah's ark have been a staple of Near Eastern lore, making it, in effect, the world's first UFO. Josephus, the first-century historian, wrote of legends that the ark landed "on a mountain in Armenia." In A.D 678, Saint Jacob, after asking God to show him the ark, fell asleep on the mountain and awoke to find a piece of wood in his arms. By the nineteenth century the sightings grew more elaborate. In 1887, two Persian princes wrote that they saw the ark while on top of the mountain, which is covered in snow year-round. "The bow and stern were clearly in view, but the center was buried in snow. The wood was peculiar, dark reddish in color, almost ironcolored in fact, and seemed very thick. I am very positive that we saw the real ark, though it is over 4,000 years old."

Base camp was dug in atop a scraped knuckle of ground; above us, Ararat remained the same, monolithic and undiminished. Dinner was set and the field cook stuffed us with a variety of tasteless carbohydrates. I had a beer and was instantly drunk. I lit a cigarette—my sixth of the day, compared with my usual fifty—and was simultaneously stoned. Ahmet and I sat leg against leg and chatted like two retarded brothers. The sun set and took the world with it. Out in the dusty central plaza of our bivouac, the staff smashed up packing crates and built a modest campfire. The Europeans meditated upon the lambent flames for a minute then burst into beer hall songs. The clock eased back several eons, and the darkness muted our many voices, made every gesture meaningful, and offered us the illusion that we were a tried and tested community, which felt nice, as illusions often do.

—Bob Shacochis, "Bob Versus the Volcano," *Outside*

In 1916, two Russian pilots claimed they saw the ark from the air, and the following year Czar Nicholas II sent two expeditions with over 150 personnel to photograph it. Because of the Bolshevik Revolution, the photographs never reached him, though his daughter Anastasia is said to have worn a cross made of ark wood. Most photographs of the ark have similarly disappeared, including dozens allegedly taken by pilots during World War II and most taken by the CIA using U-2 spy planes in the 1950s. Even Air Force One is said to have spied the ark. During a flight to Tehran on December 31, 1977, while Jimmy Carter was traveling to a New Year's party given by the shah, passengers onboard claimed they saw "a large dark boat." Said UPI photographer Ronald Bennett, who was on the plane: "It's my opinion that the president probably had Air Force One routed over Mt. Ararat and most likely saw the ark too."

Since that time, technology has only heightened interest. Dozens of books have explored the subject, and more than fifty websites track the ongoing chase. In 1988, a stockbroker from San Diego flew a helicopter along the east slope taking photographs. The following year a pilot from Chicago aired footage of an "ark-like object" on CNN. Charles Willis, who was once Charles Manson's psychiatrist, ran four expeditions, and astronaut James Irwin, who once took a Turkish flag to the moon in an attempt to butter up the Ankara government, made five. None have found the prize. As my companion and guide, the Israeli archaeologist Avner Goren, had warned, "Archaeologists won't even take into consideration that there are any remains. This story, like Creation, is crystallized from many traditions." But that won't stop the pursuit. When I asked Avner if any of the recent expeditions interested him, he said, "As a scientist, no. But as an adventurer, yes."

Which is exactly what Parachute was banking on. With prodding he explained that during a trip up the north side of the mountain in 1990, with a colleague from England, he found a piece of black wood one hundred feet long. It was located at 12,000 feet.

"But it could be a hundred years old," I said.

"We tested it."

"And how old is it?"

"When we find out everything, you'll know."

"But why wait? How much money would it take for you to bring me to it?"

He thought for a moment. "It's not the money. It belongs to us. We found the ark. If you gave me a million dollars I won't bring you to it. If you wanted the pictures I wouldn't give them to you."

"You have pictures?"

"Yes."

At this point I decided to go back to the hotel and get Avner, who had been napping. Avner had been to the top of the mountain in 1982 on a climbing expedition (no ark sightings, but lots of pure, clean snow). For the rest of the afternoon the three of us sat in Parachute's den. I asked Parachute what explained the ark's appeal.

"The ark is not so interesting to people," he said, "but Noah has meaning, like Mohammed or Jesus."

"If we can prove that any of these stories happened, then people will believe in God."

"What about you?" I asked. "What did you think when you found it?"

"I was happy. I was walking along—it was a particularly warm year—when suddenly I fell into this cavern covered by snow and ice. And there it was."

"I would like to believe your story," I said. "But I find it impossible to believe that in 4,000 years you're the first person to go into this hole."

"Around here there are only five guides licensed to go up the mountain," Parachute said. "Two are in jail, one is ill, one won't go. That leaves me."

"Will you show me the pictures?"

He refused.

"What if I tell you that you're being selfish, that there are several billion people in the world who would like to know if Noah's ark exists?"

He didn't react.

"What if I tell you that you could be the savior of the Kurdish people by bringing millions of tourists to this area?"

He didn't move.

"What if I tell you that my mother is dying"—a lie—"and that she could die in peace if she knew that Noah was real?"

Nothing.

I was stunned. "Not even for my mother!?" I said. "Do you understand what you have here? More people believe in this book, more people have died because of this book, more people are influenced by this book.... You could change the world!"

Parachute was silent for a moment and unfolded his arms for the first time in hours. "You can tell your mother that she can be happy, that in the world there is one person who has seen Noah's ark. The Bible is true."

"So if she sees your ark, will she believe in God?"

"She'll have to," he said. "And you will, too. God is real. I have seen the proof."

Bruce S. Feiler has written for The New Yorker, The New York Times Magazine, *and* Condé Nast Traveler, *and contributed to NPR's "All Things Considered." His books include* Learning to Bow, Dreaming Out Loud, *and* Walking the Bible, *from which this story was excerpted.*

IRENE-MARIE SPENCER

A Wedding in Ekinlik

This small island town marches
to a slow and sedate rhythm.

I AM SITTING IN THE CAFÉ NEAR THE FISHING BOATS, LISTENING to the fisherman with their raspy voices, to the chanting of prayers, to the wooden carts against the earth, to the high-pitched whining of the ship's engine and the churning water. I feel dizzy and radiant at the same time. I gather up my sacks of vegetables, cheese, yogurt, and supplies from the market to go find Ombashi's fishing boat for the twenty-minute crossing to the tiny island of Ekinlik. The crowd from the big ship from Istanbul, which comes every afternoon at 2:00, has finally cleared out, the machine gun guards are now gone, the Turkish street music gone, now only the lapping sea and the dark-skinned boys diving for pennies off the pier.

It is easy to spot the fishermen with their self-assured expressions and weathered faces, standing protectively near their boats on the wooden dock. Ombashi is expecting me. His bright fishing boat is painted turquoise, yellow, and red. His face betrays no emotion of any kind; but I know there is a half-smile there, camouflaged by his prominent features. Ombashi has the face of an eagle. Straddling the boat and the quay, he holds out his hand to me, taking my bag. His every movement has a purpose. I find a spot on the small bow deck. I circle it, like a cat, then sit, gathering up my arms and legs. It is warm out, a day that glistens. I feel drops of sweat in my armpits, dripping down the insides of my blouse. I stretch my legs out and arrange my faded skirt around them, then rub my feet together. The aromas around me make my head spin: the freshness of the sea air laced with wafts of heavy Turkish tobacco, grilled corn, rotting fish, the powerful body odor of these working men, and salt, the salt in the air and the skin. Blinding spots of light reflecting from the swaying dance of clear aquamarine water make me squint.

Ombashi loads on several other people, villagers returning to Ekinlik with their bags of fresh fruit and vegetables, blue propane gas tanks, and plastic water jugs. A villager unties the rope from the dock, and pushes off with one leg. We motor slowly around the huge cement pier, where the ferry from Istanbul still looms above us, casting a behemoth shadow across the water, and then head straight out for the small island about a mile across the water. Ombashi sits perched at the stern, a large angular seabird, motionless except for his arm slightly moving to steer. His sharp blue eyes dart almost imperceptibly over every roll and pitch of the Marmara Sea. I look at him and smile. He doesn't acknowledge me openly, even though I know he sees me. He looks straight ahead, to Ekinlik, but he seems to smile through the straight, immobile line of his lips. He is one who doesn't say much. But what he does say seems to matter. People listen, perking up when he speaks.

The vibration from the boat's motor enters through my heels, buzzes through my body, and reaches full pitch somewhere in the canals of my inner ears. Looking down at the churning water which turns black as we pass under the shadow of a cloud, I see exploding fireworks in the points of light shooting out from the boat's prow. I feel myself shrink, dwarfed by the vibration of the motor and the chant of the cutting water. I am feeling jubilant, and plunge my legs into the glowing Marmara Sea. The sun is warm on my arms, and I breathe in deeply. I feel myself fade away, and I melt into a place that is much, much larger than just me. This is a place full of spells and magic. I've seen blue charm beads everywhere, little beads that look like glass eyes. They ward off the evil eye. I wear them as earrings. You can buy them for pennies in the marketplace, and you see them around the necks of women, on the key chains of the men, hanging from the rearview mirrors of buses, boats, and cars. I think of the Blue Mosque, a giant blue charm, as blue as this sea.

Ombashi lands the boat at the village quay. Landing at the village is like stepping into a fairy tale, with its whitewashed, eighteenth-century stone houses, its single café with red and blue painted tables and chairs, and its small mosque with a pointed minaret off to one side. This island is from another century. As we land, there are a couple of fishermen sitting in the café. They sit and make nets, and the women sit on the porch, their faces solemn yet blissful. I can't remember any of their names, but they all remember mine. They have names which are more like descriptions: *Black Leg, Old Sailor, White One, Moonlight*. I feel embarrassed, shaking hands and embracing these warm and smiling people who call me by name. *Irena*, they call me.

The houses of the village are stone or whitewashed cement, with paisley or faded lavender curtains hanging across the doorways. The wooden beams framing the village houses are severely weather-beaten, full of gouges and splinters, and they keep their windows open, with little pots of globe oregano sitting on the sills or the front step. The women clean the thresholds to their homes daily, sweeping and scrubbing on hands and knees with soap and water, their hair tied back in scarves, and faded print shirt-sleeves rolled up to the elbows. The women smile and wave as I passed. I began to lose any desire to ever leave this island. With no cars, there is no smog, no revving engines, no car alarms going off in the middle of the night.

On Ekinlik, sounds take on a piercing and sharp quality. I can hear better, or maybe it's that I can hear at all for the first time in my life. The sounds of the insects buzzing and chirping, crickets and cicadas, even the flies that land on my arms as I walk from the village to Gülbin's house, seem enormously loud in my ears. The wind, as it heaves and pelts dust against her stone house; the black cow and its calf mooing; the chickens all around the village; the distant motoring of a fishing boat...these are the sounds of this life.

Every afternoon there is a tremendous blast from the steamship docking at Avsa. And then the sound of water, all around, a light lapping of flat waves against small beaches, always in the background. It is the prayer, the *ezan*, being sung from the single minaret of the small mosque of Ekinlik, though, which pulls me inside of this place. This is a sound which makes goose bumps rise along the back of my neck, which sends a flood of warmth washing over me, inside and out.

Gülbin is waiting for me to arrive from Avsa with the groceries. She is in the process of tying a bright scarf around her jet-black jaw-length hair as I enter the house. The glass doors which span the entire length of the front room are pushed all the way open to let in the breeze and a view of the sea, which is just down at the foot of the stone stairs. She tells me excitedly as soon as I walk in that there will be a wedding in the village tomorrow, and tonight will be the bride's special ceremony. She says it is something that cannot be missed.

We take a long time getting dressed for this special occasion, yet I have no idea what it will be like. Finally we are ready to walk to the village, at twilight. As the sun disappears behind us, to the other side of the island, we walk in the violet stillness to the beat of the evening crickets, and notice the first stars pricking through the arching cloudless sphere above us. The west wind gusts and fusses with its small hands, caresses my bare calves, and bends the enormous brim of Gülbin's hat into a near perfect ellipse.

All of the women and girls of the village are gathered in the café on the quay, in the darkness. A kind of feminine hush and smallness precedes the ancient ritual. The women gather together and begin to sing a haunting and wistful chorus. I cannot understand the words, but the meanings scrape at my bones, piercing my heart with sharp little pins. Gülbin motions to me to merge in with the women, to take part in the ceremony. We all stand touching, connected, weaving into one tapestry the voices of many unique and strangely beautiful women. They light candles, and together, the women move as a unit, an airy, wispy, floating cloud of tender hearts and open hands, we move, gliding, towards the street of the village, towards the house of the bride.

A young girl, no more than eighteen, emerges from the stone house. She is dressed in white gauze from head to toe, and a long veil is draped over her face and head like the shroud of a corpse. The women circle around her, touching and holding her, their voices melding, drawing her on diaphanous threads towards the open sky. They lead her to the café, and begin to chant and dance in circles, their song rising in pitch, their hands opening and closing like emergent, wet butterflies. The women take out pots of henna and paintbrushes, and paint round red circles on their palms. Everyone is painted, myself as well. We all surround the bride, painting her palms and soles of her feet with henna, dancing, singing, and swaying. Then we lift her up above us, in one white

Göle sees a "fundamental asymmetry" between Western and Muslim social organization: "Private spheres do not fit the same conception. 'Private sphere' in the West means 'privacy,' as far as I know, whereas in the Muslim conception the private sphere, *mahrem*, means women's world, women's place. It is sacred. It is the forbidden—forbidden to foreign men. It is basically related with the sexuality of women. It is *not* individualism. I think the basic organization of Muslim society depends on this limitation of women to the foreign man. That's why we speak of segregation of sexes. Women's veiling defines what is interior and what is exterior."

—Scott L. Malcomson,
Borderlands: Nation and Empire

flowing fountain, our movements becoming liquid, the voices separating into questions and replies. Gülbin, the village women, and I carry the young, painted bride back to her home, softly lifting her back through the door into the arms of her weeping mother. All of the women then begin to sway and sing, the tears gently making rivulets down their full, transparent cheeks. The door closes, the women stand outside in the dark, some with candles, and sing softly until the moment of separation makes itself felt in unison, wedges softly in our hearts beneath the veils.

When the women reach the dark café near the sea again, they embrace each other, quietly, sadly. Gülbin and I, united by the strong emotion and magic of the ancient ceremony, embrace the village women, and embrace each other. No words seem appropriate. Together, we walk in silence down the dark path, illuminated only by the full, effervescent moon. Together, closing our palms around the red, pulsating circles, we hear the crickets. We reach the house, still wordless, kiss, and go into our separate beds, ready to drift on the memory of the songs, to enter the magic of the red circles, in spiritual preparation for the wedding the following day.

Nothing, not even the mysteries of last night, has prepared me for the wedding day. It is a day that billows with light, a faded white day background against which the intensities of color are blinding. It is early afternoon, and all of the people of the village are gathered near the waterfront. Two of the double-decked fishing boats are decorated with tree branches and giant red bows, to transport the entire population of Ekinlik over to Avsa for the feast and celebration. The music has already started up, the musicians show gold teeth in their broad smiles. The plucked strings of the *saz* vibrate wildly, with a frenzy that jars my thoughts. The village women, dressed in their best flowered skirts and scarves, nod and flow together with a secret knowing. I open my palm. The red circle of henna is still there. It pulses with the promise of eternity in a primitive way. The circle is bloodlike and has something to do with consummation. Gülbin told me that the reason for the painted circles has to do with dreaming, or good luck, but I cannot really pinpoint it. I understand, not needing an explanation.

The men are already dancing. They dance with each other, with a foreboding abandon. The dancing men, the knowing women, move as a large family towards the pier. The boats are ready. The villagers crowd onto them, spilling out over the rails. The weight of all of us rocks the boats violently, and I am terrified that we will capsize. I imagine the entire village swimming and drowning in the sea, a mile from the shore. But the musicians, continuing to play, wedge themselves into the heaving crowd, somehow masking the effect. Gülbin and I squeeze ourselves between the circle of women, and I feel the cool, moist pressure of enormous breasts and ample bodies completely surrounding us. The women shift their bodies as a unit, moving to the music and the careening dance of the boat in the swells. I look up at the sky. It is a vibrant blue, cloudless.

The wedding is to take place in an enclosed waterfront café covered by a huge tent. A few mangy cats prowl around the edges of the outer tables. The light inside is a gaudy, fluorescent green, casting an unearthly, morbid glow on the faces of the wedding guests. Pink and blue crepe paper streamers sag from the corners of the tent, held together in the center above a huge rotating mirrored ball. Specks of light dart and swirl, and make a crazy, streaking grid on the greenish-cast canvas walls of the wedding pavilion. The street musicians are gone. Now, in the tent, there is a professional band with an electric piano, electrified instruments, and an echo chamber which gives the sequined vocalist a carnivalesque, spooky sound. A shriveled, starving dog has sneaked into the tent, and I turn just in time to see one of the village men send the bony animal flying back outside with a powerful kick.

Gülbin and I order beers. There are small bowls of sunflower seeds and peanuts on the tables. I search the expanse of people and tables with my eyes, until I locate Hakki, a very attractive young man from the village who has been visiting us at Gülbin's house. He sits at a table with some other villagers, drinking a beer and looking directly at me. Embarrassed, I turn away.

The wedding could be taking place in Las Vegas. The ceremony is very short and mundane. The bride has a tawdry look, a village girl wearing too much makeup. The bride and groom stand before a long folding table, and exchange gold rings. Nothing seems very exotic about this Turkish wedding. The greenish atmosphere gives

the whole thing a garish, cheapened unreality. The highlight of
the wedding is the money dance. The whirling, laughing couple
seems to come alive, both of them pinned from head to toe with
multicolored bills of Turkish lira. There is a traditional white wedding cake, a champagne toast, rice. This couple had apparently decided on a Western, American style wedding, something they had
admired while watching the much-anticipated, weekly broadcast
of American sitcoms on the TV perched above the village café.
After dancing to the hollow-sounding wedding music for what
seems like hours, they pack the boats and head back across the
water to Ekinlik.

I am relieved to get back. The sacredness I had experienced the
night before has been lost on Avsa, in the vulgarity of the greenish tent wedding. But back on Ekinlik, the village musicians begin
to play. The café, open and full of air and light, woos me back into
the mood. And Hakki is there, watching me at a much closer distance. The men dance together, with a visceral, sexual intensity. I
wait to see Hakki dance. When he finally does, I feel my stomach
knotting and my head lightening as I watch him move, his arms
tightly outstretched with fingers snapping, his hips undulating. I
feel small points of sweat appear in half-moons under my eyes.
Then the women dance, and I dance for Hakki. I dance, feeling the
physical force of eyes following my every swerve. I move my hips
in a circle, snaking my arms in the Turkish style. I dance with
Gülbin, and with other girls of the village. The long afternoon
light deepens, golden, reflecting gilt edges around the wooden
tables and chairs pushed to the sides of the café. Slowly, even the
gold fades into the shadows between the swells on the darkening
sea. When I stop dancing, I retreat to the edge of the quay to
breathe in the warm, black air.

When the village stops dancing, they divide down the middle,
the young men facing the young women. They start to sing a sad
and haunting ballad, the girls asking unknown questions with the
lightness of their voices, the men responding with their gentle an-

swers. I am transfixed by the profound silence surrounding the song; the voices seem to emerge from a hidden dimension. One young girl's voice seems to take on a physical form as it hangs suspended in the chasm between the village men and women; its beauty is something I can feel with the palms of my outstretched hands.

To the beat of a single drum, the group moves together to the groom's house, where the couple will spend their wedding night. The wedding couple, delivered to their bed with the song of the village, enter the stone house. To the closed wooden door and the candle in the window, the village sings outside the house. To the young bride and the honorable groom, the village sings of the heart. As the wings of the angel fold, the dark hovering form begins to move towards the sea. We walk, me with my arms out-stretched linking shoulders with village girls, as we sing, still softly. When we reach the sea, we continue to sing for a long time.

Irene-Marie Spencer writes, paints, and climbs volcanoes in her spare time. The rest of her time is taken up with her four spirited daughters, a husband, two dogs, a cat, five rabbits, two guinea pigs, and two budgies. She hails from Wisconsin, but now lives with her family in New Zealand. This story is an excerpt from a longer body of work entitled Tales of the Moon and Water, *a nonfiction account of her experiences living in a small fishing village on the island of Ekinlik in the Marmara Sea.*

TIM WARD

Encounter with the Goddess

She wears many guises,
all of them compelling.

TEN THOUSAND YEARS AGO, WHEN GRASSES HAD BEEN NEWLY
tamed into wheat and barley, wild game into goats and cattle, people clustered together on the edge of the great Anatolian Plain and
began to build houses. Between 6,500 and 5,500 B.C., 7,000 or
more lived here all at once, a massing of humankind so astounding
that the world would not see its like again until the city states of
Mesopotamia, 3,000 years later. It was the crucible of our civilization, and in its many shrines one finds the symbols that dominated
Western religion throughout the ages, and still echo for us today:
Çatal Hüyük, the first city, home of our ancestors.

There's nothing here today except the hill created by a thousand years of houses built upon houses, the only hump on the
unbroken plain. Teresa (my fiancée) and I climbed to the top, wild
grasses swishing at our knees, and looked at the trenches of the first
excavations, made barely thirty years earlier. The finds are now in
Ankara, some on display at the museum, a vivid window into the
past. You might think they would have been a simple people,
occupied with their animals, plants, basket weaving, still hunting
game on the grasslands, maybe carving rudimentary totems. Take
one look at the reconstructed shrine room in Ankara, and you see

how wrong such a picture would be, see how fruitless it is to interpret the past by drawing a line back and down from the present.

Against the smooth plaster wall of the shrine, three bull skulls line up, floor to ceiling. The heads are covered with clay, leaving the wide horns sweeping out in triplicate. Above them, sculpted into the wall, a splay-legged woman dominates the room, as if giving birth to the bulls. She looks part frog, part human. More bull skulls jut up from the floor on columns. The shrine walls were often covered with frescoes. Some are clearly scenes of a hunt: a massive aurochs bull, a stag, a boar surrounded by tiny black men holding spears, figures that seem to dance and float around their prey, perhaps even leaping over it, prefiguring the bull frescoes of Crete. Other scenes depict the great black wings of griffin vultures, flapping around headless bodies of the dead.

It's clear that the people practiced excarnation—the removal of flesh from the bones of the dead. Vultures and other carrion eaters served this ritual purpose quite well. More than three hundred skeletons have been taken from beneath the floors of the houses, where the picked-clean remains were buried, perhaps to keep them close to home. One portion of a fresco shows tall wooden towers, each with a stairway to the platform at the top. There, feeding vultures tear either at a headless corpse, or on another tower, a head without a body. The head, it seems, served as some special offering, for human skulls were found on the floors of the shrine rooms in company with the bulls. A third fresco shows a strange pattern: double rows of vultures facing each other, their bent wingtips touching each other's to form a diamond shape; and in each diamond, the body of a woman; and within each woman's belly, the dark outline of a child. I imagine a Çatal Hüyük mother and child, watching the vultures tending to their gruesome task. She explains it something like this:

"You see, the vulture eats the bodies, then she puts the life back inside the mother, where it can grow again."

Maybe this is how we inherited the story of the stork?

In a Çatal Hüyük grain bin, British archaeologist James Mellaart found an eight-inch statue of a woman seated on a chair—a throne perhaps, because the sides are two standing leopards on which she rests her arms. He labeled her the Great Goddess, and it's easy to agree. She looks old, with folds across her massive belly, folds on her knees, her breasts sagging down across her sides, buttocks bulging out from the back of her seat. The lines seem so vivid, she seems sculpted from real life, not some abstract notion of divinity. The head was broken off at the neck, and has been restored in the museum in the bland mold of another statue, so one has to imagine her without this false face. She is solid, imposing, more queen than mother of fertility and the fields, a thousand years older than her corpulent sisters in Malta.

Some observers call the roundish lump between her legs the head of a newborn child, but I don't think so. I don't think the throne's a birthing chair as they claim. There's not a single mark on the lump to identify it as a baby. And it lies between her ankles, on the floor. Unlikely that in real life it would have dropped like that. She seems to be sitting back, not squatting. Reclining, not giving birth. Given that the rest of her is rendered so true to life, I think the thing between her legs may be an offering instead: a lump of meat, a loaf of bread, perhaps a human head, like the skulls placed on the shrine room floors.

Clay figurines of women were abundant at the site, interpreted variously as household totems, fertility objects, protective divinities, or maybe even dolls. Male figures are quite scarce, but the one that caught my eye in the museum is a reclining female statue with the legs and torso of a smaller male entwined around her. From one angle, it seems to embrace her like a lover, from another, it's a resting child. Lover, son, or both? Perhaps a picture of life before Oedipus.

The aspect the shrine's interpreters find most sinister, most disturbing, are the molded shapes upon the walls, shapes identical in form to a woman's breast. Some have red-brushed, natural-looking nipples. But others contain the skull of a vulture with the beak protruding in the place of a nipple. Or the jaws of a jackal, the tusks of a boar. Writes Michael Rice in *The Power of the Bull:* "Thus the mother's breasts do not deliver life-sustaining milk but are rather the agents of death, symbolized by the animals who are her attendants. It is difficult to resist the idea that the vultures' skulls, peering out of the goddess's breasts, suggest a profound degree of psychological disturbance experienced by the priests (if priests they were)." Rice adds that it may not be coincidence that in ancient Egypt, the word *mwt* means both mother and vulture, and that the hieroglyph for mother contains a vulture's iconic shape.

To other interpreters, such as archaeologist Marija Gimbutas, the vulture is a symbol of regeneration. The vulture, jackal, and boar are all carrion eaters, and may have been special agents for transforming the dead. The symbolic beak-in-breast may represent the "eating back" of living things into the belly of the goddess to be born again. On the back of one of the vultures feasting on the towers, a double ax is clearly etched, the same symbol of regeneration the Minoans used 4,000 years later. One thing is clear: these people experienced death and transformation not in the abstract, as we do, but viscerally—as viscera, exposed and eaten.

Here is a people who still decorate their walls with murals, reminiscent of those which their ancestors painted in caves. Yet in other respects their way of life has rapidly attained an astonishing degree of cultural sophistication. Perhaps their precocious development in the end proved also to have been premature; for in our present view of prehistory, it appears to have had no immediate sequel. After the abandonment of the settlement at Çatal Hüyük, Neolithic culture relapses into temporary stagnation.

—Seton Lloyd, *Ancient Turkey*

What would it be like to enter into this world? I imagine going down the ladder into that twilight shrine, the great horns curving up around, the black wings drawn across the wall. I find that molded breast, take it in both hands, and put the vulture-nipple to my lips. As I suck, I feel the beak grasping at my tongue, the flesh of my cheeks, and as it gushes white into me, feel my red, flowing

back into it. The soft breast with the bird embedded, chewing me
as I suckle it, terror and need entwined. No way can I escape the
longing I have for the breast. Though it wounds me, I go to it as
a child. It is eternal. I rise and fall. Her nature, cannibal mother.

Teresa wondered if they ate the leopard, ate the vulture and the
jackal—wouldn't that be a religious feast, to eat the beasts that eat
the dead, to bring them back not just into the earth, but into the
community, into the family directly, once again? Perhaps the vul-
ture-mother represents the highest spiritual practice: eating one's
own. Mother Earth gives us birth, and yet from the moment of
that birth, hungers for us to return to her again. Giver of life, taker
of life. To be a woman is to understand this, I suppose. To be a man
is to be the expendable part of this cycle. Woman the vulture. Man
the bull. We are children for her womb, flesh for her lips so she can
reproduce once again. She the power. We the meat.

What is sinister about this, this perfect understanding of the
game? If the male has his hunting and aggression, does the female
not have her hunger? In the animal world (as if we inhabited another), her ferocity as a mother is far worse than any male's lust or
quest for territory. And to feed the life she brings, she is ruthless in
her killing. How I envy those of Çatal Hüyük, not to have the centuries of taboos and intelligence of modern "man" weighing heavy
upon them. They could face the most terrifying aspects of their
human nature, sculpt them, draw them exact upon their walls.
Does our fear of being food derive from coming to see ourselves
as unique and irreplaceable, of owning a soul? What have we lost
in this exchange? I think of Christ's Last Supper, the ritual sacrifice of his body and blood, and of the sacrifices of all the god-kings
before him. The ritual necessity of becoming food, food for the
people, meat with honor. A necessity before mother, the Great
Feeder, in both senses of the words.

Man, poor man, is clearly not the Feeder. Even if he eats the ritual body, he cannot convert the flesh back into life. He is a drone,
a dead stump. No life flows from his body. When I try to put on
the eyes of the men from Çatal Hüyük, I can't escape my secondary role. It may be a glorious one to celebrate in frescoes, hunt-

ing the bull, the stag. But the fact remains of being a stump, not a tree bearing fruit.

The only way to survive is with religion, by identifying myself with the bull, the grain, the vine, the symbolic return. And this may be the real birth of our religion. A woman needs no such symbol. She reproduces herself. The need for mystery begins with man wanting to be more than a stump, more than a skull wrapped in clay, a pair of venerated horns. Imagine this: a culture which says immortality for the male is linked to a sacrificial death. The others die and return to dust, but the consort who follows the path of the bull, he takes rebirth from her womb. He, mysteriously, lives. This is something entirely new, something ludicrous and poetic.

This is what I feel most strongly in the face of Teresa's urge to consume me, that I can die, as I do in sex, and be reborn, so that when she clutches at me, all pretense, all fear flees, gets burned away, scalded, and I hang, empty in space. No thought, no feeling, just the rawness of the void coursing through me. And with it, the desire for her in my arms, the ache for her in my arms. How I want this cruel mother, this wild thing. With my rational mind, I know this is not possible, this identification of the human self with infinite space, nor the sense I get that this emptiness is alive and humming. It's here that I begin to feel like Dionysus, torn apart, food for the Feeder, yet indestructible.

I have to wonder, did the men at Çatal Hüyük feel anything like it when the vulture called mother swooped down on corpses, when the frog-woman gave birth to the bulls, when they looked up at night to the horns of the waning yet regenerating moon? Was this grassy mound perhaps, during its 2,000 years of life, the crucible of all that I feel now, all religion and metaphor, stripped back to the core?

From the plains of Çatal Hüyük we drove into the Anatolian hills, a primitive, eerie land of dark forests, heavy clouds, and small stone villages where donkeys seem to outnumber cars. For long stretches there were not even grazing sheep, just black hillsides covered with a sheen of green. These hills were once the stronghold of the bloodthirsty goddess Cybele, whose rituals cured Dionysus of his madness, and there's a brooding wildness about them still. When we reach the Mediterranean coast, all this changes. The mountains become the dazzling backdrop to a string of beaches and an azure sea. The Ionian Greeks colonized this shore when the Dorians invaded their homeland, and Greek religion blended with that of Cybele and the old Anatolian gods.

In the ruins of Side, an antique Greek fishing village, fancy restaurants, flashy jewelry shops and boutiques are crammed in next to the ruins. Touts call out to us and thousands of other visitors in German, French, and Italian. It's a tourist gold rush. In vain, Turkish archaeological authorities tried to get the locals to resettle further up the coast so that proper excavations could be conducted, but the villagers clung like barnacles to the old stone temples, and everybody here is making a killing. Teresa and I stroll past the café-lined waterfront, wander through an Ionian temple, peek inside the ruins of a sixth-century Byzantine church that has been converted to a bar called Apollo's Disco. Eventually we reach Charlie's Scandinavian Restaurant, which shares a lot with a fenced-off pile of rubble identified by a sign as the Temple of Men, the Anatolian Moon God (that's "men" as in "menses," the lunar cycle, not as in males). It's built like a half-moon, still discernible beneath the overgrowth and jumble of stone blocks. It startles me to stand here in his temple, because since the beginning of this quest, I've always thought of the moon as feminine, a symbol of the goddess.

Joseph Campbell says that this was not always so, that across the Near East and Arabia it was the male who was identified as the moon because in its crescent form it resembled the horns of the goddess's bull. It's waxing and waning symbolized the death and resurrection of the sacrificial bull-god. Tammuz, Attis, Dionysus, Osiris all wear his horns. This crescent remains a potent symbol of the divine in Turkey and all across the Middle East, cast in gold on top of every mosque. Researching further, I discovered that the goddess herself accompanies the lunar bull across the heavens, appearing at his side as the morning star at dawn and the evening star at night: brightest in the sky, the planet we still name Venus. Next to the crescent horns she still appears on each Islamic country's flag. In countries where women have no vote, where they are confined in purdah, married off as property, forbidden to attend school, may be murdered by their kin if they are raped in order to erase the stain on the family name, or have their clitorises cut off to keep them sexually subdued—she still flies as the symbol of Allah.

We traveled north along the Aegean coast, headed towards the Letoum, holy of holies, the site of three temples to Leto and her immortal twins, Artemis and Apollo. The road wound through stone-cobbled villages. We passed tractors laden with sheep dung and fields of plastic greenhouses. A Roman amphitheater suddenly appeared, and next to it the temple ruins: a second-century B.C. sanctuary to the goddess, another to her children, and a third, much older, which was just a rough stone foundation. Pottery shards date it to 800 B.C but the deity is unknown, suspected to be the original mother goddess of the Leto cult. To the Greeks, Leto was just another cute nymph whom Zeus ravished in the guise of a swan. She came to the region called Lycia soon after the birth of the twins, guided to the river Xanthos by wolves, and fleeing ever-jealous Hera. Here she drank and then washed her children.

But to the Lycians, Leto was a goddess in her own right, and their culture showed some traces of ancient mother-rule. Herodotus claimed that the Lycians came originally from Crete, exiles from a fraternal war against King Minos. He wrote that they resembled the Cretans in many ways concerning the rights of women: "Ask a Lycian who he is, and he will tell you his own name and his mother's...and if a free woman has a child by a slave, the child is considered legitimate, whereas the children of a free man, however distinguished he may be, of a foreign wife or mistress have no citizen rights at all." Strabo writes that the twenty-three Lycian cities sent delegates to an annual assembly at the Letoum, where matters of mutual concern were decided on by vote; this great democratic government was always presided over by a woman.

We wove in and out of the mountains, through a strange schizo-phrenic land of ancient mysteries and concrete tourist towns: A fiery hole in the earth known as the Chimera; the weird mountaintop sanctuary of Zeus Labranda where girls were sacrificed on the altar of the god; at Demre, the tomb of Saint Nicholas, the original Santa Claus, his church built on the site of a temple to Artemis; Aphrodisias, a city dedicated to the goddess of love, but fused with bloody Cybele and served by her castrated priests; and the sanctuary of Endymion, a male sleeping beauty. As the Greeks tell the tale, the moon goddess fell in love with this handsome young man, put him into a deep sleep, and hid him in the hills so she could lie beside him every night. In this somnolent state, he still fathered fifty daughters by her. But the temple is a familiar half-circle shape, and Endymion, it seems, is just a disguise for the Anatolian moon god we found at Side.

We took one long detour down a dirt track to Lagina, a clearing on a slope above a fertile valley, site of one of the two known temples to Hecate. The foundations of the other I saw at Eleusis, for she was the old goddess who alerted Demeter to the rape of Persephone, and some identify her together with the mother-daughter dyad, as the crone-goddess of a feminine fertility trinity. There was no fence at the site, no ticket booth, no vendors selling postcards. We stopped beside the giant stone gateway to the temple, re-erected, I supposed, since every other block and stone was shaken to the foundations by an earthquake long ago and lay in heaps of rubble. But Hecate had been a goddess of desolate places and these ruins seemed to suit her well. The air around was warm and something prickled in it. Teresa said she felt a presence.

From the temple entranceway, a stone staircase led down to a pool, a poisonous milky green. Small water insects rose up from the opaque depths and sank back into it again. It's the kind of pool one has nightmares about, about something down there, where the staircase leads. Hecate, if she lives, is there at the bottom of this pool.

To the native Carians who built this temple, Hecate was their version of Cybele, savage queen of birth and death, flocks and fish, and the nursing of the newborn. When the Greeks incorporated her into their pantheon, they made her a lesser divinity of the shadowy thresholds between worlds—a goddess of crossroads, doorways, holder of the keys to the three realms, and intermediary between them. From governing the cleansing of thresholds, she became associated with the sweeping out of rubbish and of filth. These too became her province and eventually her sole domain. She became goddess of graveyards, a ghoul, queen of the witches. In this last role, pallid and rotting, her robes a shroud, she lingered on for many centuries into the Christian Era. A second century A.D. hymn sings to her like this:

> O nether and nocturnal, and infernal
> Goddess of the dark, grimly, silently
> Munching the dead,
> Night, Darkness, broad Chaos, Necessity
> Hard to escape are you: you're Moira and
> Erinys, torment, Justice and Destroyer,
> And you keep Kerberos in chains, with scales
> Of serpents are you dark, O you with hair
> Of serpents, serpent girded, who drink blood
> Who bring death and destruction, and who feast
> On hearts, flesh eater who devour those dead
> Untimely, and you who make grief resound...

Jacob Rabinowitz, author of *The Rotting Goddess*, writes that Hecate's descent from fertility to filth reveals Greek attitudes towards material existence. They yearned for the clean, heavenly air of Olympus, the purity of Pythagorean mathematics and Plato's ideal forms. Ooze and decay have no place in the life of a disembodied mind, yet the messiness of birth, sex, and death refuses to disappear. The Greeks may have loaded Hecate with filth and decay and then demonized her, but it was the Christians in their persecution of witches (those women boiling cauldrons of toads and bat wings) who finished her off. What were the witch-hunts if not a mission to eradicate the revulsion men feel when they look at women, the great patina of taboo and terror surrounding the fetidness of life so conveniently symbolized in her flesh? And if long ago we projected this onto Hecate, today we have only mortal women to be the repositories of our loathing, and who trigger in us this danger and this fear.

I get a flicker of something vile. Hecate repels me, she draws me, holds a secret for me inside her rotting mouth. A flicker of truth about our revulsion at feminine flesh. I remember a friend of mine—he was only in high school at the time, and yet he understood this all so well. He told me he had found an easy way to break-up with girlfriends after he no longer wanted them. When they started making out, he said he would keep his eyes open, and he would just look at her up close, as if through a microscope. He'd stare at the glistening pores, pimples, blackheads, the creases, hairs, erupting moles, and folded skin. He would feel nauseated, and that would be the end for him. He could dispose of her then, treat her like dirt.

A Turk in a baseball cap stood up from beneath a tree, stretched, and thumbed two tickets off his pad for us. He spoke few words of English but nimble as a cat, led us through the ruins, showing us markings in the Carian script and here and there the sculpted head of a lion, a floral motif, a live snake in its lair. He pointed out a gray stone trough, big as a bathtub. He drew an index finger across his neck to mimic a slit throat, and made as if to pour his blood into the trough. I imagined it filled with frothing red. "Of bulls," he said, making horns with his fingers on his head, "of bulls." He ended the tour at a clear stream that welled from a nearby spring, Hecate's Spring, which had irrigated fields since classical times and still feeds the crops today. We thanked and tipped our guide, and I went back to gaze once more in the fetid pool.

It was there, down deep, that revulsion I feel like instinct, that says, "Don't touch! Don't touch that water! Something, something will wrap itself around you and pull you in and suck you down." It's not death that makes me tremble at the water's edge. It's the moment before death, the moment when the living consumes the not-yet-dead. The maggots, the scum, the crawling things that cover the skin. The decay that is life at its most primitive. It's the knowledge that she is hungry for me, that I am prey to something I can't escape, and when I look into the green ghoul-eyes of her face, I feel the fear of it right through me. Not the simplicity of annihilation. That seems almost sweet by comparison. No, this is the spider that eats my flesh alive, tears me from consciousness, back into earth. That slow consumption by the septic force, dissolving and sucking, that is man's fear, the fear he senses behind every woman's smile and stockinged leg. But we don't know it. It's underneath, as if it's frozen in ice. Yet we feel the hatred that this fear arouses, hatred like a hot brand our forefathers seared into us for a hundred generations back: Eve the deceiver, responsible for our fall from grace, the one who brought us death disguised as lunch; or Pandora, the beautiful woman, designed to inflict on man every evil released from her unlucky box.

What hope do men have of getting past this fear, this hate? How can we approach a goddess after centuries of making her the wicked witch? So much hate. I feel it in myself, gazing at her in the pool. Hecate's is the face I see on Teresa sometimes when we're in the throes of passion, the sucking jaws, the appetite for my flesh. The she-beast unleashed, gnawing on my neck. So starved for me. Mouth on my body, everywhere sucking like the void. She strikes terror into my heart, as if she will tear me to pieces. Maenad, succubus, ghoul, witch, thing of the earth, consuming my flesh—no, my immortal soul, the thing of the heavens my forefathers fashioned to escape her clutch. Woman the spider, woman the leech, woman the parasite, the maw, and this slow emptying of my vitals into her.

Why is it, then, that I hold her close when Hecate glimmers at me from her face? Exactly for this, exactly because she fills me with terror. My little self flees in horror, the shell disintegrates, fails, and in its place, I am. The darkness arises, still scared of her, but alive. Then I notice that though she is totally possessed—I believe the strength in her could no doubt rip me apart—she does not hurt me. She loves me in some strange sense. And I feel something more, when my shell is gone, and it is just her and me, I feel her hunger for me like an infant, rooting for its mother's breast.

The green pool, it's like looking at a picture of a face that only exists inside of me. How I envy the Carians, envy them for knowing Hecate well enough to build a temple to her, for being able to spill blood and worship her terrifying nature. Still she lingers in Lagina. I lean in over the pool, and long to see her shadow.

The silversmith Demetrius called an emergency meeting of his guild and warned the men that the two things they cherished most were under attack: their goddess, and the income they derived from selling silver statues of her to the pilgrims who thronged to visit her great temple in Ephesus.

"Men," Demetrius declared, "you know our livelihood depends on this trade. You can see and hear what this fellow Paul is doing. He says gods made by human hands are not gods at all. Not only here in Ephesus, but all over Asia he has managed to convince people that this is the case. Now there's a great danger that our trade will come into disrepute. More than that, there is also the danger that the temple of the great goddess Artemis will itself come to be despised and even She, Artemis—whom not only Asia but all the world reveres—will be stripped of her greatness and come to mean nothing."

> I could hardly believe it. Here I was entirely alone, free at last to walk through history. Vegetation pressed in on the flanks of the boulevard, blocking out everything else; it felt like I was entering a time tunnel. The wind was hot, coming in searing gusts through the dry bushes; it sounded eerily like the squeaking of masts and rigging of the ancient port that had once existed at the end of the avenue. The face of Medusa leered at me from a column, eyes rolled back in her head, the mane of poisonous snakes flailing.
>
> —Tony Perrottet,
> "The Medusa Beckons"

When they heard this, the men began raging through the street, shouting "Great is Artemis of the Ephesians!" They found one of Paul's traveling companions and hauled him into the theater. The mob had grown huge and wild. People shouted accusations and chanted over a Jewish representative's attempts to speak to them. But then the city clerk arrived. "Men of Ephesus," he chided, "doesn't all the world know that the city of Ephesus is the guardian of the temple of the great

Artemis and of her image, which fell from heaven? Therefore, since these facts are undeniable, you ought to be quiet and not do anything rash." He added that if the silversmiths had a grievance against these men, they could take it to court, and reminded them that they were in danger of being charged with rioting, which would bring down the wrath of Rome. It was a masterful blend of appeasement, reason, and intimidation, and they all left meekly.

But the clerk was wrong. Demetrius had it right. Within a few centuries Christian emperors would ban all pagan practices. The temple to Artemis, four times the size of the Parthenon and one of the seven wonders of the ancient world, would be sacked, obliterated, its marble quarried to build churches, its statues ground to powder for making plaster. In 1860 it took a team of archaeologists nine years just to find it. Today, only a single pillar has been re-erected. It stands in a swamp, like a lonely marble redwood with a bird's nest on its crown.

Walking the excavated streets of Ephesus, less than a mile from the temple grounds, it was easy to imagine what the city must have been like in the first century A.D. when it was the Roman capital of Asia. These days it's packed again with foreigners, the entrances lined with souvenir shops and money changers, kiosks selling banal and erotic postcards and, after a gap of 1,600 years, statuettes of Artemis—plastic now, instead of silver. At the time of Paul the city had broad boulevards, public baths, gymnasiums, fountains, mansions for rich merchants, a port, the famous library that rivaled Alexandria's, and the great theater—quiet now, but once filled with a bloodthirsty mob. A footstep carved in stone next to a bawdy drawing points the way to a local whorehouse. With half a million inhabitants, Ephesus was the New York of the ancient world. "Devoted to dancers...the whole city was full of pipers and effeminate rascals and noise," writes the ancient tourist Philostratus.

Paul urged his Ephesian converts to shun the city's licentious ways. "Be like God in true righteousness and holiness," he wrote to them. "Among you there must not be even a hint of sexual immorality, or of any kind of impurity.... Nor should there be obscenity, foolish talk, or coarse joking.... No immoral, impure or greedy person—such a man is an idolater—has any inheritance in the kingdom of Christ and of God."

The goddess, she was not so harsh with humankind. No divine appearance is more moving than that of the Great Goddess to Lucius, the poor soul transformed into a donkey in the Apuleius tale "The Golden Ass," written in the second century A.D. After suffering humiliation and brutality, fleeing from a deathtrap, poor Lucius sees the full moon above the ocean, and he brays to the goddess for help. She rises up to greet him from the waves:

> All the perfumes of Arabia floated into my nostrils as the goddess deigned to address me: "You see me here, Lucius, in answer to your prayer. I am Nature, the Universal Mother, mistress of all the elements, primordial child of time, sovereign of all things spiritual, queen of the dead, queen also of the immortals, the single manifestation of all the gods and goddesses that are. My nod governs the shining heights of Heaven, the wholesome sea breezes, the lamentable silences of the world below. Though I am worshiped in many aspects, known by countless names, and propitiated with all matter of different rites, yet the whole round earth venerates me.... I have come in pity of your plight, I have come to favor and aid you. Weep no more, lament no longer; the hour of deliverance, shone over by my watchful light, is at hand."

His salvation is simply to eat the petals of a rose. Freed from a donkey's shape, Lucius enters the goddess's priesthood in Corinth, and spends his days "enjoying the ineffable pleasure of contemplating the goddess's statue." Apulieus's contemporaries in Ephesus would have understood exactly what he was talking about, and certainly they would know poor Lucius was not the only man who had to make an ass of himself before turning to the goddess.

In the Ephesus Museum an entire hall is devoted to three life-sized statues of Artemis recovered from her temple. I sat on the cool marble floor and gazed up at her, my shot at that "ineffable pleasure." The room is dim, the soft lights playing on the idols' curves. Her face is impassive, her posture rigid, skirts flowing down making a single column of her legs. In the crooks of her out-stretched arms she cradles two lions. Her hands reach out to her adorers as if to fold them into her. On her chest, beneath a zodiac necklace, she has rows and rows of breasts. Twenty, thirty, it's hard to count them all. They hang from her like clusters of grapes. She takes my breath away. It strikes me suddenly as so wrong-headed, the scholars who claim she is a goddess of fertility. Fertility—that great archaeological fallback for describing every statue of the feminine divine, as if to explain her and dismiss her with one word. But this Artemis does not remind me of birth. She's a goddess of abundance, of breasts overflowing, enough for all of us to suckle.

This promise of the abundant breast, this is what I fear in her. Why? Because I'm a member of the cult of scarcity, that tribe that believes there is never enough to go around: not enough food, not enough money, sex, or love. I grew up in a prosperous middle-class family. I have a job, a child, a lover, and a hundred times more security than any other human generation has ever known. And the fear's still there, the fear that it will all be snatched away some-day. So it's better not to take too much, not to want too much. Luxury is abhorrent to me. I call it thrift, but it's fear. Sometimes I envy members of that other tribe, the cult of abundance for whom life is overflowing, and they can easily reach out and grab that teat, and suck, and trust that there will always be milk.

Her breasts—to see them clustered there between her arms in-toxicates me. It is the thing we were born to ache for. If Jung is right and there are archetypes hardwired into the brain, then the breast must be the most important: to press against it, latch, suck, and gulp is the most primal human instinct next to drawing our first breath. Artemis, she opens it up in me, and I feel the need like a pang. I remember that the Spartans used to put male babies on a mountaintop for seven days after birth, then weaned survivors early. It made better soldiers, they said, gave them a kind of anger. If we are made to long for the breast, does not having it twist some-thing in us, create an anger and a craving we must carry all of our lives—especially men like me, from a bottle-nursed generation, suckled with the taste of a rubber nipple? Is this the root of our culture's grand obsession with large breasts?

At age eleven I was flipping though catalogs in search of brassiere ads. I tore out pages of *Life* magazine featuring topless Las Vegas showgirls or half-naked African tribeswomen, and hid them in my closet. At thirteen, I was thumbing through *Playboy* magazines in the back of the local variety store, terrified I was going to be discovered in my depravity. I touched just the edges of the pages so as not to leave a sweaty fingerprint. I still remember the first time I softly placed my hand on a girl's blouse. The ecstasy shivered in me that short instant until she gently returned my fingers to her shoulders. In a crowd, my eyes still find the woman in a low cut blouse. My head swivels on the beach. I feel the thrill to see the swell of them, the bounce of them, the gorgeous raspberry tips of them though a light summer dress. I think of pornography, strippers, advertising, the breasts pushed in our faces in the rush to get our cash. I remember sitting in strip bars, watching girl after girl expose her breasts for all to see, and me soaking it in like a drunk at his liquor, each pair revealed leaving you wanting to see the next pair and the next and the next, though almost all were pumped and artificially rounded, an identical army of Barbie dolls. In the raw magazines, women's breasts are distended until they are grotesque, and it seems there is no limit to the flesh men crave. Imagine if Artemis of Ephesus could be our pinup model now, if multiple breast enhancement became the newest fashion, each woman sporting one dozen, twenty, thirty breasts or more. Would that assuage this need we have, we of the cult of scarcity, for more, more, more?

Strange how all the breasts we see today never fill us up. They leave us wasted, yet still wanting more. What happened that we turned them into a commodity, a silicon pillow to be possessed? In the act, we lost them, or they eluded us, because what they provided was never in the breasts themselves. Artemis symbolizes a kind of giving we no longer understand. Not an exchange, not love returned for love or money, but a flooding from out of plenty. This is the goddess that Lucius turned to, a goddess so full that our need, our "depraved and sinful nature," is not an obstacle to her blessing. She gives because she is that giving, that flowing out of the gift. What was my life, but a craving for this flowing out once more, a longing for it and a belief that it doesn't exist?

The Ephesus guidebooks say that these days most archaeologists don't think the lumps on Artemis's chest are in fact her breasts at all, but rather the severed testicles of sacrificial bulls—fertility offerings that were part of her sacred rites. Historically, severed testicles were intimately associated with Artemis; her priests cut off their genitals to honor her, and only a man thus unmanned could preside over temple rites. Some scholars believe these eunuch priests originally conned their way into the hierarchy of priestesses, eventually gaining power and taking over. The robes of Christian priests and the vow of celibacy may be relics of this revolution. Others interpret ritual emasculation as a rite of gender-change: men so drawn to the goddess that they rend themselves to attain her image. The Romans called them Galli, and their cult flourished in the heart of Rome. During Cybele's festivals there, scores of men in frenzies of devotion would slice their manhood off, and throw the severed organs in a great bloody heap. This rite of self-castration appears again and again in the Near Eastern myths of Attis, Adonis, Tammuz, and Osiris, the severed penis a fertile agent of rebirth. In this way the priests of Artemis reenacted, bloodily, the sacred sacrifice of the ancient kings, whose death brought new life to the land, and in this they earned their role as counterpart and eunuch consort to the Goddess of all abundance. Breasts or testicles? An icon may have many meanings. Looking at the goddess now, I see her with disturbing double vision—both with breasts and swinging testicles around her neck. The gift, and the brutal price that gift demands.

To receive that breast—was that to be her eunuch slave? I had to laugh. Too many of my past relationships had been with the likes of Artemis. Sooner or later, I would be cutting off my balls so she could sling them around her neck. I believed with each relationship that this act would lead to some epiphany. But I just lay there bleeding. And so I hardened my heart to Artemis's kind. Her offer of the breast took too much of me. I wonder if Paul hit a chord with the Ephesians of his day when he wrote to them: "Wives, submit to your husbands as to the Lord." Once the woman submits, once she is property, then you own those breasts, those clusters of abundance. Own them. And yet it has not worked for us men, these past 2,000 years. They hang there still, a promise and a torment, ours to possess in marriage or the marketplace, and yet strangely out of reach.

At times when Teresa is naked within my grasp, I feel such hatred for her breast. I clutch it in my hand like a dove about to take flight, and want to squeeze the life out of it. I want to possess it and tear it at the same instant, want to make it mine and to hurt it. This breast, the thing I want so much, the thing I believe I will never have. And when I reach my frenzy, there are times when I'm suddenly the boy again, the boy at her breast, and I want it with a fierce craving, I clutch it and I am stricken with terror that it will go away. It's worse than the vulture's bite. I hate her then, I hate her most when I want her breast like this, hate the helplessness of the need, the helplessness I feel in her arms then, because nothing matters like the nipple in my mouth, and I disappear into it and suck so hard I know it hurts her, hurts her with the pleasure of the sucking need in me. They make me savage, craven, dependent. And what bliss it is, locked in Teresa's arms, to feel that hate and let it pour out, while I lie pawing at her breast.

From the ruins of Ephesus, Teresa and I drove up a wooded hillside to a large gravel parking lot crammed with a dozen tour buses and perhaps a hundred cars. The crowd swarmed around us, tour group leaders shouted for order and waved their pennants as a steady throng pushed through the entrance and past the many kiosks. But on this hilltop, the statues and portraits that the vendors sell are not of Artemis, but of the final form the goddess took at Ephesus: as Mary, Mother of God.

According to early church tradition, John came to Ephesus before Paul's crusade and brought Jesus' mother with him. She lived here for many years, died and was buried in these hills. A seventeenth-century German invalid named Anne Catherine Emmerich had a series of visions describing the exact location of the house where Mary lived. In 1891, members of the Lazarist order of Izmir followed the directions of those visions and uncovered a sixth-century house with foundations dating back to the time of Christ. Today it's venerated as a Catholic shrine, Pope Paul IV having certified its authenticity.

As the Turkish director of the Ephesus Museum subtly put it, "Since the Virgin Mary possessed many of the virtues of Artemis, the most magnificent goddess, the new religion gained popularity in Ephesus." In fact, the edicts of Theodosius banned all pagan practices and closed the temples by the end of the fourth century A.D. Under threat of death and torture, practitioners of the forbidden old ways changed the goddess's name to Mary and then carried on. The first church in all of Christendom dedicated to the Virgin was established in the shell of an old medical school in Ephesus. In A.D. 431, a great church council was conveyed at this site

We hurried by, feeling like intruders. Outside the church we stopped to drink little glasses of hot tea. Amid souvenir stands offering holy cards and plastic statues of the Virgin, I noticed something startling about the trees. White dots covered their dark bark like little stars, high as hands could reach.

"Bits of paper," Eshber explained. "People write prayers to the Virgin on tissue paper and stick them on the bark."

"Why?" I asked.

"They believe Mary comes here every day to read them."

Tree after tree was covered this way. So many scraps, so many sorrows.

"Prayers for what?" I said.

Eshber shrugged. "What if a woman can't have a baby? What if somebody is ill? It could be lots of things."

—Candace Dempsey,
"Our Lady of Electricity"

to settle a controversy that was ripping the newly powerful religion apart: Was Mary the mother of God, a quasi-divine being to be revered, or was she merely the mortal mother of a fully human Jesus, who only received the spirit of Christ upon his baptism? Two hundred religious authorities debated the issue for three months, in the end declaring Mary both mother of the human Jesus and the divine Christ. As a footnote, they declared officially that Mary was buried here, though the tomb has not been found. So in Ephesus, the ancient cult of the virgin-mother Goddess and her dying-to-be-reborn son was successfully grafted onto the cult of Mary. As the gospel spread, more by decree than personal belief, local goddesses all across Europe assumed new identities as Madonnas and blessed virgins.

Teresa and I joined the crowd along the wooded path to Mary's house. We passed a fountain, flower gardens, and eventually arrived at the humble brickwork dwelling, fully reconstructed. Two Franciscan monks with tonsured heads and hooded brown robes—but not quite eunuchs—guarded the door, preventing overcrowding or entry without the proper dress. Inside, a simple black statue of the virgin stood surrounded by fresh flowers, her arms outstretched to the believing masses. These people were not tourists like the ones at Ephesus, they were pilgrims, pressing to the front with prayers of supplication, praise, and gratitude. They lit candles, put offerings in the box. Some wept, some gazed in silent rapture. What was the difference between this scene and the worship of Great Artemis that Saint Paul decried? Nothing but the size of her temple and the clothes she wore. And if one were to pull aside the modest robes the Blessed Virgin always wears, how many rows of breasts might we find hidden on the inside?

And yet, though I could contemplate Artemis in a museum with a sense of awe, I found the shrine of Mary stifling and false, the gatekeeper priests oppressive. A house found through a sickly woman's dream? Come on, I said to Teresa, what did that prove? And look at all these people flocking to it. At least the temple of Artemis was marked by her image which fell from heaven—a meteorite of some sort, an actual event. But this was simply superstition. Teresa, however, lit two candles. One for her daughter, one for me. Her eyes questioned my scorn, and I had to laugh. The old

Protestant in me has more trouble with Mary than with Artemis, it seems. Or was it that I was far more comfortable sitting at the feet of a dead goddess than a living one, one who might answer my prayers, but in return place her demands on me?

Tim Ward is a Canadian author, journalist, and media consultant. He has written three books about his travels through Asia: What the Buddha Never Taught, The Great Dragon's Fleas, *and* Arousing the Goddess. *This excerpt is from his new book,* The Savage Breast, *about his travels through Southeastern Europe and the Aegean in search of ancient goddesses. He lives in Maryland.*

* * *

Çay in Çankiri

Looking for a respite from a rough journey,
these travelers get both less and more
than they expected.

LATE IN THE EVENING THE CROWDED BUS GRINDS TO A HALT
in Çankiri. Two hours and eighty miles north of Ankara, we are
the only passengers dismounting onto a sidewalk almost as wet and
muddy as its Ankara counterparts. Fog swirls above the deserted,
ill-lit streets.

It's not quite what we expected.

Back in Ankara, that afternoon, we'd explained to the cheerful
woman at the capital's Tourist Information Office what we were
looking for: a twenty-four-hour layover in a thriving, cosmopolitan city, on the way to the Black Sea. She recommended Çankiri.

"How big is it?" we asked.

"Smaller than Istanbul," she had replied. "Smaller than Ankara.
Less than a million people. And it has a great mosque."

It sounded perfect. We badly needed cheering up after endless
days of bus and train travel across inland Turkey, plagued by melting snow, muddy streets, and a country introverted by a long winter. Our best moments had been glimpses through steamed-up
windows—a woman washing a sheet in a stream, stretching out
her arm as the train roared by, looking up for a moment; a man
leading a donkey to a brook to drink.

From the Tourist Office we'd walked back to the Otobüs Garaj with a newfound optimism. Çankiri would have busy cafés, music, and conversation spilling out onto colorful streets. It would have the exuberance of Istanbul. We'd floated above the knee-deep mud, shrugged off the weight of our heavy bags, and ignored the filthy water flying up from the wheels of taxis. In the warmth of the bus station we'd drunk beer and eaten chocolate biscuits.

But now it looked as though the blue town sign we had glimpsed in the bus's headlights was right and the Tourist Office was wrong. Not strictly—the population was less than a million (by something like 961,000 heads)—but in all the important details, and explaining why there is only one hotel recommended in our pamphlet; it's probably the *only* hotel.

We find the place easily enough, and check in to our five-dollar room—though if they'd asked fifty dollars we'd still have had to take it—setting out immediately in search of dinner. Fortunately, one of the town's two recommended restaurants is right next door.

Inside it's selectively crowded—all the tables along one wall are fully occupied, with the rest of the vast room empty, save for a canary in a cage by the window, and several huge plants, including potted palms and a giant free-standing rubber tree. Palm-side, we are seated in splendid isolation from the other diners. We order a selection of Turkish salads, pita bread, and beer, and wolf it down, hungry and tired after twelve hours on the road.

Nickie goes off in search of a washroom, and while she's there a sweet old man pops over to our table and puts a baked potato on each of our plates. I smile at him and he rubs his two index fingers together gleefully as he returns to his table, bubbling away incomprehensibly in Turkish. Once again I wish I had any Turkish words beyond *lütfen, mersi, su, ekmek, çay, and bira.*

Already full, we eat the potatoes out of politeness and toast the old man across the way. While we're doing this, a plate of peeled fruit arrives—bananas, chopped oranges, sliced apples, mandarin segments, and a small bunch of grapes (these, washed locally, will later be my downfall). The fruit is delicious; a fitting end to a full day, and we eat it quickly and greedily.

Perhaps too quickly. For as soon as the first plate is finished, a second, larger version arrives, along with our benefactor. He toasts us with raki; we return the compliment with beer. As if to test our stamina, a waiter is summoned, and a mountain of freshly made potato crisps and mustard is brought to our table.

More rubbing of fingers, and laughing, and we suppose this means we are good friends, since we have no common vocabulary with this smiling-eyed genie.

In a continuing effort to be polite we force these down—they are delicious; it's a tragedy we're not hungry—and I make a foolish comment about how nice the bananas were. An entire bunch arrives from nowhere, shortly followed by more beer, a platter of sweetmeats, sticky cakes, and more raki for monsieur.

We do our best, but we're feeling as plump as Thanksgiving turkeys, and worrying too about this uncalled-for generosity. In a fit of guilt—there are still mounds of food left on the table, even after our valiant efforts—we ask for the bill; it seems the only avenue of escape, and escape we must, or we shall burst.

The bill comes to around ten dollars—expensive compared to what we're used to—and the old man insists on paying, despite our protests. He says he'll see us tomorrow and we part in regal style, much bowing, waving, kissing, and smiling; we don't dare say that we're leaving tomorrow.

Knocked out by generosity, we head up to our unheated room, after cadging four extra blankets apiece from the management. Through plastic-sheeted windows—poor man's double glazing—we can dimly see and hear a stream gurgling pleasantly past, overshadowed somewhat by a huge siding and shunting yard, in full operation from dusk to dawn. There is much clanking and whistling throughout the night; though it doesn't interrupt my sleep, it merely disturbs it—the train shrieks transposed into minor nightmares, the stream to imagined rainfall.

At 7 A.M. we check out and walk to the train station; the streets are wet and muddy still, but attractive now with shafts of weak sunlight washing through the fog and turning the dirty cobbles pale gold. The ticket office is closed, however, and we're told to come back at an unspecified later time—though there is a train, it seems, heading to the Black Sea at midday. We knock on the stationmaster's door and ask for left-luggage in nearly fluent sign language. He offers us a corner of his office—a treat, as everyone else in town is staggering around with what look like sacks of potatoes, and nowhere to put them.

As we are walking out through the waiting room, trouble arrives in the form of one brown and two gray uniforms. Brown points at me; the grays approach. One flashes ID. *"Polis,"* it says, and so does he. This seems serious. Hard-eyed and tight-lipped, the other one says "Passports!" Nervous as always before the law, I fumble for them. One of the officers unfolds a piece of paper. My name is on it, misspelled, and I'm already searching for a loophole. But the passport number is indeed mine. A sick feeling settles in my stomach, probably fear—though conceivably an early grape twinge. By nightfall I will be very ill.

We are asked to sit, while Authority passes judgment. The man in brown—who turns out to be the local sheriff—stands guard, with his hand on his holster. Time passes. Nickie is convinced it's something to do with not paying for dinner. I insist it's a routine check—but like Josef K. in Kafka's *The Trial*, I can't believe we're innocent. The seconds tick deafeningly past on the station clock.

And then, with no explanation at all, we're handed back our papers and dismissed. We burst outside, suddenly aware of the meaning of freedom.

We search for picnic food, finding the untouristed streets of Çankiri less rewarding for shoppers than the market square in Ürgüp. You could buy anything there—fruit, vegetables, pots, pans, copperware, rugs, carpets, blankets, detergent, cosmetics, toiletries, clothes, bread, any kind of tinned food, tea, coffee, water, alcohol, pasta, rice, and dried wheat. Anything, that is, except Turkish Delight. So it's with real delight that in Çankiri we finally find what we've been looking for—softer and sweeter than any yet.

Our pamphlet says we must see the mosque, the museum, and the castle—so we do.

The Ulu Cami—Great Mosque—was built by "Turkey's most famous architect," according to our pamphlet (presumably Mimar Sinan in the sixteenth century). It turns out to be a quiet place— they have to unlock it for us. Inside, it's richly decorated and full of stunning carpets.

The municipal museum, not far away, turns out to be a dusty collection displaying everything from crocks of coins to a marvelous two-foot-long Roman vase, to Ottoman costumes and embroidery. The "ruins of the eleventh-century castle"—vestiges, really—are a steep, stiff walk, out of town. There's not much to see, but the exercise does us good.

As we walk back down the partly cobbled dirt street a door opens, and from it appears a woman bearing the night's slops, held well forwards, steaming vigorously in the morning light. With no further ado, and having reached the middle of the road, she sloshes the contents into the street and retreats indoors. It's the real thing, lumps and all. So much mud, I had thought, and so unusually fragrant. The streets serve as open drains, running down to the pleasantly gurgling stream outside our bedroom window...

We're distracted from our malodorous reverie by an old woman waving a teapot and cackling "*Çay! Çay!*" Feeling adventurous, we accept the offer—it's not often you get the chance to meet Turkish women at all, and it's a nice change from the all-male teahouses.

Carefully removing our shoes—the custom suddenly makes perfect sense—we crowd into a toasty room and sit where we can, on a pair of beds set at right angles in the corner. The eight-by-eight-foot room is also the kitchen—a basin with ramshackle cupboards underneath and a pipe stove, which doubles as the cooker, complete the furnishings. The kettle goes on to boil.

We are joined first by a thirty-year-old woman and three children, then, as word gets around, by four women in their early twenties, five more children, two young men, and an ancient fellow with a knobby walking stick. With nineteen of us in the room it's crowded but convivial. We speak no Turkish and they no English, so instead we share sign language, cigarettes (still universal currency in Turkey), postcards of home, and drawings from our notebooks.

They offer us *çay* and *kahvalti*, a delicious breakfast of bread and pale homemade cheese; we break out our biscuits and Turkish Delight. And we finally understand with an awful certainty that the rubbing together of fingers is Turkish for "Just Married!" On this trip Nickie's been wearing a wedding ring to fend off unwanted advances from young Turks—even though we're not a couple, let alone married. But last night we were treated like honeymooners.

As we make choo-choo noises to let our hosts know we have a train to catch, there's a knock at the door. It's the sheriff. We cower. But no, he may be the sheriff, but he's also the husband of one of the women. He laughs and smiles, shows off his sheriff's badge, and walks us back to the station. Whilst done in the friendliest of ways, it's still like being run out of town. The sheriff stops and chats to various people; we suspect he's telling them "Don't worry; I'll see that they're on the next train out."

And indeed we are. The sheriff buys our tickets and hands them to us for two dollars apiece, helps us recover our bags from the stationmaster, and waits with us for the train. A small and curious crowd forms around us, and we field their questions as best we can.

Finally the train steams in, all screeching brakes, disgorged smoke and swarming passengers, a once-a-day theatrical moment for Çankiri. We climb on board, and finding no seats we eventually settle guiltily for a pair in first class—only to discover that the sheriff had bought us first-class tickets.

As we heave out of the station on the start of the endless journey to the Black Sea, we see the sheriff strolling up the platform. On either side of him are the two gray-uniformed policemen. All three are laughing.

Piers Letcher has been traveling for twenty-five years and travel writing for twenty. British-born and educated, he has spent most of his adult life in France eschewing alliteration. He has published more than a thousand newspaper and magazine articles and a dozen books, including Croatia: The Bradt Travel Guide *and* Eccentric France, *a guide to France's bizarre buildings, ridiculous royalty, quirky collections, impossible inventions and peculiar people (both published by Bradt Travel Guides).*

BARBARA BOWEN

A Step in the River

Remain open, and all will be well.

I'm riding the ferry to Kusadasi after a stop on Samos, a Greek hub off Turkey's coast. Coincidence has me aboard with Mike, a fellow New Yorker I'd met in Patmos, the last island of my Greek visit. We've both heard tales about travel in Turkey—stolen credit cards, con men, nightclub mishaps, solo women accosted—but we're committed. Mike is due to catch a flight from Istanbul, and I'm meeting friends for a sailing adventure at Marmaris, down the coast. The twilight sky begins to drape a soft curtain over Kusadasi Bay, filled with ugly tankers looming like steel cattle. The city is a profusion of shabby buildings packed like crowded teeth. It's a drastic contrast to Patmos, where pastoral charms—enchanted hills, grazing sheep, luminous multicolored stones—die hard, as my mind is taken hostage by a new mise-en-scène. The thought of traveling alone here fills my heart with vague dread.

I've read that Kusadasi is noted as a popular resort town. One of few Aegean passageways from Greece to Turkey, it's also gateway to Ephesus, the mysterious ancient city dating from circa 10 B.C. Most of Ephesus's remarkably intact ruins are from its heyday in the Roman period. By then a metropolis, it allowed religious freedom for all inhabitants: Jews, Anatolians, Romans, Egyptians, and the first Christians. I'm drawn to ancient relics, especially those proffering clarity on the present day. Turkey is full of such riches. I plan to make stops in search of them on my journey south.

At the border crossing, Mike and I laugh nervously, then hold our breath as we squeeze past a throng of travelers. We hit the street. Turks accost us, selling their hotels, rugs, and jewelry. Barely audible, we yell goodbye amidst the din.

I'm looking for a bank. A Turk shouts and tugs at my sleeve, demanding I get into his car. "Here, here!" he shrieks, pointing to a feminine figure in the back seat. "American woman, right here! You come, you come, too!" I whip my bags off the ground and gallop, full throttle, to the other side of the street. The man sends a shiver up my spine, and so does the entire spectacle. I look for a place to hide—feeling like an alien pup among wolves—bathed in a meteoric shower of fluorescent glare from the shops. Brassy trinkets, Turkish rugs, and handbags scream at me from all directions.

In Athens, I'd bought a ring from a young sultry Greek woman with profuse hair and equivocating black eyes. I bought the ring, an onyx, wondering if I really liked it. At this moment, it seems to leer at me like The Evil Eye.

We started to dread going outside and got a negative feeling about Turkey, but after analyzing the touts' responses, my husband and I realized that by not speaking to them we were hurting their self-esteem. We had perceived them to be unfeeling, unscrupulous, aggressive forces trying to push us into shops. We felt like tourist dust being brushed this way and that by human brooms. But we didn't realize that the touts were human and that their job was difficult. They are constantly rejected and they only make money if they get tourists to go into the shops.

—Donna Schilder, "Hawkernyms: Out-Touting the Touts"

A British woman taps me on the shoulder. Her calm, empathetic manner is balm for stretched nerves. She too was accosted upon first arrival in Kusadasi. She suggests I take a room in her hotel. It's close by, she purrs. We proceed down a dirt lane through the main square with a dizzy array of merchants and vendors. Shop fronts and outdoor stands are packed in solid rows. Vacationing Turks are buzzing past, the foreign traveler being a rarity here in September.

We walk and walk, until, it seems, we've walked forever. We enter a quaint but tattered lobby. Who's there but the Turk—the one with the car. He owns this hotel. Stout and compact as a bullet, his energy commands the entire room. He'd sent the Brit to snag me, sneaky devil. Sitting nearby is my American counterpart, as advertised. The Turk, I'll call him Osman, brings us "ahpel tee" to smooth our feathers. Mine are not smooth. But I tell myself to relax. Here, respect for personal boundaries will not equal what I consider normal. I hear the rate: about ten dollars. Rough rooms by American standards, but decent.

I reluctantly speak with Charmaine, "The American." She is also a victim of the coup, after all. She's twenty-something and lively. Defiance is loosening. I take a room, as Charmaine has, and we decide to brave the streets for dinner.

We wander the streets in awe. The men, and even the Turkish women, dispense airs of aggression. The square exhales the brash winds of Western commerce entangled with the exotic East. We amble up a street full of nightclubs. Like incensed roosters, men taunt and tease us toward their watering holes with the lure of discounts. It's all a game, circus-like.

One man leaps at me, grabs my arm, and shouts one inch from my ear, "Scooz me plez, con I haahsel you?!" He snatches a 5 million lire note, out of my hand. When I snatch it back on impulse, he turns beet red, shaming me for thinking he was stealing my money. He was trying to help me count it, he says, storming about like a peacock striving for take-off.

"Look, my friend," I say. "We Americans think it rude to snatch things out of one's hand. I know you weren't stealing my money (yeah, right). I have been in Turkey for only two hours now. Forgive me, eh?"

He nods his head with stern approval, watching to see who's watching him, now satisfied a woman hasn't appeared to best him.

One glass of sewage-beer later, Charmaine and I already feel like caged animals in a frenzied zoo. We commit to leaving Kusadasi in the morning. We are no longer eager to suffer the crowds at Ephesus, nor to rest complacent under Osman's rule. We attack Charmaine's travel book for a refuge south, where we both are headed. Back to the evening streets, amidst the mayhem. Crass commerce. Fevered invasion of personal boundaries. Kusadasi—fascinating and dreadful.

Near a clothing shop, we encounter a young Turk sitting with a sickly kitten, nursing it with a syringe. He is kindly stroking it. He talks with us softly, mourning the town he'd known as a child. "Kusadasi was a good place once," he says.

Charmaine and I amble back to the hotel, trying to comprehend how economic hardship might elicit this jarring ambiance. Chronic weakness and corruption in banking, inefficient agricultural subsidies, flawed energy policies, and a slow pace of structural reforms, all contribute to Turkey's poverty and complex growing pains. I hate to admit, excepting the boy with the kitten, I'm uneasy in this vortex of raw confusion.

Charmaine and I make our getaway early. Turkish travel infrastructure is well-developed, especially the bus system. The bus to Soke, with one change, will lead us to our destination, Altinkum, a beach resort favored by Brits. Sadly, we leave the Ephesian Temple of Artemis and her statuary behind, unseen.

The countryside is mountainous with myriad pines. It recalls the Rockies, though the trees are spaced apart, exposing rich colorful topsoil. A surreal tableau of stunning green and burnt sienna rolls off to infinity. Mysterious wooden boxes line the hillsides, looking like crude urns for cremated ashes, a kind of cemetery. We later discover they hold beehives for the harvest of honey. We ride through peaceful hamlets engulfed by pink oleander and silvery olive groves. Out here, one is able to breathe a sigh of relief. The country is revealing its beauty. We pass a line of young, armed soldiers along the road. Charmaine assures me they're simply guarding the basalt mines we passed a few minutes ago.

On our next bus, we meet Matthew, an Austrian bar owner from Altinkum. His breath is afire with spirits. He's funny, helpful, and probably in the right business. Thanks to him, we find a nice hotel, near the beach. Altinkum seems diametrically opposed to Kusadasi. It's small, slow, and quiet this time of year. We loll in the sun, serenaded by British accents floating above an expansive beach. Later, we eat waterside, engaging in conversation, as language barriers allow, with gentle Turks. Turkish women seem to disappear altogether outside larger cities. The vacancy is odd and extreme. Still, I'm cautiously warming up to Turkey. Charmaine is smitten, having a foundation of study to ground her. We've grown grateful that fate tossed us together.

The next day, Charmaine joins me in a motorbike campaign to three ancient sites. One of them, Priene, boasts an ancient Temple of Athena I've wanted to see ever since Athens. Viewing the Parthenon I had recalled the goddess Athena, in whose name it was built. I saw photographs of her thirty-nine-foot statue, moved long ago to Constantinople, now Istanbul. With helmet, spear, and bulging eyes, Athena's wisdom is projected as a warrior's, amazon-like. Centuries before the Olympians appropriated her, Athena's essence was of deep knowledge and regeneration, symbolized by the owl. The ruins of Priene date from this earlier era.

We rent an old bag-of-bones motorbike on the beachfront and set off, swerving and guffawing like a couple of drunks. Exiting the town limits, we enter an entirely different world. Rolling hills give way to long straight roadways, again giving way to rocky curves. Up ahead, cresting waves are licking the sky. Into the bracing air, we ride the coastline where the Aegean and Mediterranean Seas meet. We are dwarves amidst the azure expanse. Scant traffic consists of mostly old-style tractors driven by salt-of-the-earth men with leathery skin. An occasional modern car passes by, looking ghastly and out of place. Even Ed, our fondly named motorbike, seems too advanced for this scene. The hills unfold into a vast alluvial plain, as the road carries us further inland. We witness billowing white tents in the distance, appearing at once feeble and majestic. Cotton fields are coming into view. We didn't know they were so beautiful, fluffy white balls bursting forth on jagged branches. Draped in heavy garments for warding off the sun, migrant families are harvesting them. Their swollen loads protrude in odd juxtaposition to their bodies. Impulsively, we begin to wave hello. Waves returned, we feel a tinge less awkward about our entry into their world. This little bike is a time machine, pushing us deeper into the past. Many families live packed into those tents. There is a simplicity out here—a bare earth struggle for survival—that Charmaine and I will never know.

Miletus protrudes in the distance, like an ancient spaceship on a flat plain. By the eighth century B.C., Miletus was the principle Greek City State of the Aegean. It produced the world's first

---

As we sped off into the country, the pension manager shouted, "Fill up with gas!" A quick glance at the gas gauge showed a full tank, so we took his caution as a simple reminder to bring back a full tank. We took turns at the helm, no destination before us other than excitement and adventure. And we found both about fifteen kilometers outside of Ürgüp, when the scooter began slowing just past the village of Aksilur. As we sputtered to a stop, we remembered the pension manager's last words. Even though the gas gauge was still looking mighty "F", a glance into the tank revealed a shiny and stainless steel bottom. Bone dry.

—Ryan Forsythe, "Friends I'd Never Met Before"

Western philosophers, including Heraclitus. A poetic fragment of his reads, "It's not possible to step twice into the same river...it scatters again, comes together, and approaches and recedes." We are literally the only tourists here today. It's dead quiet, and the structures loom large. Portions of the great city are intact, like the Roman-Era theater seating 24,000 people. Roman baths, a beautiful old mosque and Hellenistic stadium, are also well preserved.

Two young Turks, Yesil and Aydan, escort me to an olive grove to see temples too far gone for the camera. But their Turkish hospitality is endearing. Aydan points out, in shyly chopped English, that he's getting married in the spring. He shows off his horse, the one Yesil is now riding. As we saddle Ed, they fill our hands with tasty roasted grains, on the order of peanuts. Leaving Miletus, we pass young women hauling cotton. They turn their backs, pretending they don't see us. Soon, however, they peek from behind their loads, beaming smiles, playing to the camera.

On the road to Priene, our main and furthest destination, a flatbed truck passes by. On the back, a huge load of workers is packed like blades of grass. We're a stone's throw away from the truck. With each of them facing us, the eye contact is near embarrassing. Still, we are compelled, as if magnetically, to stay close. We're awkward intruders, trying to veil our conspicuousness. That's hopeless. We surrender and relax on the wind. Tensions between truck and bike start to give way, and we extend our hands up. A few of their hands move upward. More go into the air. Some eyes are lighting up, ours catching fire on theirs. White teeth are gleaming under sheer iridescent scarves in pastel colors that float like chiffon across the women's faces. The craggy, sun-beaten skin, the multicolored wraps, the children's pigtails and overalls, ivory palms riding the air...suddenly look unspeakably beautiful. We wave and flow and wave and flow, until every face has opened, and we have become simple spirits wafting on breezes that lie behind the ravages of time, deep inside the strangeness of ourselves, where we are familiar. The present moment expands into immeasurable lifetimes.

Priene is at least another thirty minutes away. The books make the three sites sound like hop, skip, and jump. They are not. Ed putts along, but is showing his age. We cross our fingers. The plain stretches to forever. We are virtually alone on the road. Finally we reach Priene, most spectacular of the ancient Ionian cities, literally perched on a rocky bluff overlooking the Meander Valley.

Priene was designed in the fourth century B.C. by Pytheos, who inspired the famous mausoleum. Largely unchanged since Hellenistic times, it was built in a strict geometric grid. The site is vacant except for a few other straggling tourists. Ghosts, eager to tell their stories, seem to hover among the giant rubble. Gigantic steps lead up to the Temple of Athena. It's located high on the bluff over the valley, once the seafloor in ancient times, before the silting of the Meander River filled the harbor. We try to imagine how this still awesome sanctuary looked with the endless blue sea expanding outward, dramatic waves lashing at the heels of the cliff.

Charmaine and I don't speak much. My camera dwells on the golden afternoon light. I shoot, unhurried. Charmaine writes in her journal. Time freezes on the colossal Ionian columns, broken, but no less powerful. Athena's original and purest essence seems to be lurking. The temple bears an inscription noting that Alexander the Great financed its completion. He also liberated the Prieneans from the Persians. For this, they devoted a small shrine to Alexander, considering him in league with the gods.

We need to photograph Didyma, our last city, in the fading rays of today's sun. We jump down the mammoth steps, an old design, for lack of sophisticated weapons, to intimidate intruders. Ed awaits. We pack him up and retrace our path in the amber light, a play of glow and shadow.

Soon Ed begins to cough and spit. We plead with him that his death could well be ours, or at least cause unthinkable problems. The sky dims over the endless valley. A new chill enters the air. Thankfully, Ed obliges. As twilight falls, we reach Didyma.

Didyma was holy ground long before the Ionians ever arrived. The Greeks rededicated the site to their god, Apollo. The oracle was continued and intimately connected with the ancient city of Miletus.

The site is closing, but I quickly shoot what I can of the elegant structures. The Temple of Apollo is the dominant focus. It encompasses over 100 stone columns in a double row, and seventy-foot walls. The design was so highly advanced, it needed work intermittently for 500 years. Though never finished, it was considered the greatest architectural feat of the ancients. Many columns have been re-erected. What's left of the structure is pure drama and a sight to behold at sunset, but there's little time to savor it.

I find Charmaine across the road, talking in her friendly manner with several Turkish men. They enjoy her with no trace of disrespect. The rural Turkish woman is tucked away at home, living the purely domestic life. Western currents pull hard in Turkey, but deeply rooted Islamic tradition drags like undertow, away from the larger cities. An infant country groping upon a land of deep and layered history, Turkey overflows with paradox.

Dusk creeps in and ushers us onward, back to Altinkum. Ed chugs along, giving us the last of his life. Entering the town limits, I feel myself crossing a threshold. At Athena's temple, we entered stillness, a wisdom deeper than a warrior's. The workers on the flatbed truck brought us wholly alive to the present. With them, the spirit of Artemis broke free. Turkey is undeniably raw—in her torrid struggle for identity and survival, yes. But also in her sheer power to touch eternal bone, in her elegance as ancient portal to the nerve center of being. The river called Meander once led through Priene, Miletus, and Didyma, all those years ago. The day was like a step in the river, as Heraclitus wrote, never to be repeated. Despite all expectations, Turkey has warmed in my bloodstream. I glance at my ring. It now appears benevolent.

Barbara Bowen is a writer of drama and creative nonfiction, with twelve years experience in professional photography. Her work is inspired by travel and mythology, and is focused on the intersection between art and spirituality. She has written theater reviews for New City Magazine, Chicago. *Her prose and poetry have been published in journals and reference books across the U.S.*

TIM CAHILL

Anybody Seen a Tiger
Around Here?

The Caspian tiger might still be out there,
wandering the hills of eastern Turkey.

I WAS SITTING IN THE OWL, A SMALL BAR IN A SMALL TOWN
in Montana, when I was lifted bodily from the stool—no small
feat—and kissed exuberantly on each cheek. "Doctor C.!" Tommy
the Turk said by way of greeting. He is a barrel-chested man, bald
as a billiard ball, and he wore a blue-and-white woven wool cap,
like a yarmulke. I assumed that he was back from one central-Asian
war or another. People who know these disputes know Thomas
Goltz. A war correspondent and author of certain distinction,
Goltz is one of the few Americans who have met and interviewed
the players in several shadowy and little-understood conflicts. He
lectures frequently and once spent a day making the rounds briefing the spooks at the CIA. "I've got a quest for you, Doctor,"
Tommy said.

He showed me a clipping from the London *Sunday Express*. The
lead sentence said that high in the mountains of Turkey "could lie
a secret which will stun scientists: the return from the dead of a lost
species." The article quoted Dr. Guven Eken of the Society for the
Protection of Nature: "The Caspian tiger is considered to be extinct, but in southeast Turkey local hunters claim to have seen
tigers in the mountains."

We toasted Tommy's safe arrival back in Montana and discussed the idea of searching for the ghost tiger. As I recall, this involved a great many toasts. The next morning I woke up with some fuzzy recollection about an agreement to go to Turkey and search for the Caspian tiger with Tommy the Turk, a guy famous for covering wars. Was this a good idea? Would we get shot at? And what the hell did I know about tigers?

One week later, Tommy and I were in Istanbul, along with photographer Rob Howard, who is nicknamed—for reasons impervious to investigative reporting—the Duck. We were sitting at a café overlooking the Bosporus and talking with the afore-mentioned Dr. Eken. He was an Art Garfunkel-looking guy who confessed that he had never actually been to southeastern Turkey, didn't know the first thing about tigers, and didn't really actually have the names of any hunters who'd seen one. He'd only heard rumors.

So now we were tracking *rumors* of a ghost tiger. The less-than-helpful Dr. Eken sought to dissuade us. The southeastern part of the country was "sensitive," he said. "Security" could be a problem.

The problem, in a nutshell, involved the long-running Kurdish insurrection. Twenty million Kurds live in four separate countries, making these folks the world's largest ethnic group without a homeland. (The de facto statelet that has existed in northern Iraq ever since the United States made the area a no-fly zone doesn't really count.) The two dominant Iraqi Kurdish groups are largely sympathetic to Turkey and the United States. A third group, the Marxist-Leninist Kurdistan Workers Party, or PKK, which also op-erates in Turkey, advocates using whatever violent means are nec-essary to establish an independent Kurdish state. The PKK has been largely defanged by the arrest of its leader, Abdullah Ocalan, in February 1999, but pockets of resistance still exist, especially in the remote, mountainous, little-inhabited areas of southeastern Turkey. The day before, for instance, two insurrectionists had been killed by soldiers in a prolonged gun battle outside the town of Semdinli, near the border with Iraq.

It was Tommy's impression that things were winding down in the southeast and that we could talk our way through most military tary checkpoints. Eken insisted that we at least talk with the Society's big-mammal man in Ankara, Emry Can, a man who knew even more about tigers than he did, which seemed, on the face of it, to be pretty much a slam-dunk.

The rest of our brief stay in Istanbul involved sitting around in innumerable offices, smoking lots of cigarettes, while Tommy talked about tigers in exchange for press passes and letters of introduction. Foreign journalists assured us that we probably couldn't get to certain towns in the southeast. Mostly, we were given to understand that the authorities didn't want to see another story in the foreign media excoriating the Turks for oppressing the proud and noble Kurds. This story is written and broadcast so often it actually has a name: the "cuddly Kurd/terrible Turk" angle. The Turkish military and police strove to suppress such reports, and only weeks earlier American and British TV crews had been expelled from the area. Our quest, we explained to our friends in the press corps, was about cuddly, terrible tigers, and as such, a different matter entirely. They were dubious.

In the past week, in fact, I had done some research on the Caspian tiger. Its dossier was fascinating, but surprisingly thin.

Tensions have eased significantly between Kurds and Turks in recent times. Most fighting in the southeast has ended, and speaking the Kurdish language in public is no longer outlawed. Turkey's current elected president, Ahmet Necdet Sezer, has called for many reforms, including ending the ban on teaching Kurdish in schools. In the 1999 elections, Kurdish candidates won the mayoral seats of all major cities in southeastern Turkey, whereas before, Kurds were not even allowed a political party.

—JV

Historically, the animal once ranged from western China through the central-Asian "-stans" to Iran, Iraq, Azerbaijan, and Turkey. It was this Caspian variety that gave the striped cats their name: Romans supposedly captured them on the banks of the Tigris, called them tigers, and took them back to the Colosseum for their circuses. This subspecies of *Pantera tigris*—one of eight to walk the earth over the past few millennia—looked a good deal like the Bengal tiger, with khaki fur and black bands on its back and legs. It was a big animal; only the endangered Siberian tiger is larger. Males measured up to nine feet from the nose to the tip of the tail, and weighed in excess of 500 pounds. In winter, it developed a distinctive bushy coat, which surely added to the various misgivings of travelers considering going mano a paw with one in the snow of a mountain pass. A carnivore status survey conducted in Iran from 1973 to 1976 failed to turn up any evidence of the creature. The last known Caspian tiger was shot in 1970 in the southeast-Turkish town of Uludere.

We took the night train down to the capital city of Ankara and talked with the big-mammal expert, Emry Can, who interrogated us fiercely—he thought we were hunters, looking to knock off the last tiger. Finally satisfied of our innocence, Can admitted that he himself had not been to the southeast, but was planning an expedition "next year, or perhaps the year after."

Anything we might find—tracks, confirmed sightings—would be of great significance, he said. Unfortunately, he had no idea where we might start our search.

And so, with no firm destination in mind, we flew to the major town in the southeast, Van, on the shores of Lake Van, the largest freshwater lake in Turkey. There we met up with Saim Guclu, chief engineer of the National Forest, Eastern Anatolia Region, a big, jolly man in his early sixties with a white mustache. Saim would provide a driver and transportation: a small Nissan truck with an extended cab and a forestry-department decal. We would pay for gas and fork over $300 for each day we shot pictures in a national forest. In other words, Saim seemed to be what he claimed, a forestry official, albeit one with his hand out, not an intelligence officer assigned to keep an eye on us. "I am ashamed to admit that I have never been to Uludere, where the last tiger was shot," he said. "We have done no inventory of the animals in these places. Of course, our department has existed only since 1994. Your presence here is very helpful to me, you see."

Saim said he had pored over books and documents in the forestry department for information on the Caspian tiger and had found little there. It was dawning on me that it didn't take much to be an expert on this animal, and that I was getting to be right up there. "If we find evidence that the tiger exists," Saim said, "it will be a great thing, not only for Turkey but for all the world. Wildlife doesn't belong to any one country."

Unfortunately, not everyone shared Saim's enlightened views.

"How dare you!" Tommy was saying to the soldier at one of the military checkpoints on the road to Uludere. We were in the forestry-service truck with Saim and his driver, and we'd been stopped at the summit of a pass. The soldier had just said, "Why don't you stay home? Why come here and stir up trouble?" By which we knew he meant, "We don't want to read any more cuddly Kurd/terrible Turk stories."

"How dare you speak to me in that tone of voice before you know what my mission is?" Something about this gave the soldier pause, and Tommy took advantage of the lull to trot out the passes and letters we'd smoked so many cigarettes to obtain. He explained about the tiger, and the conversation settled down into friendly banter and an invitation to tea. We soon found ourselves in the wooden guard shack, smoking more cigarettes and laughing about one thing or another. My name, for instance, was a matter of great hilarity. In Turkey, no one is named Tim, but many are called Timur, in honor of the fourteenth-century Mongol who conquered much of this part of the world. He was known for his cruelty; he is said to have ordered the deaths of 17 million people between the Black Sea and Delhi. Historical mass murder was looked upon with a degree of respect. It was my last name that was the problem. Cahill is pronounced *Djaheel* in Turkish and means "ignorant." So Tommy and the soldiers sat around drinking tea, smoking cigarettes, passing around my passport, and laughing out loud at my name. Timur the Ignorant: It was like being called Attila the Dope.

We left the guard shack and plunged down a paved two-lane road onto flatter land and then drove parallel to the border with Iraq until we reached the turnoff to Uludere. The narrow road meandered up alongside a flowing green creek lined with white-bark poplars, and we passed an abandoned village of quaint stone houses, each with at least one wall leveled by artillery fire. "We don't know who did this," Saim said, "the PKK or the military. Whoever it was, let Allah strike them blind."

And then we were in Uludere proper, passing ancient houses made of river rock and winding our way through streets crowded with tall, generally slender people with imposing hawk-like faces: Kurds. We stepped out of the truck and were immediately surrounded by men, all of them answering our questions at full volume and at the same time. No one knew the man who had shot the tiger in 1970, but there had been a fellow who shot one in the sixties. He was dead. Forty years ago, the paved road we'd driven had been a mule trail. Uludere was now a big town. No one had heard anything about tigers for years.

An old man said there had been lots of tigers in the early sixties. He had heard them at night while he tended his sheep. They made a sound like the bray of donkey. Not the *heehaw* sound, but the *ahhhh* noise they make. Someone else said the animal was so heavy it took three men to carry a dead one, that its track looked like that of a domestic cat, but bigger, with claws as long as a man's index finger. The big cat, he said, seemed to seize the snow: When its paws flexed, the pads would leave little snowballs in the middle of the trail.

We had been talking with the men for about ten minutes when the sub-govenor of the province arrived, along with several policemen. This self-inflated little turd threatened to confiscate our film and detain us until he could ascertain the nature of our business in Uludere. Saim, the Duck, and I retreated to the truck behind a solid wall of Tommy-talk while our driver fired up the engine. A cop put his hand on Tommy's shoulder, but he shook it off, jumped into the truck and said, "Go, go, go!"

Back in Van, we were out of ideas. But it was a nice sunny day, and we drove to a dock about twenty-five miles outside of town and hired a boat to take us to the old Armenian church on Akdamar Island.

We'd heard rumors of a Loch Ness-type monster in the lake and we asked the boatman about it. "There are no monsters," he said, "but there are some very large snakes." I assumed he meant eels. "I have never seen one. My father did: He said it was as big around as a fifty-five-gallon oil drum and as long as this boat." The boat appeared to be forty-five feet long. "But," Saim said, "you are describing a monster."

The island was rugged and rocky, and it rose out of the clear blue waters of Lake Van like a shattered sculpture. The domed church, built in the tenth century by the Armenian king Gagik Ardzouni, was surrounded by almond trees, the branches bare and gnarled in the winter sun. The lower walls were covered over in bas-relief. There were depictions of a naked man and woman in a garden, eating something that looked like an apple. There was a knight on horseback spearing something that looked very much like the Lake Van monster. Another sculpture showed a man being tossed from an open boat into the mouth of what could, once again, only have been the Lake Van monster.

More to the point, there were tigers all over the walls. Before the Armenians were eventually driven from the church by the Turks, they had painted animals around the upper dome: goats and wolves and tigers. Lots of tigers.

I sat in the sun, looking out across the lake at the shining, snow-clad mountains, and thought how, at least in historical times, there'd been tigers here. Also apparently present had been Saint George, and Adam and Eve, along with Jonah and the Lake Van monster.

That night, we walked through the maze of cobblestone alleyways off the main street of Van and finally found a shop where one of Tommy's boots could be resoled. The cobbler, Mustafa, talked as he worked. He had never seen any evidence of a tiger around Lake Van, and he hunted birds in the mountains quite often. Still, Mustafa said, if we liked, he could call the most avid hunter he knew and invite him down to the shop to talk. Halim was a man of fifty-six, a Jack Palance look-alike with long arms and hands the size of canned hams. He agreed that there were no tigers anywhere nearby and hadn't been for many years. He had heard rumors about tiger sightings to the east, however. We should talk to his hunting partner, a baker named Hamid Kaya. "Where does Hamid Kaya live?" Tommy asked.

"Semdinli," Halim said.

We drove southeast, passing from checkpoint to checkpoint and moving ever deeper into the mountains. The road took us over a pass in what could easily have been the Swiss Alps with snow several feet deep. Far below, a narrow valley stretched out as far as the eye could see, and at its farthest extent, hard up against the mountains rising abruptly behind it, was the little town of Semdinli. Tiger town, terror town; take your pick.

We drove down the main street, an amalgam of two- and three-story buildings of the type that collapses during earthquakes. Small patches of sooty gray snow lay in the street. We parked next to the bakery and asked if Hamid Kaya, the bread maker, was there. Once again, we were surrounded by Kurds, a dozen or more of them, all wearing some variant of the tribal costume of baggy pants and a cummerbund.

Were we here to talk about the terror, they all wanted to know, and we said no, we were here to talk about tigers. We had read reports that there had been several recent sightings. Hunters, the paper said, had seen the animal in these mountains.

"Then they lie!" one man shouted. "No one hunts here." The dangers, men on all sides explained, were simply too great. The mountain trails were mined. A hunter could be mistaken for a terrorist and shot by the military, or he might be mistaken for a military commando and shot by the terrorists. Since the insurrection began in 1984, more than 30,000 people had been killed. "No one hunts here," a man repeated.

"*I* have been in the mountains," said a distinguished-looking older man wearing a wool sport coat over a pink sweater. Musa Iren, seventy-two, said he had seen a tiger in the mountains not far away, near Yaylapinar. That was eight years ago, and he had tracked it through the snow for two days.

"Do they make a sound?" Tommy asked.

"Like a donkey," Musa said. He made an *ahhhh* sort of sound.

"Describe the tracks."

"The tracks were like that of a cat, but as big as my hand, and the claws were as long as my index finger," Musa said. Tommy and I passed a significant look. "Anything else?"

"Yes," Musa said. "When the tiger walks, he seizes the snow and leaves small balls of packed snow in the middle of the track."

"This is true," said another older man, named Cirkin, who said he shot a tiger, also near Yaylapinar, forty years ago. It required thirteen rounds from a shotgun to kill the animal, and three men to carry it.

"These animals are not extinct," Musa said. "I guarantee you they are up there. Not just one or two, but many."

There was some general scoffing about this but another man came to Musa's aid. "Because no one hunts—it is sixteen years now—the animals are coming back. Even here, near town, we see more bears and wild goats and wolves and wild pigs. Why not tigers?"

There were now fifty or sixty men gathered about, all shouting out their opinions. "Listen to me," Musa said. "You know the village of Ormancik, on the border with Iraq? Four years ago, a man of that village, Haji Ak, killed a tiger. He brought me the skin, and I had it in my shop for two years. I could not sell it and gave it back to him."

I was wildly excited as I wrote place names in my notebook: Yaylapinar, Ormancik, Ortaklar. It was at precisely that moment, of course, that we were arrested by the police.

Tommy the Turk—in a typical effort to seize control of the

situation—refused to get in the police car. "We'll walk, thanks," he said, as if the officer were a pal who'd just offered him a ride. The crowd had melted away, and we trudged slowly behind the police car as it moved past a green army tank and down a steep hill toward the station.

Inside, the two-story cement bunker was a maze of corridors, with cops coming and going every which way, but down the longest hallway was a central office where a man in a stylish suit sat behind an imposing wooden desk. This had to be the chief, and Tommy bulled past the cop who had detained us, rapped once on the open door, and strode in. "Please tell me exactly what is going on here," he said in Turkish. "We need to know," the chief said in near-perfect English, "what you are doing in our town." As it happened, the chief was a sucker for Tommy-talk, and we left with his personal phone number in case there was any more trouble. He also called the military commanding officer of the province, Colonel Eshrem.

We were escorted to the army post that dominated the town, and then through a leather-padded wooden door studded with brass tacks, and then through a second padded door, like a kind of air lock. Certain military and police officers we'd met had regarded our mission as a highly laughable cover story for some nefarious activity or another. The colonel, however, not only believed us but thought the search for the Caspian tiger was a worthy goal. He was a man given to folksy aphorisms. "You search for the tiger," he said. "We say time spent searching for treasures lost is never time wasted."

Regrettably, the colonel could not allow us to travel any farther down the road to Yaylapinar and Ormancik. The two PKK insurgents killed recently had been shot between Semdinli and Ormancik. That was just last week. The rebels were all over the area, and a military strike was planned against them within days.

Still, the colonel thought it would be a grand thing if tigers still existed in the midst of war. There was, he said, thinking aloud, a military exercise the next day. Several village guards, armed Kurds loyal to the government, would be meeting up with his soldiers and continuing on to Yaylapinar. "So, you could get to Yaylapinar with them," the colonel said. He didn't think the danger would be too great.

"And tonight," the colonel said, "you will please be my guests. Sleep here, in the barracks."

And so I spent a night in a Turkish military barracks, which, I know, sounds like a fantasy out of a John Rechy novel. (Actually, our private rooms were better than those of any hotel we'd seen.) But the next morning, we were finally on our way, searching for the tiger…with a military escort. We rode with a Captain Milbray in a Jeep Cherokee, between a truck full of uniformed soldiers and an armored personnel carrier, as the convoy made its way along the side of a ridiculously steep slope. Hundreds of feet below, a river churned over the floor of the gorge, and burned-out military vehicles littered the banks.

Captain Milbray didn't buy our tiger story, not even a little bit. "I've been out in these mountains for four years," he said. I've seen bears and wild goats and wild pigs, but never a tiger. And none of my men has ever seen one."

"Have you ever looked for one?" I asked.

"No," the captain said. "Well, two days ago I shot one. But I ate it. Even the skin."

"What a good joke, Captain," Tommy said.

Presently, the road branched off to Yaylapinar. We stopped for a moment, and suddenly a dozen heavily armed Kurds appeared out of nowhere. They came pouring down the slopes at a dead run, swathed in baggy pants and turbans and cummerbunds, carrying knives, grenades, and automatic weapons. In the space of thirty seconds we were surrounded, and even though I knew they were with us, it was a little unsettling. This is how fast it can happen to you out here, I thought. And then the Kurds piled into a truck, and we were moving again.

The road dropped into the valley of the Pison River. There were patches of snow on green grass, and cows grazed in the fields. As we pulled into Yaylapinar, dozens of people converged on the Jeep. Someone put out white plastic lawn chairs, and Tommy and

I sat down and interviewed a man named Zulfigar, who'd shot a tiger, a female, perhaps ten years ago. "The mark of this animal," Zulfigar said, "is that when it walks, it seizes the snow. The claws are as long as my first finger."

Other men were butting in now, talking about tigers in the old days, and even Captain Milbray seemed to catch the fever. "When you shot the tiger," he asked Zulfigar, "was it before or after your military service? Before or after your first child was born?" In this manner he ascertained that the tiger had been shot not ten years ago, but more like forty.

Still, Captain Milbray was no longer mocking us. "Why," he asked Zulfigar, "did you shoot the tiger?"

"In those days, he who shot a tiger was a hero."

"These are not those days," the captain said. "Today, he who shoots a tiger is my enemy. I will see that he goes to jail."

As quick as that, I threw an arm over the captain's shoulder, and we thanked each other in the manner of Alphonse and Gaston.

We went to another village, Ortaklar, then returned before dark to the army post at Semdinli, where the colonel was waiting to debrief us. About that time, there was a knock on the padded door. A young officer stood at attention and reported that some village guards in Umurlu had seen a tiger. Word about our visit had apparently spread. "When was this?" the colonel asked.

"Five days ago."

"Ahh, I don't believe this," the colonel said. "I was there three days ago. They would have told me."

"Not," I suggested, "if they were out hunting when they should have been guarding the village."

"Just so," the colonel said. "Have the men come to Semdinli."

There were three of them. And yes, they'd been hunting wild goats instead of standing guard, which is why they hadn't said anything to the colonel.

It had happened about four miles north of the village, in a labyrinthine area called the Honeycomb Cliffs. The youngest of them, a thirty-year-old named Nuri Durmaz, had moved off to the west alone. "There was a little snow," he said, "not a lot. I was about halfway to the peak. There was an overhanging wall, like a cliff, and I saw something 100 meters away. I couldn't see its head, but it was big. It would have taken two, maybe three men to carry it."

"What color was it?" Tommy asked.

"Like my pants," Nuri said. He was wearing khaki pants. "It had black stripes on the legs and resembled a large cat."

"Did you shoot it?" I asked.

"No. I was in a bad place. If I only wounded it, it could have torn me apart."

"What did you do?"

"I went to get my friends."

And here Nuri's friends chimed in with descriptions of the tracks: claws as long as a man's finger, the little ball of snow in the center of the print. It wasn't the only such creature up in the Honeycomb Cliffs, said one of the men. He'd seen the same tracks in about the same place almost exactly a year ago.

I brought out some pictures I'd copied for just this purpose. There was a drawing of the Anatolian panther, also thought to be extinct; a photo of a lynx, many of which still roam these mountains; and one of a Caspian tiger, taken decades ago in an Iranian zoo. Nuri discarded the panther and the lynx. "This one," he said, holding up the picture of the tiger.

"What do you think?" I asked Saim.

"I'd say 50 percent credibility."

The Duck and I both put it at a 70 percent sure thing. The colonel said, "I don't have an opinion to be expressed in a percentage, but I believe in nature. This is a wonderful thing for Turkey and the world. I will inform my lieutenant in charge of the area to monitor the situation. I will give him a camera and ask him to use his night-vision goggles whenever possible."

Nuri said, "The next time I see this animal, I will kill him for you."

"I don't think you should do that," the colonel said. This was expressed as an order. But then the colonel softened his voice. "If these men publish an article, and if peace is established, you will find that people with cameras will come here, and to your delight they will put much money in your pocket."

"This is true?"

"This is true."

"I can almost smell that tiger," Tommy was saying. We were now on our way to Iraq to try to enter the Honeycomb Cliffs from the southern side of the range.

The colonel had been kind enough to give us a glimpse of a classified map. Unfortunately, the cliffs were also ground zero in the war against the PKK, and there was no way he was letting us get anywhere near them. But Tommy and I had noticed that the cliffs stretched into northern Iraq. So we'd bidden goodbye to our military friends and started driving along the border with Iraq toward the town of Sirnak. Saim was in a state of high excitement. The colonel, he said, had told him that if he were ordered to do so, he, Colonel Eshrem, could use his resources, including helicopters and substantial manpower, to search for the tigers. If Saim, acting as a forestry-department official, were to write to the colonel's superiors, that order could come through in as little as three or four months.

"I asked him what was the best way to word such a request," Saim said, "and the colonel even dictated the letter for me." I gathered that forestry agents couldn't always count on enthusiastic cooperation from military officers.

At Sirnak, we parted in an orgy of embraces and kissed cheeks. Saim refused to accept any money, despite our agreement. He was a man of great honor and emotion, and he wouldn't take our lucre, "for the sake of the tiger." He said, "You have done a wonderful thing."

We hired a car and driver in Sirnak, then made a run for Ormancik and the border. Tommy was confident there would be no problem getting into the Kurdish-held territory: He had worked with several aid agencies, helping Kurdish refugees when Saddam Hussein rolled his tanks on his own people after the Gulf War. Tommy still had friends among the former refugees, and, in fact, the cap he wore, the one I had always thought of as a yarmulke, was a treasured gift from an Iraqi Kurdish general.

At the border, however, a Turkish official refused to stamp us out of the country. We spent two days there while Tommy worked the public phones, calling his friends in Ankara in an effort to, in his words, "find someone who'll squash this little prick for me."

For two days, I sat against a wall while Tommy stood at the phone, talking Tommy-talk as only Tommy can talk. "Look," he was saying to some English-speaking Turkish official in the capital, "We're not actually going into the mountains." (Not unless we could get into Iraq, he failed to say.) "We'll just be doing what we did in Turkey. We talk to the police and to the military and to the people in the villages. We raise people's consciousness, get them thinking about what it means if this animal still exists."

Day two at the border was now slipping into day three. "All we really want to do is make people aware of this magnificent creature," Tommy was saying.

Sitting there, listening to all this, it occurred to me that maybe that was enough. For now. Maybe, as the colonel and Saim had said, we actually had done something wonderful. People should be made aware. Because, in my almost-expert opinion, the tiger is out there.

Tim Cahill is the author of seven books, mostly travel related, including Jaguars Ripped My Flesh, Pecked to Death by Ducks, Pass the Butterworms, *and* Hold the Enlightenment: More Travel, Less Bliss. *Cahill is also the editor of* Not So Funny When It Happened: The Best of Travel and Misadventure, *and the co-author of the Academy Award nominated IMAX film,* The Living Sea, *as well as the films* Everest *and* Dolphins. *He lives in Montana, and shares his life with Linnea Larson, two dogs, two cats, and a host of friends.*

$_\star\ ^{\star}\ _\star$

Remzi's Curse

*A travel romance can have
lasting consequences.*

WHEN I SET OUT TO CIRCLE THE GLOBE ALONE, MY FAMILY was certain I'd return in a coffin. Their only hope was that I'd pick up a man along the way. My mother in particular was very keen to see me matched up, and actually encouraged me to pick up strangers. "Girl, why don't you find some nice, strong guy along the way to help you carry that big ol' bag?" she said. I rolled my eyes, but secretly I hoped—was sure—I would, actually.

At the core of my heart, I knew God had plotted a Harlequin Romance ending for me. He had already X-ed the spot where I would bump into a Rugged, Sensitive, Intelligent, and Handsome Wayfarer who would take one look at me and say "At last." And then we'd walk hand in hand through the dusty Arabic market, oblivious to the flies landing on our faces, shopkeepers peering out from their fruit stalls to proclaim, "*Ill'hamdu l'illah!* Thanks be to God!"

But it was slim pickins at the hostels where I stationed myself. Shaggy, boozy boys in Tevas and the same shirts they'd worn since the overland journey from India didn't figure into my Hollywood fantasy. I can't respect a man who bargains down the price of a fifty-cent beer. They didn't seem to notice me much either, being in need of a haircut myself and always hunched over tea and a journal.

216

My blue eyes drew the lusty brown locals to me like a magnet, however, especially in the Middle East. "Beautiful! I love you!" "*Ishta*! Cream!" they'd yell, hissing and clicking their tongues as I crossed the street. Sometimes they'd even snatch my breast, or worse—I was told that racy American movies were to blame. The walls around my heart quickly hardened. "No, no, no; *imshee, gidiniz*, go away," became my relentless mantra through the Middle East and Mediterranean, especially in Turkey, where the boys are clingier than sweaty clothes on a sweltering desert day.

Then I met Remzi.

Tired of the bikinied beaches and liquored discos of the Mediterranean, I had journeyed to Turkey's far east, to Kurdistan. The guidebooks warned me that PKK terrorists nab tourists there and make them eat raw snake and hedgehog, and that women should never travel to Eastern Turkey, especially alone.

So I expected to land in cultural outer space. Instead, I made instant friends who took me into their homes, schools, villages, businesses, and lives. When I refused to stay any longer, they passed me on to acquaintances in my next destinations, the hospitality building up like fireworks on the Fourth of July. I had never felt safer.

Two middle-aged Dutch women I met along the way gave me a card for the Büyük Asur Oteli hotel, and told me to ask for Remzi, the hotel manager. "Say hello for us," they said as I boarded a bus for Van, a historic city near Turkey's Iranian border.

The women didn't know my type, or even that I was on the lookout, but Remzi fit the script. Kind, witty, and expressive. Hazelnut eyes, almond skin, and raspberry lips. Remzi took me into his office, we struck a fair bargain on a room, and sealed the deal over dinner.

Remzi took me in so quickly and smoothly that I didn't have a chance to say no, or even know what I was saying yes to. My second day there, Remzi gave me a tour of Van and took me out for lunch, gestures I marked up to brotherly Kurdish hospitality. Still I wondered, was he really just being nice, or was he after something else?

That night I got violently ill from the cold cucumber soup his sisters made with unpasteurized yogurt. Remzi sent me up toast, cherry jam, and peaches with pink carnations on the side—"roses," as he called them. Suddenly I knew he was courting me.

While my stomach recovered, Remzi took me to lakeside restaurants, abandoned islands, and tea gardens. We watched sunsets, laughing at the big orange as it slipped into Lake Van, and darkness left us huddling against the wind.

Remzi introduced me to the famous cats of Van, snowy Persians with one blue and one green eye. At his family's apartment, Remzi's sisters served tea to us, and his widowed mother welcomed me in a voice gruff from hand-rolled cigarettes. I played with his henna-fingered nieces, who took to me like an auntie. Back in his office, Remzi strummed jangly chords on the *saz*, serenading me with mountain legends in a booming cowboy tenor. "Whatever you want, boss," Remzi joked. A week became a century.

One evening, we climbed to a crumbled hilltop castle a thousand-some years old. I gasped at the pale green of Lake Van, crisp against the violet sky and zebra-striped mountains. Sitting at the bluff's edge, we peered down at goats, mosques, and merry makers, tiny and innocent beneath us.

In such slow spaces, Remzi unfurled his life and boyhood for me. Stealing eggs from baby birds, being frightened by the big talking box when the village got its first TV, struggling with school because he spoke no Turkish. To fulfill his military duty in Ankara, Remzi flipped burgers and played in the army band. Working for his family's hotel, Remzi learned English and how to be gentle. Now he dreamed of opening his own tour company and traveling to "Indiana Jones" places like Africa and Arizona.

I also learned about Remzi's culture, how it's been pushed undercover by Turkish nationalism. I was as fascinated as I was horrified by his stories about Kurdish life. Until the last decade, Kurdish culture was outlawed; speaking the language or listening to bootleg cassettes meant a trip to jail. Politics is still a taboo subject for fear that the wrong someone might hear. Remzi could rarely visit his home village because the military closes the roads at sundown. Even when they're open, the passport checks and pat-downs every mile often keep people from their destinations.

At night, we slipped out onto the terrace on top of the hotel and swayed our bodies together under the stars. We promised to look at the night sky once we parted and to remember we were seeing the same moon. "*Seni seviyorum!* I love you so much!!" he'd say. He interpreted my silence as not "feeling free with my feelings," which was somewhat true. I couldn't tell him that the feelings weren't really there.

Remzi was a welcoming oasis for a lonely wanderer. But with each hour, I fell deeper into his heart, an awkward place I couldn't quite seem to leave. Beyond the deep voice, broad shoulders, and sculpted face, Remzi was still a boy, far too delicate for my rough, fickle hands.

That didn't stop me from enjoying Remzi's bed, an ink-blue, anti-evil-eye charm staring out from the wall as our bodies heated up. But though Remzi got so aroused the veins on his forehead bulged, I refused to take my pants off. It had all gone too far already. Instead, I let him escort me back to my room and kiss me good night, hearts and groins thumping.

Every day I tried to leave, Remzi gave me spaniel eyes and I gave in for another day. "Thank you, thank you!" he said, twirling me in the air. He thanked me again with gifts I didn't want but couldn't turn down, including his Nazar Boncuk, the blue-eyed talisman. Remzi said it would protect me from unwanted attention.

But I had to pluck the stars from his eyes eventually, moving on to the green meadows of Romania, the sandy beaches of Thailand, the snowy heights of Tibet, every day falling in love with a new corner of the world. When I left, Remzi was in such bitter despair that I swore off travel romance for the rest of my trip. "You drank me like a cup of tea," he said when we parted, literally hitting his head against the wall.

He was right. I devoured his life story, his culture, and his love mainly to satiate my curiosity.

Three years later, Remzi's phone calls still haunt me here, back in my San Francisco apartment, reminding me to be careful what

I wish for. The azure eye looks out from my wall, now watching over my solitary sleep. In spite of my mother's continued prayers, I've yet to find a man. Remzi's cursed kiss was the last to cross my lips.

April Thompson is a travel writer whose work has appeared in such publications as Walking, Lapis, Moxie, Passionfruit, Alaska Airlines, *thingsasian.com, and the* San Francisco Bay Guardian.

STEPHANIE ELIZONDO GRIEST

Tears from Turkey

*In a place like this, chivalry
is far from dead.*

THERE WAS A TIME WHEN I PRIDED MYSELF FOR HAVING TEAR ducts of steel. I was the only kid on my block who could watch *Bambi* without bawling; *Beaches* made me snicker. Graduation. Weddings. Breakups. Disappointments. I endured it all with neither a sigh nor a whimper.

Until, that is, I went to Turkey.

Istanbul had been a destination point on my atlas for ages. After working in Beijing for a year, I finally made it, with loose plans of selling carpets by day and belly dancing at night. My plans changed my fifth day there, however, during a visit to the Archaeological Museum. As I gazed at a row of headless statues, my hand happened to brush against the spot on my thigh where I always strapped my money belt. Instead of a reassuring bundle, I felt only bare skin.

My heart stopped. I threw down my backpack, hiked up my ankle-length Guatemalan skirt, and gazed in horror.

The money belt was still there.

Its contents were not.

I stumbled about the museum in a state of shock. I had used my passport and American Express card only an hour before and

221

deliberately sealed them both back into the belt. What happened? Did everything somehow fall out? How could I not have noticed? I remembered reading about thieves who tossed powder into tourists' eyes and robbed them blind in a matter of moments. Did that happen to me?

Panic set in as it dawned on me what I had just lost: money, credit cards, passport, airline ticket, traveler's checks, visa. In short, all forms of identity—except my Beijing work permit, which said I was American in Chinese—and all my finances, save for thirty dollars in Turkish lira.

I bolted for the museum's exit, nearly knocking over a museum guard in the process. "My passport!" I shrieked over my shoulder. I raced through Gulhane Park and the Topkapi Palace grounds, darting in and out of tourist patches, frantically retracing the casual stroll I had taken only minutes before. I was nearing the towering minarets of the Aya Sofya when I spotted a Turkish policeman. I scrambled over.

"I lost all my stuff!" I wailed.

He looked at me, amused. A couple of his buddies joined us.

"Money! Passport! Gone!" I told them.

One of the officers pointed with his rifle toward a building labeled "Tourism Police." I scurried over, dodged the security guard, and barged in on five officers settling down to an afternoon smoke.

Something I'd learned quickly on the road is that tactics differ from country to country. Vodka bribes had taken me far when I was an exchange student in Russia; I'd yelled a lot that past year in China. But what about Turkey?

When I approached the men with determination, not a one raised an eyebrow. Realizing that pushy women may not be well received in Turkey, I took a deep breath and tried reasoning with them.

They lit up another round of smokes.

I pleaded for their help.

One got up to make apple tea.

I was about to ask if they preferred Johnnie Walker Red Label or Black when I remembered that I was broke. I collapsed into a chair in despair, and—beyond my knowledge or control—a tear rolled down my cheek.

That did it.

I was instantly surrounded. One officer dabbed my eyes with a tissue; another handed me a phone. The third took to patting my shoulders and murmuring "No cry, no cry, no cry," while the fourth gave me some vital instructions: "You can get everything replaced as long as you say it was stolen. Understand? Not lost. Stolen." The fifth officer pounded away at a typewriter before handing me something written in Turkish that appeared important. With that, I was dismissed to the city police department.

I walked out of the building in a daze. I had never seen tears work outside of a B-grade movie. Surely Gloria Steinem would not have approved of what I just did. NOW would revoke my membership. I felt like a coward, an anti-feminist, the world's biggest wuss.

But then again, I was a wuss with an important-looking document in her hands on her way to the city police. I was going places.

I handed over the document with feigned confidence to the officer behind the desk. He looked it over carefully, eyebrows raised, before handing it to another officer, who walked it downstairs. I was wondering how someone could have possibly reached inside my money belt without my knowledge when a new police officer joined me. We made small talk for a couple of minutes—Where are you from? Texas? Do you have a horse?—before he stopped abruptly, looked straight into my soul, and said: "I saw you by the Aya Sofya. You said you *lost* your passport."

I tried not to blink. Was he bluffing? If not, should I? Then I had an idea.

"But all my stuff is gaaah-hnn," I blubbered as a fresh wave of tears dampened my streaked face.

Within five minutes, I had an official "Declaration of Theft" and directions to the American Consulate.

And then I just got shameless.

In the forty-eight hours that followed, I cried for the consulate and bawled for the bank. At first, I waited for a rejection before raising the floodgates. Then I got the tears flowing before I even walked through the door. My tear ducts got a little crusty, but I still managed some sobs for American Express. Not only was I ushered to the front of every line, but all emergency processing fees were summarily waived. My passport was replaced in three hours as opposed to three days; my traveler's checks were replaced in a matter of moments. The guys at the airline agency gave me a discount on my new ticket; a bank teller bought me lunch.

I never did figure out what happened to my money belt that day. But I've since learned that the Vietnamese sometimes hire professional criers for funerals.

I'm considering a career change.

A Chicana from South Texas, Stephanie Elizondo Griest has volunteered at orphanages in Moscow, edited propaganda in Beijing, and danced with rumba queens in Havana. Her stories have appeared in The New York Times, Washington Post, Latina Magazine, Travelers' Tales: Cuba *and* Her Fork in the Road. *Her first book, an account of her journey across the Communist Bloc, is forthcoming from Villard. She spent the past year of her life traveling some 45,000 miles across the United States in a nineteen-year-old Honda hatchback named Bertha, documenting history for kids at http://www.ustrek.org.*

JOHN KRICH

Allah Hit Me

On Turkish back roads, the author discovers
that the oneness of humanity is inescapable.

WE FILED INTO A VILLAGE TAVERN WHERE THE FOOD SIMMERED
forever in giant pots. Each of the passengers pointed at the stew of
their choice. While we ate, half-dazed, we saw the dim outlines of
peasants lingering in the town's one cobblestone square. Hands
jammed down their pockets, watch-chains showing from their vest
pockets, pancake-shaped caps overhanging flesh-buried eyes, the
men were submerged in silence. They seemed to be holding a tortuous vigil, waiting for a drawing of lots that would determine the
next one to lose his crop, his land, his best mule, or his wife. Or the
next man to sneak away in the night for America.

Before re-boarding the bus, while Iris searched out a toilet, I
wandered off into the square. The night offered a sweet sheep-
herding darkness, though it was lit by stars as plentiful as prophets'
oaths. The villagers smoked strong cigarettes; they fiddled in syn-
copation with strings of sorrow-polished worry beads. I did nothing but drift, circle, and watch. From the way their wide-brimmed
caps shielded their weary faces, from their formidable recalcitrance,
they could have been Sicilian Mafiosi. Any of them could have
been my grandfather, a guarded and suspicious greenhorn, getting
off the boat at Ellis Island. And I realized *I* was wearing my Mao

cap from Hong Kong to the same effect; slung over same eyes, same anxieties, same gratitude for night. Hunched over, in their black vests, the Turks were coughing and whinnying and worrying. They carried the burden of the stars. In my homespun white vest, I whinnied and worried and hunched over, too. When I tried to turn away from my likeness with them, I noticed how all of them seemed to turn away doggedly from their common likeness. The turning away was part of the likeness itself.

Then Allah hit *me*. A genetic chill struck, more strongly than it had with the yiddisher mommas of businessmen on the bus. I knew that I was getting as close to my beginnings as I was ever likely to get. In silence, I communed with these brethren of mine, with a peasant's legacy of grieving and furtive strength that I carried in my bones. What difference did it make if I moved up and down these well-traveled routes from one hiding place to another? The planet spun and held me to it along with these crumbling walls and broken men. I would always be found in the village square.

Together, under the stars, under our thinking caps and our planning caps and our working caps and our yearning caps, clinging to our glorious separation, my colleagues and I brooded over the unyielding terrain we'd been placed on, and over our identity, which came hard, which also had to be sown and reaped, all of us pondering long journeys, and what purpose we might serve on this earth.

Award-winning writer John Krich is the author of a novel about the private life of Fidel Castro, A Totally Free Man, *and well as three nonfiction books,* Why is This Country Dancing?: A One-Man Samba to the Beat of Brazil, El Béisbol: Travels Through the Pan-American Pastime *and* Music in Every Room: Around the World in a Bad Mood, *from which this story was excerpted. His travel and sports writing, reportage and fiction, have appeared in* Mother Jones, Vogue, Sports Illustrated, The Village Voice, The New York Times, *and many other publications. He lives in San Francisco.*

PART FOUR

IN THE SHADOWS

Turkish Knockout

Come as a guest, but keep
your eyes open.

WHEN THE DATE-RAPE DRUG FINALLY WORE OFF TO THE POINT where I could think and function, I found myself facedown in a darkened park not far from Istanbul's Blue Mosque. For an instant, it was as if I'd been born all over again, erased and re-rendered. I remembered nothing: who I was, why I was there, what I'd ever been doing before that moment.

Instinct told me to stand up. Shaking like an addict, I drew myself up to my haunches and pushed with my legs. I rose to my full height for just an instant before something malfunctioned and my whole body veered rigidly to one side. I fell over like a windup toy on a rumpled bedsheet; my shoulder hit the pavement first, then my face.

Blood welled on my cheekbone as a hazy understanding began to form. I patted down my pockets: my petty cash was gone, as was my wallet, my leather belt, and my Swiss Army knife. I felt along my belly for my hidden money belt, but it was gone too—passport, traveler's checks, and all. Oddly, my red spiral notebook and my recently purchased Penguin anthology of Middle Eastern mythology were still jammed into my back pocket. Pulling myself into an upright position, I took a few deep, deliberate breaths.

Sitting there, drugged and dazed in the dim park, I strained to reconstruct what had just happened.

Up until the moment I lost consciousness, my day in Istanbul had already been exceptional—enlivened by unexpected camaraderie, by uncommon novelties. In one afternoon, I'd met more strange people than the rest of my brief days in Turkey combined. Trying to determine at what point I went wrong would be no easy task.

Technically, I wasn't supposed to be adrift in the city that day, since I'd been scheduled to join a preplanned Cairo-bound overland trip the day before. However, when the truck and trip leader never arrived for the pre-departure meeting, I found myself with an extra day to kill in Istanbul.

Since I'd already spent three days touring Istanbul's marvelous historical attractions—from the lavish Ottoman halls of Topkapi Palace to the crowded dagger-and-hookah-pipe stands of the Great Bazaar—I decided to devote my extra day in Istanbul to random wandering. Strolling the parks and alleys of the Sultanahmet

---

※

"Be careful," people would say, "those Turks are such scam artists." Inundated by such cautions before my first trip to Istanbul, I have now come to view the subject as more comic than tragic. Sure, there are cases of rough mistreatment, like the English lad I met who had been given a syringe-injected Coke and later woke up in a warehouse, stripped of his belongings; or the oft-repeated tale of the lamentable visiting Romeo, who is forced to pay for the drinks for a whole table of Turkish vixens who, however suspiciously, seemed rather friendly in the beginning. (And this is not to mention the inevitable heckling suffered by all blond foreign females.) Yet in most cases, unless one is a soccer hooligan, defaming Atatürk, or trespassing on military property, finding real trouble in Turkey is difficult.

—Christopher Deliso,
"Making a Buck in Istanbul"

tourist district with no particular goal, I spent my morning taking in the details I'd been too busy to notice when I first arrived.

Istanbul has long enjoyed a reputation of mystery and intrigue, of East and West mingling in grand palaces and smoky alleyways: a place where dreamers, schemers, and pilgrims go to lose themselves. As I walked that day through the ancient neighborhood where the Bosporous and the Golden Horn meet the Sea of Marmara, everything I saw seemed to contain a hidden currency. When a tout in Sultanahmet Square bullied me into his carpet shop, I was interested less in the Persian-styled rugs than the 1,500 year-old Byzantine column that slanted crazily through the recently-poured concrete floor of the showroom. When I asked an old Turkish man how I might find an *"eczane,"* he gave me directions to the pharmacy in shrill, German-inflected English that made him sound like Colonel Klink from *Hogan's Heroes*. When I walked past the earthquake refugees camped out in the grass along the Hippodrome, I noticed that several of them clutched cell phones. A little gypsy girl selling candy near the tram station wore an oversized Metallica concert shirt cinched at the waist like a dress. Cats crouched in doorways and alleyways; seagulls soared over the minarets of the Blue Mosque. A neatly dressed Turkish boy sitting on the tram grinned shyly at me and whispered "Fuck you," as if in greeting.

Sometime around noon, I was approached near the Galata Bridge by an African teenager. His skin was as black as coffee, and he flopped after me in a loose-fitting pair of rubber sandals. "Hey man," he called to me. "Where are you going today?"

Since this same guy had already approached me two other times in the past three days, I decided to yank his chain a little. "I'm going to Senegal today," I said. "Don't you want to come with me?"

A look of confusion came over the boy's face. He'd told me he was from Senegal two days before, but no doubt he'd told dozens of other people since then. It was a few beats before he smiled in recognition. "Oh hey, I remember you. You're Mr. America. You're always alone, and you never want to meet any girls. Maybe you could meet a girl today, huh? You have a place to stay?"

"Yes, I still have a place to stay," I said. "And no, I don't need to meet any girls. I'm just looking for some place to eat lunch."

"Why don't you go to McDonald's? American food for Mr. America, yes?"

"But Mr. America is in Turkey now," I said. "So maybe he'll eat Turkish food."

"Turkish food is for Turkish people. McDonald's is better for you. Maybe you can buy me a hamburger, O.K.? I want to try a McDonald's."

"You've never eaten at McDonald's before?"

"McDonald's is for Americans. I am so poor!"

Against my better judgment, I decided to indulge him. "What kind of hamburger do you want?"

"A big delicious one. And a Coca-Cola. I will wait right here until you come back."

"If I buy you a hamburger, you have to come to McDonald's and eat it with me."

The Senegalese boy seemed to hesitate for a moment before falling into step with me. On our way to the restaurant, he told me his name was Ahmad. "Do you think I am very handsome?" he asked.

"I'm just buying you a burger, Ahmad. I don't want to be your boyfriend."

Ahmad let out an embarrassed laugh. "No, no," he said. "I want to know, am I very handsome? Could I go to Sweden do you think?"

"What does Sweden have to do with whether or not you're handsome?"

"I think rich Sweden women like boys from Africa. I want to go to Sweden with a rich woman."

"Sweden is cold, Ahmad."

"But I think rich women are very warm!"

At McDonald's, I ordered two Big Mac meals. Ahmad temporarily forgot his hustler persona as he devoured the food in silence and stared around at the spotless, mass-produced interior. "That was my best food ever," he said, somewhat dispassionately, when he'd finished. "Now I will help you find a pretty girl."

"I was thinking of something else, Ahmad. How would you like to go out for a smoke?"

Ahmad's face lit up and he leaned in toward me. "You smoke hash?" he said in a loud whisper. "I will find some for cheap price!"

"I don't want to smoke hash," I said. "I know something better."

In the heart of the Sultanahmet tourist area—not far from Emperor Justinian's 1,400-year-old Church of the Holy Wisdom—I'd recently discovered a back alley waterpipe joint called the Enjoyer Café, which was run by a man who called himself Cici (pronounced like "G.G."). Though the café was wedged between Internet rooms and kilim vendors, Cici's home-spun, adage-spewing charisma more than made up for the lack of authenticity. Thin, lazy-eyed, and companionable, Cici would make his rounds as customers from every stripe of the tourist spectrum sat on cushions and pulled on the bubbling blue-glass pipes.

I'd first visited the Enjoyer Café (named for Cici's mantra: "Enjoy your life!") the night before, along with a few other clients from my postponed overland tour. Though my companions left when the tramlines closed, I stayed on the outdoor cushions and chatted with Cici about Islam and America until the cafe closed. Since Cici had sincerely asked me to come back, I'd decided to treat Ahmad to an afternoon at Cici's waterpipes.

Ahmad looked dubious the moment he saw Cici's café. "Those are apple-smoke pipes," he said. "Apple smoke doesn't make you feel good. I will find some hash instead."

"The smoke is not important," I said. "I think it's just a good place to relax and talk."

"I am sorry. I must make an appointment with my brother. I can't smoke with you today. I will find you a girlfriend later, O.K.?"

"Whatever you say, Ahmad." I watched as the Senegalese teenager flopped off down the alley.

At the Enjoyer Café, Cici greeted me with a nervous smile. "I am glad you returned to talk to me," he said. "But I am sorry to worry. Maybe it's none of my business, but was that black boy your friend?"

"That was Ahmad. I wouldn't call him a friend, necessarily. He's just someone I know from walking around Sultanahmet. I just bought him a hamburger."

Cici looked at me like I was crazy. "You must be careful, my friend. He is a bad boy, I think. Many Africans are not honest people. They come here only to cheat and steal."

"I'm careful. Besides, I know Ahmad is a hustler, and Ahmad knows I know that. I think he's harmless."

"I am sorry. You are right. I only warn you to be careful because many people come to Turkey like blind men. Tourists, they come to take photos, but they don't see past their cameras. Businessmen, they come to Turkey to trade, but they are blind to everything that doesn't carry a price. Travelers, they look around, but they only see what is already in their mind. Do you know how you must come to Turkey, my friend?"

I already knew the answer (he'd given me a nearly identical spiel in a different context the night before), but I didn't want to throw off his rhythm. "How's that?" I asked.

"You must come to Turkey as a guest. Then you will look with your eyes and you will see. Not as a tourist with his camera or a traveler who looks and sees his own dreams. Be a guest of Turkey. A guest knows he is safe, because his hosts love him."

"I'll be your guest then, Cici. Do you have a pipe for me today?"

"Of course, my friend." Cici said something in Turkish to Mustafa, his sleepy-eyed assistant. When Mustafa had ducked into the small indoor hut to prepare a pipe, Cici shot me a sly grin. "Did you meet Mustafa yesterday?" he asked.

"Sure," I said. "But I didn't talk to him much."

Cici laughed cryptically. "Mustafa is too tired to talk. After the earthquake, he is afraid to go back to his apartment, so he sleeps here. None of his girlfriends want to sleep with him in the café, so he is very sad."

"Just how many girlfriends does Mustafa have?"

"Not very many, since his girlfriends cost 10 million lire for each night." Ceci laughed heartily. "Mustafa is only twenty years old, so of course he is crazy for sex. Tell me, must Christians take a bath after the sexual act?"

"No, not that I'm aware of."

"Well in Islam, a man must wash after sex. If he dies before this bath, he will not be pure before Allah. So you see, when the earthquake hit Turkey in August, Mustafa was not pure; he had not yet washed."

"Had he been with one of his girlfriends?"

"No," Cici said. He grinned and made a wanking motion. "He was watching porno movies."

"Watching pornos counts as sex?"

"A man is impure whenever he, well, whenever he finishes." Cici made another dramatic wanking motion to underscore his point. "And Mustafa was impure, so when the earthquake came, he did not know whether to run outside and be safe, or to first take a bath. Because, you see, if he was killed trying to run outside, he would not be pure before Allah."

As Cici told me this, Mustafa came out and placed a blue-glass water pipe before us. I watched as Cici spooned a few hot coals into the small brass bowl. The damp apple tobacco let off a curl of smoke. Mustafa took a seat beside me and handed me the pipe's wooden mouthpiece.

"So what happened?" I asked, choking a bit on the thin, sweet apple smoke.

"What do you mean, my friend?" Cici asked.

"What happened during the earthquake? The 'choice' you were talking about."

Cici laughed. "This is not a secret," he said. "You do not need to talk like a spy. In Turkey, there is no shame for men to talk about sex and purity. If you want to know what Mustafa did during the earthquake, ask Mustafa."

Mustafa gave me a puffy-gummed grin. "I ran outside," he said. "No bath." He blushed, then turned to Cici and asked something in Turkish.

"Mustafa wants to know something about America," Cici said. "He says he heard that in America, girls do not want money for sex. Is this true?"

I thought for a moment, thinking of the best way to phrase my answer. "In America, men and women are social equals," I said. "Sex is a free choice for both sexes."

Cici translated this for Mustafa, then laughed at the reply. "Mustafa says he will move to America, so girls will pay him for sex." Cici gave me a sardonic look. "I think he will never make any money."

I stayed at the Enjoyer Café with Mustafa and Cici for nearly two hours that afternoon. Mustafa asked me lots of baffling questions about sex in the West ("But what do you say to a woman to get sex if you have no money?"), and Cici preached for a bit on the values of Islam: how a gift to the poor is like a gift to the Creator; how everything in life beyond basic human needs is a matter of ego; how the Creator has ninety-nine nicknames, but only answers to Allah.

As I got ready to leave, Cici again warned me about Ahmad, the Senegalese boy. "I only mean to be careful around those black boys," he said. "I don't mean to worry about the future. Do you know why we must not worry about the future?"

"Why's that?"

"Because the future is the next moment. Who knows what will happen in the next moment? Who knows which of us is closer to death? This is why I say: enjoy your life."

That was the last time I would talk to Cici. Before that day was over, however, I would see both Mustafa and Ahmad again.

I left the Enjoyer Café at about half past three that afternoon. Unbeknownst to me at the time, I had only three waking hours left in my day.

The simultaneous charm and risk of travel is it shakes up the paradigms and habits that help you simplify and interpret day-today life. Life on the road, for better or for worse, vivifies a muted aspect of reality: it makes you realize that random factors influence your life just as much as planned ones.

On page eighty of the *Lonely Planet* guide to Turkey, there is a passage entitled "Turkish Knockout" that reads:

"Thieves befriend travelers, usually single men, and offer them drinks which contain powerful drugs which cause the victims to lose consciousness quickly. When the victims awake hours after, they have a terrible hangover and have been stripped of everything but their clothes. The perpetrators of this sort of crime, who are usually not Turkish, often work in pairs or trios."

Bad fortune tends to magnify and mythify these innocuous little details and oversights. That I never read page eighty of my guidebook during my first four days in Istanbul is one of a thousand factors which, in retrospect, seemingly conspired to leave me unconscious and penniless one night in the middle of the city.

A certain 101-level existentialist (Kierkegaard, I think) once suggested that life is lived forward, but understood backwards. This in mind, I have recalled and re-recalled the three hours

---

One report was of foreign (non-Turkish) thieves from another Islamic country befriending a British subject and riding by bus with him across the country to Istanbul. The thieves offered him a soda in Gülhane Parkı. When the victim awoke, his camera, wallet, and passport were gone, as was his luggage from the hotel where they were all staying.

If you are suspicious of newfound friends, eat and drink only from your own supplies or those bought fresh in sealed containers from the hand of a waiter or shopkeeper. (It's possible to inject drugs into a sealed container using a syringe through the seal.) True Turkish friends may offer to pay for drinks to satisfy the requirements of traditional hospitality. They needn't deliver the drinks themselves.

—*Lonely Planet Turkey*

preceding my robbery so many times that, now, the event itself almost seems like a miracle—a divine shroud woven from 1,000
thin, perfectly converging threads of chance.

Of all the factors that contributed to my demise in Istanbul,
perhaps the most damaging variable was also the most innocuous:
Shortly after purchasing a book of Middle Eastern myths at a shop
near the Sultanahmet tram stop, I met up with a couple of
Australians from my postponed overland truck trip. They informed
me that our trip leader had finally turned up in Istanbul, and was
due to arrive with the group in Sultanahmet at around seven that
evening. Figuring this would be as good a time as any to register
and pay my trip fees, I returned to my hotel and took my passport,
traveler's checks, and $400 in petty cash from the lockbox.

Thus, for the first time since I'd arrived in Istanbul, I was personally carrying all of my money and identification at once.

I emerged from my hotel to find Mustafa, the sleepy-eyed
assistant from the water pipe café, waiting there for me. "I see
you inside," he said. He pantomimed smoking a waterpipe.
"You remember?"

"Of course," I said. "You're Mustafa, right?"

Mustafa nodded. "We eat now?" he asked.

At the time, I wasn't sure why Mustafa had pegged me as a
dining companion. Initially, I thought he was going to tout me to
some expensive restaurant, but instead he took me to a street ven-
dor for flat bread and meat sauce. He briefly dug for pocket-
change, but made no protest when I paid for the food myself. In
an inspired flourish, I even stopped at a storefront market and
bought two Efes Lager tallboys—one for each of us. Mustafa led
me to a park bench near the Hippodrome, and we ate our meal in
the late-day sun.

Since Mustafa wasn't much for conversation, I took out my
Middle Eastern myth book and began to read. After a few minutes,
Mustafa took the book from me and started to flip through the
pages. Whenever he saw an illustration, he would ask me what it

was. "I don't know," I would tell him each time. "I haven't read the book yet."

At some point during this charade, Ahmad flopped up out of nowhere and sat down beside us. "Mr. America!" he said, startling me a bit. "We go to McDonald's again?"

I looked over at the African teenager, who was already peering around for other tourists to hustle. "No, I think once a day is enough, Ahmad."

"You need a girl now?"

"Not right now. Maybe Mustafa wants one."

Mustafa looked up from the book, laughed, and handed his beer to Ahmad. Ahmad took a polite sip, and the two of them paged through the illustrations in my myth book.

"What's this?" said Ahmad, pointing at a Babylonian drawing.

"He don't know," Mustafa said authoritatively.

For a moment, I felt perfectly happy to be perched on a park bench in Istanbul with a teenaged Senegalese pimp and a homeless Turkish onanist. Sitting there, basking in the first blush of my beer buzz, I felt like I'd rediscovered a couple of misfit little brothers.

After a few minutes, Mustafa made like he had to leave. "I work now," he said, pantomiming a waterpipe again.

"Sure," I said. "No problem."

Mustafa held up the myth book. "You give to me?"

A part of me wanted to let Mustafa keep the book, but I'd just paid $13 for it and had barely read the first page. "Can you read English?" I asked.

"No."

"Then I think I'll keep it for myself," I said.

Mustafa stood up to leave. "You come?"

"No," I said. "I have to meet someone at seven. Maybe later tonight."

After Mustafa left, it didn't take long for Ahmad to get bored with both me and the myth book. "Will you stay here today?" he asked.

"Only for about forty more minutes," I said. "Why?"

"Because I will leave now. But maybe I will come back with a beautiful woman for Mr. America."

"Whatever you say, Ahmad."

Ahmad flopped off, leaving me alone on the park bench. Since the folks from the overland trip would be arriving on the tram, I moved fifty meters over to a bench within view of the tram stop. I wasn't there for five minutes before a round-faced, olive-skinned man came up and asked me if I would take a photo of him and his friend. I set down my beer and took a couple shots of them standing together. Even with their touristy hip-packs and sunglasses and cans of Efes, the pair looked awkward and out of place.

"Where are you guys from?" I asked.

"You try and guess!"

I've always been awful at guessing nationalities, but I looked them both over. The round-faced man looked vaguely like an old Puerto Rican friend of mine. His friend, a skinny, brown-skinned fellow with intense eyes and smoke-stained teeth, looked Persian. I decided to place my guess somewhere in the middle. "Are you from Spain?" I said.

"Close: Morocco."

The Puerto Rican Moroccan introduced himself as Mohsin and said he ran a pizza parlor back home. The Persian Moroccan's name was Hasan, and he told me his parents were diplomats in Malaysia. They were on their way to visit Greece, and—since I'd recently arrived from Greece—I decided to offer a few travel tips. Paging through the maps in their French-language Greece guide, I gave them the kind of hearsay advice and half-digested guidebook information that travelers always share with one another when they cross paths: which mountains are supposedly good for hiking; which islands are supposedly good for partying; which historical sites are supposedly worth their while.

"This is great," Mohsin said as I briefed him on various attractions. "How do I thank you?"

"No worries; sharing travel secrets is a time-honored tradition."

"We are new to traveling, I guess." Mohsin held up his can of Efes. "Maybe you want a beer?"

"I already have one," I said, pointing to my own can.

"How about food? We can go to the waterfront and eat fish. Please. You are our first American friend."

"I don't much like fish," I said. "Besides, I really don't have time to eat. I'm meeting some people here in about thirty minutes."

Mohsin seemed distressed at the thought of me not liking fish. "You don't like fish only because you don't know fish!" he exclaimed. "Moroccans are the best fisherman in the world, and I know how to choose the best fish. I can look a fish in the eyes and know if he's a good fish or a bad fish. I can teach you!"

In the previous weeks, I'd had a Finnish girl teach me how to read palms and a pair of Hungarians instruct me on tasting wine. Learning how to size up a fish seemed almost too weird and charming to pass up. Still, I had other priorities. "I'm sorry," I said, "but I really can't miss my appointment."

"I will give you a ten-minute lesson to looking at fish. You will be back here before your friends, and when they arrive, you can teach them also about fish."

I pondered this for a moment. "We'd better hurry, then," I said.

I jammed my myth book into my back pocket as we trotted off toward the waterfront. Halfway across the Hippodrome, I spotted Ahmad chatting up a couple of unenthused-looking Germans. In good spirits, I yelled over to him: "Where's my girlfriend, Ahmad?"

Ahmad looked over at me distractedly. "Hello!" he said, as if trying to place me.

"Do you wanna learn how to buy fish?" I called to him.

A look of mortification came over Mohsin's face as I said this. "No!" he hissed. "Don't bring that boy with us."

"It's no problem," I said. "He's a friend."

"He's an African. Africans are cheaters and thieves."

"You're African too, Mohsin."

"Yes," he laughed. "But I'm not black!"

By this time, Ahmad had returned his attention to the Germans, so we kept walking. "You shouldn't judge people that way," I said to Mohsin. "You have to judge people as individuals.

There are good and bad people everywhere you go. That's one of the things you learn when you travel."

"Americans are crazy," joked Hasan. "They like everyone."

Mohsin laughed and took a package of cream-sandwich cookies from his daypack. "Life is all we have." He popped a cookie into his mouth and handed another to Hasan. "Maybe it's good to like everyone."

Mohsin and Hasan had played their roles perfectly. When Mohsin tossed me one of the cream-sandwich cookies, I didn't even remotely suspect that it had been laced with (most likely) Rohypnol. I didn't think much of the slightly bitter taste as the cookie went down, nor did I think it suspicious when Hasan stopped to take a leak in the bushes near the waterfront. Mohsin suggested we sit on a park bench while Hasan did his business.

The last thing I recall that day is Hasan furtively poking around in the foliage along the old stone retaining wall that overlooks the Sea of Marmara. The very next instant in my memory is one of night and solitude—of me drugged and disoriented, momentarily trying to remember how to walk again.

Anyone who's been robbed clean overseas will know that the days following your robbery provide a kind of masochistic therapy. Amidst the tedious hours of down time in various police stations, consulates, and traveler's-check offices, you have ample time to re-examine each individual thread of your demise.

To retrospectively pluck any one of these threads is to watch the robbery neatly unravel into some idealized parallel future. It's a torturous, yet irresistible exercise.

In time, this exercise of memory renders things relative: it makes you realize that things could have been much, much worse; it makes you realize that bad experiences, on the road or otherwise, help you appreciate good experiences otherwise forgotten. You come out, in the end, with a sense of wonder at all those other, unseen moments when the threads of chance fluttered—nearly connecting, but not—just past the periphery of your life.

And then—once you have replaced your passport and filed away the lessons learned—you resume weaving.

Because you now know there is a certain holiness in the notion that those threads exist at all.

Rolf Potts writes an independent travel column for National Geographic Adventure, and his work has appeared in Best American Travel Writing, Condé Nast Traveler, National Geographic Traveler, Travelers' Tales Greece, Not So Funny When It Happened, *and Salon.com. He is also the author of* Vagabonding: An Uncommon Guide to the Art of Long-Term World Travel. *He feels somewhat at home in Bangkok, Cairo, Pusan, and Wichita, Kansas. His virtual home can be found at http://rolfpotts.com.*

NICK DANZIGER

* * *

Where's the Outrage?

At the height of tension between Turks and Kurds,
the author witnesses brutal treatment
of Kurdish refugees.

WAITING FOR MY BUS AT ADANA I SPOKE TO A TURKISH
schoolteacher who was keen to practice his English on me.
Beneath his contempt for the Kurds was a vein of distrust and fear.
"They're so dirty, they have too many children, they're under-
developed and indifferent to the civilizing things in life." He couldn't
understand why I was interested in their plight, although he admitted that the chemical attacks on the Iraqi Kurds were "unfortunate."
I concluded that, to the Turks, the Kurds were the bringers of pol-
lution and ill fortune.

From Adana I traveled through the night and the best part of
the morning by bus to Cizre. The dramatic scenery of soft rolling
barren hills like worn velvet, plains to the south and mountains to
the north, bespoke a harsh, impoverished existence. Here and
there, choking dust tracks led off the main road to small mud-
walled settlements scraping by on subsistence living. When the bus
stopped in towns we were besieged by eager children working as
street vendors. I shopped well from my bus seat and, likewise, for
the locals the bus stop is a lifeline.

It was with a mixture of anticipation and trepidation that I arrived at Cizre: the thrill I always experience on arriving in a new

244

town tempered by the horror of what I might find there. As we approached the town I was greeted by a scene from biblical times: men in the fields with their flocks, women down by the river washing clothes. The town was half asleep in the wide, littered and dusty street where men dressed in baggy trousers sat amongst their produce. Within minutes of the bus disgorging its passengers, I was alone at the bus station. I walked into the main road and asked directions to the hospital. Eventually, I was taken there on the back of a horse-drawn cart.

The resident doctor, a Turk from Ankara, was one of only a handful of Turks in the town. Yes, he had heard of casualties from the chemical attacks but hadn't seen any. It remained a mystery as to where the victims were being taken. The doctor had nothing to hide; he showed me around the grim and dilapidated wards and invited me to take lunch with him in the lower ground-floor canteen, where our view was restricted to the hoofs of cows as they rubbed themselves against the hospital's outer wall.

After lunch the doctor escorted me to the edge of town and directed me towards the refugee camp at Silopi, only a few miles from the border with Iraq. Silopi, like Cizre, is on the main highway to Iraq where daily hundreds upon hundreds of oil tankers trundle back and forth carrying precious Iraqi oil to Turkey and its Mediterranean ports for export. I hitched a lift on one such tanker. No sooner had I told the driver I was from England than he proceeded to talk football:

"Gary Lineker—good footballer, Shilton, Anderson, Robson..." The Turkish truck driver knew the whole England team by heart.

We passed Silopi and were closing in on the border with Iraq when the refugee camp came into sight. The driver put me down 500 meters from it; he didn't want to be seen dropping me too close.

It had been wise precaution. The camp, normally a rest stop for pilgrims *en route* to Mecca, had been transformed into something of a military base with the army at one end and the refugees at the other. Two guards in military fatigues blocked my entrance. A senior officer was summoned. He checked my credentials: my passport and a very battered fake press card. I signed my name in a registrar's book and then the officer escorted me across the camp to a handful of Turkish relief workers who sat in the shade of an outhouse, drinking *chai* and looking bored. They didn't want to be photographed. The military officer quickly tired of me and returned to the temporary barracks. I walked across to the infirmary where a doctor and two nurses were besieged by a tide of exhausted and wretched refugees. Women and children were asleep on the floor, mothers were nursing their babies. The makeshift infirmary's small rooms and hall echoed to the sounds of coughing and cries. The small team of medical workers were processing the refugees in conveyor-belt fashion with vaccinations. With 16,000 refugees already packed into the camp without proper hygiene facilities, contagious diseases and diarrhea were a real danger.

These people had fled their valleys and villages in panic. Families had become separated; wives had lost their husbands; children had lost their parents. Uncertainty shrouded their missing brothers', sisters' and husbands' fate.

They had no vehicles to help them in their escape and their livestock had either perished or been left behind. They had trekked for several days across 2,200-meter (7,500-foot) mountains; shoeless grandmothers, old peasants haggard and bent double from years of toiling in the fields, and children as young as five carrying babies strapped to their backs. Terrorized and chased from their country, they entered the unknown with nothing but the clothes they wore. Surrendering to the Turkish authorities, they were promptly shepherded into refugee camps. Some considered themselves lucky; the Iraqi army had now created a *cordon sanitaire* along the border: anyone attempting to cross would be shot on sight. Those Kurds who lived too far from the border remained trapped inside Iraq with no means of escape.

The Kurds are non–Arab Muslim people. Over 20 million of them are spread through Turkey, Iran, Iraq, Syria, and the Soviet Union. Most had been shepherds raising sheep and goats. They had lived in the mountains as far back as their communal history could be recounted, although the moments they had lived in peace were admittedly rare. Life under Arab, Turkish, and Iranian rule had never been easy. Following the collapse of the Ottoman Empire after World War I, the Treaty of Sèvres in 1920 promised them an independent state, but this was never ratified. Instead Britain annexed the oil-rich Kurdish region of Mosul to Iraq, then a British mandate. The Kurds had lost many campaigns for autonomy and are treated with hostility by most of their host governments, who have prohibited the teaching of their language, razed their villages, denied many of them citizenship, and forcibly deported others. During the course of the twentieth century, the world's largest stateless minority has on several occasions been betrayed and neglected by foreign governments. In recent years Syria, Iran, and Turkey have given military aid to Iraqi Kurds. Syria has also supplied military aid to Turkish Kurds, as has Iraq which has also given military assistance to Iranian Kurds. In each case the assistance to rebellious Kurds has only been enough to create a nuisance, never enough to enable them to break loose and become independent.

In the last few years, since the beginning of the Iran–Iraq Gulf War, they had been chased, persecuted, decimated, forcibly deported, expelled, and exterminated on political, racial, and religious grounds by the Baghdad regime. Some had correctly predicted that, when the war between Iran and Iraq ended, Iraq would set the might of its armed forces on its irrepressible Kurdish population.

Nothing, however, had prepared them for the venom of the slaughter that was to take place. The refugees recounted how the first sign had been the smell of the acrid gas, even before they heard the jets and helicopters and the explosions releasing their deadly toxic charge. I was given an account by a woman who had watched her father die as he stood by a stream with his grazing flock. Others recounted how they had fled up the mountainsides and watched the onslaught of phosphorus bombs. Civilians had been deliberately targeted. The fields and villages were strewn with corpses. Two women told me they had watched their children killed by strafing as they tried to join them on the mountainside. No one knew how many had been killed in the attacks.

Here in the clinic were the agonized cries of the survivors, and the grief and trauma of having been brutally uprooted from their homes and valleys for reasons beyond their understanding. Bewilderment and incomprehension surrounded the events that led them to flee their birthplace and homelands. Very few had ever left their tightknit communities—some had been to Baghdad, slightly more had been to the Kurdish and oil-rich city of Kirkuk.

Access to their lands had been difficult at the best of times. The steep and narrow valleys had always given them a certain degree of protection and enabled them to continue a way of life unhindered by central authority. The aerial bombardment had, however, irrevocably altered the equilibrium that had been in place for centuries. A people who had never been subdued by land forces and had, up to this day, maintained a formidable guerrilla resistance that had held the invaders at bay, suddenly found that the odds were changed.

As I walked into the main area of the camp, I found a vast amalgam of tents and shelters improvised from blankets, carpets, clothes, and strips of material and sections of plastic held together to form crude protection against the elements. Many slept in the open. The tired and frightened refugees were grouped together in pathetic bundles of exhaustion, often fast asleep, huddled together in domino patterns. Each represented the misery of a broken family, an abandoned home, a flight into the unknown, pain, despair, and destitution.

A curious thing happened as I entered this part of the camp: the tranquility was abruptly shattered. News of my arrival had traveled quickly through the camp and a massive, heckling crowd came storming towards me. My camera captured the mob as it approached and finally engulfed me. The children were in the vanguard, shouting and chanting battle cries; they waved their arms and clenched their fists, their wild blue eyes unfocused with frustration, anguish, and rage. I continued to photograph the sea of faces. People were pushing, shoving, and jostling, and I was finding it difficult to stay on my feet. The grown-ups tried to offer me some protection from the crowd, but were themselves jostling and shoving to get to the front. Emotions were running high, the deafening screams now at a startling pitch. Several men created a small distance between me and the seething mass, but the distance kept breaking down as the mass pushed forward. Whichever way I moved, the crowd moved with me; there was a serious risk of tents and shelters being trampled underfoot. The women and smaller children sat impassively throughout the disturbance. I decided to put as much distance as possible between myself and the main area of the camp in the hope of losing the crowd, and partially succeeded by reaching a mound at the far end.

My feeling of relief was momentary. Quite suddenly the sound of semiautomatic gunfire reverberated all around. Terror and panic swept through the camp. Old men stood bewildered and lost, women and children were screaming and crying hysterically. Clutching my cameras, I ran towards the Turkish soldiers who were indiscriminately shooting the defenseless refugees. There was no escape.

The refugees were dragging the dead, dying, and injured away from the barracks and back into the camp. In the background above their heads I could see the soldiers lined up, holding their guns ready to shoot again. Sprawled on the ground in front of me was a man whose head had been partially blown away. His friend picked him up and cradled him, looking at me despairingly, his face pleading and full of anguish. I photographed. There was nothing I could do. The man was dead.

Another man lay injured not far away, surrounded by enraged men. Some of the children had caught sight of his horrific wounds. A young girl screamed uncontrollably, she *screamed* and *screamed* and *screamed*.

There was a steady train of injured; a man was swept along the ground on a blanket, blood gushing from a wound. I was taken to a tent where a man had a bullet wound in his stomach. He lay on an improvised bed; as he breathed, part of his intestine moved through the wound. I felt sick. I also feared for my own safety; the soldiers knew I was in the camp and they wouldn't relish a journalist broadcasting the barbaric treatment they had meted out to the refugees.

A Kurdish man grabbed me by the arm and led me back through the camp. I hid amongst the Kurds and was moved from tent to tent. Children were posted throughout the camp to warn me of approaching soldiers. I thought of escaping, but by the time I had devised a plan to get over the compound wall, Turkish commandos had been brought in and we were surrounded. I set about hiding my film, crucial evidence of their fatal aggression.

I thought desperately about the various possibilities of hiding the film and decided to dismantle my telephoto lens and hide the film in the lens casing. I was sweating profusely and had the greatest difficulty with the miniature screws. The sweat poured from me, clouding my vision and making it all but impossible to work with my hands. It was a ridiculous choice anyway; you could see the film inside the lens. As I searched for an alternative hiding place my publishers' words came back to me: "Be careful, don't get into any trouble." I didn't want to die! I thought how often I had said that to myself and also, after each dangerous journey, "That was the last." Yet here I was again. But then I thought how lucky I had been. I considered the humility of these extraordinary people and the dignity they had maintained under such inhumane and trying circumstances, compared to which my plight seemed insignificant. And so with renewed effort I searched for a way to hide my film. •

I thought back to customs and airport security checks. What had they considered the most and least obvious hiding places? I looked through my camera bag and remembered that they had checked the unwrapped cartridges of film but not the forty rolls of unexposed film which remained intact, still untouched in their original boxes and thin cellophane sleeves at the bottom of the bag. I set about carefully opening the cellophane sleeves and replaced the virgin rolls of film with exposed rolls. Now I needed to reseal the boxes and the cellophane. I explained to the woman in the tent that I needed some glue. I tried everything to make her understand "glue," but to no avail. However, as I worked with the boxes of film, the woman, her two children, and the man who had brought me to the tent became fascinated by my attempts. With no glue I decided to use my masking tape to close the boxes. I began by folding the tape over onto itself, making it double-sided. The woman immediately stopped me from proceeding any further. She left the tent and minutes later returned with a tiny roll of cellotape. Now everyone was engaged in the spirit of the task. "Glue" was concocted from sugar and water, and the job was completed. The cellophane didn't look perfect; there was a small tear down one side, but it did appear as though it had never been opened, which was the desired effect.

Before surrendering to the authorities I walked around the camp, taking in all I had seen. I was escorted by several men in turbans and the traditional brown overalls and distinctive waistbands of the Kurdish resistance fighters, the *peshmerga*, which means literally and, after the day's events all too prophetically, those who face death. Their despondency was total. As they saw it, their struggle for self-determination or independence was over; with no friends and no defense against chemical weapons they felt crushed. Now their immediate concern was that the Turkish troops should refrain from further indiscriminate shooting. They had massed in the open clearing to protest against the arrival of two Iraqi agents in the camp; the soldiers' answer to the demonstration had been to open fire on the protesters. Once again they felt embittered and forced into submission by a brutally hostile force. Their future was bleak, their choice stark: they could return to Iraq; Saddam Hussein had appealed to them to come home and promised an amnesty whilst he continued to strafe lines of fugitives and bomb and shell their villages, or they could accept Turkish hospitality and remain at the mercy of the Turkish army. They pleaded for international help that would never arrive.

The *peshmerga* took me to a man injured in the chemical attacks. As I entered the tent a young man propped him up.

"Look at his eyes," said the young man, who spoke some English. The whites of the victim's eyes were no longer visible— they were completely bloodshot. I had no way of knowing what had caused this.

"Why is he here?" I asked.

"We are keeping him here because when we first arrived they took all the injured people away and they won't tell us where they have been taken."

"What about the men injured in today's shooting?"

"We had no choice but to ask the Turkish authorities to help, otherwise the men would most certainly die."

I was curious as to where he had learned his English. "I speak French as well; I studied tourism in Baghdad." He looked up at the group of gaunt, strong, unshaven faces lost in the uncertainties of exile.

We passed young children, some still crying inconsolably for their lost parents; other children cried because they heard others cry. A twelve-year-old girl sat alone in a tent; hopelessly vulnerable, she looked forlorn and melancholic, a statue of robbed innocence. Some mothers began to cook bread, their dinner, on hot plates resting on stones. The men had agreed to go on hunger strike to protest against their treatment and the massacre.

I took some last pictures in the fading light, but neither my mind nor my heart was in it. I was thinking about what the authorities would do to me. Several rows of tents before the open ground and the barracks, the *peshmerga* and a group of children bade me farewell and wished me luck.

As I crossed the open ground, two uniformed soldiers came forward and arrested me. They took me to a clearing next to the barracks. One of them took my camera bag away and I was given a seat before being questioned by five men in civilian clothes, all of whom were armed. They weren't

---

           ⚹

The PKK—Kurdistan Workers Party—is the name of a Kurdish guerrilla force which, in essence, declared war on Turkey.

—JV

---

soldiers. They were almost certainly the much-hated special Interior Ministry police force, the Ozel Tim, formed to fight the Turkish PKK insurgency.

"*Sprechen Sie Deutsch?*" one of them asked. A tall brutish man kept his submachine gun trained on me.

"No."

"*Parlez-vous français?*"

"*Oui.*" They questioned me in French.

"What are you doing here?"

"I came to take pictures," I explained.

"Who do you work for?" This was a question I knew was going to come up. I worried about the fake press card I had presented to the officer when I entered the camp. I told them I worked freelance for a photographic agency. My interrogator was unimpressed.

"What pictures did you take?"

"The tents, families, children, the infirmary."

"Nothing else?"

"No." My interrogator didn't sound convinced.

"What did you see in the camp?" he asked.

I tried to give what sounded like an honest but naïve account. "At one point there was a commotion, I heard some bangs, I was at the far end of the camp. Later, I saw a man with a stomach wound."

"Did you take any pictures of him?"

"No," I lied.

The questioning stopped. They went through my camera bag and took all the opened rolls of film, but they left the two packages of "unused" film in the bag. There was a long silence punctuated by groups of soldiers passing to and fro in quick marches. Close by, five or six Kurdish men were standing in a shallow open pit guarded by some soldiers. I sat gloomily as the night chill began to cut through me like a knife. The tall man pointing his gun at me ordered me to stand against the barracks wall. I braced myself. After what seemed an eternity I began to shiver under the eerie glow of stadium lights. My heart was pounding wildly; I was terrified. As I was being searched a military officer joined the group. He looked at me contemptuously and scowled what sounded like an order to the man questioning me.

"What did he say?" I asked.

"He said you should be shot in the interests of national security."

I blurted out, "What about my companion?"

"What companion?" my interrogator demanded.

"The one I arrived with."

I made up a story to persuade them to believe I wasn't on my own. I had to establish that it was known I had come to the Silopi camp and that if I disappeared people would come asking all sorts of difficult questions.

I invented a name for my nonexistent companion and embellished the cover story as I went along. "Paul Davison, he works for an American newspaper.... He dropped me near the refugee camp.... We agreed to meet later."

Abruptly a sense of urgency overtook my inquisitors. They wanted all the details: my companion's age, his nationality, the type of vehicle he was driving, and where and what time we had agreed to meet.

We were going through the details when all of a sudden a flurry of activity transformed the camp and halted the questioning. The soldiers started to line up in formation and my five interrogators stood to attention. A helicopter and a cavalcade of black limousines and military jeeps brought the province's governor and military commander to the camp. The governor and commander made a cursory inspection of the soldiers, conferred with several officers, and left as suddenly and in the same sweeping cavalcade as they had come. I had tried to appeal to the governor, one of the interrogators trying unsuccessfully to stop me: nonetheless, my pleas to be released fell on deaf ears.

The questioning resumed. They wanted to meet Paul. "At what time are you going to meet your friend?"

It was now around eight o'clock. I told the Ozel Tim that we had agreed to meet at about six o'clock.

"Where?"

"At the bus station in Cizre."

In the distance, as we walked to a car, I could see a hundred or more Kurdish civilians sitting on the ground in rows, their hands on their heads; they were being herded silently into two open trucks.

I sat in the back of the car sandwiched between two of the men. One man in the front left his submachine gun resting on the hand brake. On the outskirts of Cizre we were stopped at a roadblock. The driver wound down his window, conferred with the soldiers, and we were waved through.

The bus station was deserted. "There's no one here," they remarked angrily. "Where is he?"

"I don't know," I said weakly.

"Why isn't he here?"

"I was meant to meet him three hours ago. He probably gave up waiting and is wondering what happened to me."

"Where do you think he went?"

"Our plan was to head for Hakkari or Diyarbakir; we hadn't decided. Maybe he checked into a hotel for the night," I said helpfully.

"Which one?" they asked.

"I don't know, we hadn't planned on staying here." They checked all the hotels. I didn't think there would be many hotels in the small town of Cizre, but surprisingly there was a handful, and they were determined to find him. I sat back in the car—I was going to enjoy this charade of chasing a ghost for as long as I could.

At each hotel three of my jailers entered the reception area clutching their guns. One remained in the car guarding me. As they checked the hotel registers they grew increasingly impatient. At one hotel they kicked the young receptionist out into the street.

When they had finished we drove back along the road towards Silopi. At one of the first dust tracks beyond Cizre they pulled off the main road and headed towards the hills. My heart began to beat faster. They stopped the car and made me get out. One of them pulled me around to the back of the car and placed a gun to my head. The only light was from the car's headlights.

"You say you are a photographer."

"Yes."

"Who is this American friend of yours?"

"Paul Davison, he's a journalist."

He paused. "Apart from your American friend, who else knows you are here?"

It was a menacing question. My heart began to pound again. Amongst themselves I heard them talk about the PKK—the Kurdish *peshmerga*. Out here the Ozel Tim could do anything they wanted. I realized they could easily put a bullet through my head and dump me in the mountains, and if I was ever found they could blame the Kurds. Foreigners had been kidnapped and shot by Kurdish separatists elsewhere, and the United States Department of State has for many years issued a caveat advising travelers not to leave the main highways in remote rural areas of Turkey or generally to drive at night.

"Does your embassy know you are here?"

They didn't, nor did anyone actually know I had gone to Cizre, but I wanted the Ozel Tim to believe that there was quite a list of people.

"There's my picture editor at the photographic agency, the newspaper that sent me on this assignment, my family—in fact they will already be worried because I telephone them every evening and they'll wonder why I haven't called." I suggested they let me telephone them so that they wouldn't worry about me. They didn't answer.

One of the men opened the boot of the car and pulled out my camera bag. Were they going to leave me here? He walked with the bag towards the light and began to rummage through the contents. They had already confiscated all my loose film but the re-wrapped film was still in the camera bag.

Holding all the unwrapped film in their hands, they asked me again, "Is this all the film you took?"

"Yes," I replied.

"What about these?" One of them returned to my camera bag and began to unpack it.

"What are you talking about?" I swallowed hard.

He reached into the bag and pulled out the cameras. "Is there any film inside?"

"Inside?"

"The cameras."

It was an obvious place but one they had overlooked. They opened the cameras and pulled the rolls of film from them.

I was driven to a military barracks where an army officer took charge of me. The Ozel Tim seemed angered that they had to release me into the army's custody.

I had no idea what time it was. The major took me through a garden to a veranda where the province's military commander, the governor, and various high-ranking officers had gathered. There was plenty of food and drink and I was told to eat. I had only eaten a small lunch in the past two days, but I wasn't hungry, I had no appetite. The officials sat around the table hardly speaking except to ask me questions. Who was I working for? What had I seen? Had I taken any pictures? I was to spend eighteen hours under repeated interrogation. I stuck to my story that I had seen only a single wounded man. I said I hadn't taken any pictures of him; besides, the Ozel Tim had taken all my film from me. I also said I was

The brutality of these tactics is indisputable, as is the brutality of the PKK's rebellion. Yet the eagerness with which some foreign governments have condemned Turkey, justified as condemnation may be, is more than a little disingenuous. Turkey was facing a threat to its very existence as a unified state, and it responded the way other countries in the post-war world have responded when peoples under their sovereignty rose in rebellion. The Turkish campaign against the PKK was comparable in various ways to those waged by the Dutch in Indonesia, the British in Malaya, the French in Algeria, the Americans in Vietnam, the Serbs in Bosnia, and the Russians in Chechnya. Turks understandably react unpleasantly when those former imperial powers condemn them for using tactics they themselves perfected not so long ago.

—Stephen Kinzer, *Crescent and Star: Turkey Between Two Worlds* worried about my friend who had driven me to Cizre. Did they have any news of him? I asked to call my family or my editor or the newspaper—they knew I was here and would be worried if I didn't call. I asked the governor what they were going to do with me. Solemnly he said, "We haven't decided."

I spent the night incarcerated in another barracks. While I was being driven there in a jeep, an argument broke out between two officers. "What's your name?" one of the officers had asked me. "Nick—and yours?" I answered politely. When the officer told me his name his companion severely reprimanded him for doing so. Such petty behavior didn't give me cause for the slightest optimism. Once locked into a room I dared not sleep.

I was released the following day. No explanation was given and I considered it prudent not to ask for one. The officials returned my film, which they had processed, but the developed film was cloudy and failed to reveal any images. Which must have surprised them. They even arranged a seat for me on the bus out of Silopi to Ankara. I thought I was free but, having been driven into Silopi, I was told not to leave the bus company's ticket office. Outside, across the street, were two of the Ozel Tim who had interrogated me; they were talking to three men I hadn't seen before. A sickening feeling returned to my stomach. The army had been positively pleasant compared to the Ozel Tim. I sat in my allocated seat on the bus only to discover I was being followed by one of the men who had been talking with the Ozel Tim. He sat one row behind me across the aisle. I could see the butt of a revolver sticking out from the bottom of his shirt.

As the bus pulled out of Silopi I remained nervous. They had said I could go, but was this some kind of trap? I turned around and looked at the man who was following me. I searched for clues and played a hundred and one scenarios over in my mind. I was overcome by tiredness but was fighting to stay alert. I kept thinking they might try to shoot me and dump my body somewhere. I tried to convince myself that there were too many witnesses. They would have to get me off the bus and to do so we would have to stop in the middle of nowhere. As we traveled across the bleak stretches of barren hills along the border with Syria, what I feared most was the noise of the engine decelerating. Several times we slowed to a crawl and I wondered each time whether it was the moment I had been anticipating. When the bus began to decelerate in jerky movements and I could see the driver pumping the brake, I began to panic and the adrenaline started to flow. Was this the moment I had steeled myself for?

The bus came to a stop close to a car that had been flattened in a crash. I was drenched in sweat and as I stared out of the window I thought how clever and convenient it would be to make my disappearance look like a road accident.

After a long delay, we re-boarded the bus. I didn't return to my allocated seat; instead I went to the back where the man who was following me couldn't see me. No sooner had the bus driver moved into gear than my guard leapt from his seat screaming at him to stop. "Where's the foreigner?" he shouted. I peered up from behind the back seats; the relief driver next to me was highly amused by my simple ruse and I asked him where we would be stopping enroute to Ankara. He told me Mardin, Kiziltepe, Gaziantep, and Adana in the early hours of the morning. "Are there any buses from Adana to Alanya and Antalya?" I asked.

He laughed, "From Adana there are buses to everywhere." I hoped to use the Adana airport as a quick gateway to Istanbul, and the information was just what I wanted to hear. A false trail would allow me a few extra hours in which to seek help.

When we reached Adana, I disembarked like most of the passengers, but then re-boarded and disembarked several times, as is quite normal during lengthy stops. At one point, choosing my moment carefully, I disembarked with my bags and asked a rival bus company to hold them for me. The bus from Silopi blew its horn signaling our departure for Ankara. I had other ideas. I re-boarded and walked past my original seat in front of the man following me so that he could see I was on the bus. I then made a show of retiring to the back of the bus, but just before we pulled away from the parking bay I left the vehicle by its back door praying that my "shadow" wouldn't notice, ran to collect my bags, and headed for the airport.

It was a nerve-racking wait. The first plane departure from Adana wasn't until eight o'clock. I had two hours to kill, so I bought a ticket for the first flight and joined some American soldiers. To calm my nerves, I asked, "Where are you guys headed?"

"To get us some ass," said the air force engineer. From what I gathered, their base to the south of Adana was a backwater in a sea of abstinence.

I reached Ankara and called the British embassy to tell them what had happened but, more importantly, that I was leaving Istanbul the same afternoon and wanted them to check that I had got on the plane. I called Trisha to put her in the picture and to expect me back that evening.

In London, mentally and physically exhausted, I had the film processed immediately. The images of the dead and dying civilians were all too graphic. The editor of the newspaper that had sent me on the assignment explained that their readers didn't want to have their breakfasts ruined. Two other national newspapers bought the pictures, but neither was prepared to carry them.

Back in New York, the picture editor of a leading magazine looked at the photograph of a refugee clutching his dying friend who had been shot in the head. "It's a pity that the man's head isn't turned a bit more away from the camera," he said.

Nearly three years later, some of these Kurdish refugees were still languishing in Turkey, interned in temporary settlements and forgotten by all.

Award-winning photographer/writer Nick Danziger has often found himself in dangerous predicaments. He is the author of Danziger's Travels, Danziger's Britain: A Journey to the Edge, The British, *and* Danziger's Adventures: From Miami to Kabul, *from which this story was excerpted.*

JEREMY SEAL

* * *

The Fairy Tales of Van

Turks cope with the ghosts of Armenia
in a variety of ways.

THE THREE HAD GONE TO SCHOOL TOGETHER. NOW THAT they were in their late thirties, only those friendships reminded them that they had once been children, and the short holiday that they took together every spring grew in importance as each year passed. For a few days, they would laugh until the fading memories were returned to them as if new, and the laughter would soothe the rapid passage of the years.

For a few days, amiable Sadi would no longer feel lonely in the space of his Istanbul bachelorhood, with his thinning hair and ballooning paunch. A generous light would fill Mustafa's cloudy eyes, and the pains in his chest that fed on worry and cigarettes would not trouble him. With his thick black beard and hawkish features, he resembled the gunmen of Beirut, his two friends joked, but he enjoyed the teasing. Ismail would welcome his old friends from distant Istanbul, almost a thousand miles away, and in their company the longueurs of his life in a frontier town of southeastern Turkey would be temporarily lifted. For the school friends, summer was four spring days in Van.

It was a beautiful afternoon in May. In the darkness of his ground-floor office, hemmed in by buildings and passing traffic, it struck Ismail that he had not heard the glockenspiel sounds of the Aygaz delivery van, the song of the Turkish winter, for days now. After the rigors of a winter at 5,000 feet, he noticed these seasonal indicators. Like a flower with an instinct for sunlight, Ismail had sought out the town's vantage points until he knew by rote every street corner with a view beyond the city limits, every second-story office and café where he could watch the snow on the mountains receding day by spring day, sidling up the valleys and screes as the sunshine pushed back the evidence of winter and mud smoked in the bright warmth, feeding roadside rivulets of melt.

Today his friends were in town, and the vantage points were not enough. Ismail called up Sadi and Mustafa and suggested an outing to the lake. They took Ismail's red pickup. The radio played the theme from *Love Story* as they sped along the water's edge, and they let it play despite their suspicions that deep inside each might be laughing at the others for listening to it. To the right, the lake ran to the distant feet of snowcapped volcanic peaks. To the left, the hills rose more gradually from the lakeshore, permitting a few snatches of yellow-green, spiky young trees in early leaf before the contours bunched together into a mean, unrelenting ascent.

I was standing at a nearby jetty a few miles down the road, eyeing a boat suspiciously. I was the only prospective passenger and the skipper was talking an extortionate price.

"I'll wait for some other passengers," I told him.

"Not this time of day you won't," he replied, flicking away the stub of a cigarette. "They all come in the morning." Just then three men drew up in a red pickup from which sounded the tinkling notes of the theme from *Love Story*. One of them, I noticed, was fat. Another looked as if he had taken hostages in his time.

We met on the boat to Akdamar Island, a favorite escape for the people of Van. Now that summer was on the way they would soon take to the boats with their picnics and barbecues and clamber ashore for a day in the sunshine. While the children swam in the icy water and the men smoked cigarettes and took their ease, the women would cook, turning kebabs on skewers in the shade of the almond trees.

The old cutter drifted toward the island across water in which was mirrored in perfect detail the mountains, the snow, and the lilac-colored blossoms of the almond trees, which partially concealed the sunlit terra-cotta ruins of a conically domed building. The prospect was so beautiful that it seemed improbable, as if only a dream. We were crossing a great volcanic lake so filled with mineral sodas that the clothes our helmsman trailed from the stern emerged transformed, bleached clean. Where the bow of the cutter disturbed the reflection, throwing out great ripples, we could see between them into a depth unknown and a darkness without end. Lake Van did not have many fish, but cats that did not believe this were known to prowl the shore; it was said that each one had eyes of different colors. We stepped ashore among the whisperings of birds and insects, the air freighted with the scent of blossom. Once upon a time, they had called this place Vaspurakan. So unearthly was it that no other name would have done.

Then the plane came, so low that I did not hear its thunderous engines until it was overhead, casting over the island on its approach to the airport a black shadow that chilled long after the plane was gone. It was a military transporter; I could clearly make out the markings among its camouflaged, khaki confusions. As it disappeared, reducing to a black spot far down the lake, I sensed a reminder being served: that even among the blossoms of Vaspurakan, real life was liable to intrude.

I had flown into Van only that morning. Military transporters were parked on every side of the airport. As we walked toward the tiny terminal building, two distinct groups were taking shape on the tarmac. To one side, some thirty men stood uncertainly, hoping that they might regard themselves as a welcoming committee but realizing that they should have prepared themselves for inspection. They were falling into line, running hands through their hair for the last time, and patting at rumples in their jackets. Government employees, they fixed their eyes upon a mandarin of apparent consequence and the attentive retinue that scraped and bowed its way across the tarmac around him. The mandarin reached the employees and worked his way down the line, cursorily shaking hands with each of them as they inclined toward him. Then he was gone, spirited into the warm interior of a waiting black Mercedes, leaving the thirty men to break into puddles of unmotivated manpower, reach deep into pockets of cigarettes, and wonder how their handshakes had gone. So their morning passed.

The other group was of younger men. They were conscript soldiers headed for military service. They all had been given cropped haircuts and uniforms that did not fit well, but their luggage remained pathetically their own. Some had suitcases that were tied shut with blue twine; others flaunted pirated status symbols such as Benetton duffel bags. One forlorn character carried two plastic bags, one blue, one pink, with a single trouser leg hanging sorrowfully from the top of the pink one. They were waiting for nothing as grand as a handshake, only the barked order from their commanding officer to board the transporter.

In front of them a pair of green-shrouded coffins that had been lowered from the hold of another transporter was being shouldered by a duty of soldiers and borne slowly to a waiting military ambulance. As the coffins passed, the fresh conscripts stiffened to attention as if by instinct, all except the boy with the plastic bags, who bent respectfully to tuck away the errant trouser leg.

I wandered up the jetty at Akdamar, the place of Turkish forgetting. The island was a sunlit fairy kingdom with trees in blossom and tall headstones inscribed in an unfamiliar script. The friezes on the walls of the domed building standing on a shoulder of the island were like a text from a fabulous story that had nothing to do with the pathetic significance of handshakes in the pursuit of modest preferment or with the coffins of young conscripts. Instead, there were lions, snakes, angels and dragons, horses, dogs, gazelles, oxen, eagles and turkeys, cocks and bulls. There was a problem in fairyland, though: the building, its pink sandstone walls absorbing the warm sunlight, was a church, and it was Armenian.

Even those around me who had recently ignored the military transporter, I thought, would surely have to acknowledge the awkward realities enshrined in this building. But jovial Sadi, whose portly presence accompanied me through the ruins of the church, taught me a lesson in forgetting.

"Seljuk," he said, identifying the architecture of the building to his satisfaction and, at the same time, neatly delivering his mind of any Armenian problem. By simple extension, the nearby headstones and the bodies that lay beneath them were no longer Armenian connections. Sadi had airbrushed Armenia out of his life.

How had it come to this, that decent Turks like Sadi could re-fashion the evidence of bricks and mortar so that their absolving view of national history would prevail? The Armenians, perhaps 3 million strong in the nineteenth century, had lived under Ottoman sovereignty for hundreds of years. Their tragedy was to be located on the Ottoman periphery, where the Christian Russians were always seeking to gain influence. In the nineteenth century Russia increasingly portrayed herself as champion of the oppressed Arme-nians. During the Great War there were those Armenians who in-trigued to advance the Russian cause. The Russians captured Van and held it from 1915 to 1917.

Then the Bolshevik Revolution radically reshaped priorities in occupied Van. Suddenly, atheist Russia was no longer interested in old-fashioned notions such as Christian solidarity. Her new credo being workers, she promptly withdrew from Van, leaving the way free for the Turks to return, slaughter at their leisure what they saw as its fifth-column residents, and torch the place.

In my exasperation, I wondered what I could say to Sadi about the well-documented charges against his country, which alleged that between 1915 and 1918 some one-and-a-half million Armenians had been slaughtered by Ottoman troops in eastern Turkey. I guessed that Sadi was too well entrenched in his forget-ting to acknowledge the testimony of surviving Armenians, those who had witnessed victims being tied together as if in a necklace and then thrown into one of eastern Turkey's fast-flowing rivers after one had been shot to become the millstone by which all, eventually, would drown. I chose not to tell him that the accounts of all those beheadings, those firing squads and rapes, were widely believed in the West. I did not tell him what was known of the deportations, forced marches through the Anatolian Mountains that ended in mass graves deep in the deserts of northern Syria. I told him only that the building on Akdamar was actually built 300 years before the Seljuks. Besides, if he was right, he could explain why the Muslim Seljuks had built themselves a church—assuming he accepted that it *was* a church in which we were standing. After a long pause, Sadi nodded slowly. It was a church.

> For a deeply disturbing first-hand account of the Armenian genocide in Turkey, read "Dovey's Story" in Peter Balakian's book, *Black Dog of Fate.*
>
> —JV

There is a conspicuous innocence in the Turkish spirit, a sincere belief in the highest of ideals that cannot countenance the possibility of such a holocaust. The Turkish refrain most sincerely expressed, "We are all people," articulates a fervent belief in common humanity. Nineteen fifteen is remembered as the year of Atatürk's defense of Gallipoli, the anvil of heroism on which the Turkish state was later forged. Turks find quite unpalatable the idea that in the same year the blueprint for the Final Solution was being fashioned at the other end of their country. And so Sadi and people like him have picnicked on Armenian islands until the islands appear Turkish and history is reordered to their satisfaction.

In libraries over the years, among travelers' diaries and memoirs, moldering pages of dog-eared print and sepia photographs, I had found unsensational accounts that had served to convince me. These were not accounts that detailed atrocities against Armenians; they were cameos, compelling in their very ordinariness, told by priests and adventurers, mercenaries and writers, painters and eccentrics, old soldiers and aristocrats. The simple accumulation of unexceptional references to Armenians living their lives in nineteenth-century towns and villages all over eastern Turkey led to the question where, then, are the Armenians now?

For there was a time when Armenians lived all over Turkey, particularly in the east, as every nineteenth-century traveler remarked.

There is the Armenian banker in the central Turkish town of Afyon, or Opium, who affronts the writer Professor Ramsay in 1883 by charging 5 percent of the value of a check to cash it (*Impressions of Turkey*, 1897). There is Frederick Burnaby's Armenian doctor in Tokat, educated in the States and speaking with a Yankee drawl; the peasant hosting a wedding party north of Van; the woman by the edge of Lake Van stitching a shirt for a passing sergeant; the young shopkeeper jailed in Erzincan for a married woman's love of him (*On Horseback through Asia Minor*, two volumes, 1877). There is Lord Warkworth's Armenian host, who suffers in his home near Erzurum the threat of a beating from a Turkish officer intent on interfering with his lovely daughter; there is his Armenian priest with a flowing jet-black beard (*Asiatic Turkey*, 1898). There is Edward Vizetelly's Armenian peasant, who helps the writer to a bag of wild duck on a bitter moonlit night by a stream near Erzurum, and his tall, gaunt Armenian, the landlord of a drinking den in the border town of Kars who wears baggy breeches, a bolero jacket, and a threadbare fez and sells Bain-Bruel cognac that has suffered a fortnight's journey on the back of pony or camel to reach the throats of his motley clientele (*The Reminiscences of a Bashi-Bazouk*, 1897). There is the Reverend Joseph Wolff's Armenian pipe-maker's son who puts him up in a town of 200 Armenians and 200 Muslims and bemoans the fact that the town's Armenian schoolmaster has just packed his bags, leaving them with a school but nobody to teach in it (*Mission to Bokhara*, 1846).

Where were all these Armenians, their stories peppered with the tellingly ordinary details of real life that combined to condemn? Now there were only the Armenian enclaves near the Syrian border, those in Istanbul where I had found Garbis Bey and his daughters making a last few fezzes in a sweatshop, and an Armenian church on an island in blossom.

The boatman had made a fire from twigs by the water's edge and was brewing tea as we returned. His assistant was offering up prayers to Allah in the shadow of the church. As we sat, Sadi told me his own story of Akdamar, a tale of forbidden love between a beautiful girl called Tamara and a young swain whose efforts to reach her on the island were thwarted by those who stand in the way of high passion. It all came of course to an unhappy conclusion, the young man drowning from his efforts and sighing, "Ah, Tamara," as he disappeared under the waves, his last utterances supplying the island with its name. Even after his slow nod in the ruins of the church, Sadi evidently preferred his history thus.

Jeremy Seal also contributed "A Visit to Soapmakers" in Part One. This story was excerpted from A Fez of the Heart: Travels Around Turkey in Search of a Hat.

THE LAST WORD

SCOTT L. MALCOMSON

On the Bosporus

*Adrift on the waters where East meets West,
the author takes time to remember.*

ON A MILD SUMMER EVENING, AFTER DINNER, YOU WALK DOWN
the slope of Üsküdar toward the Bosporus with Dina. The root of
her name means "religion." "That makes it easy to remember," she
says, which is true if you know Arabic (she's a historian, from
Lebanon). You walk down darkened streets to the quay and board
a motorboat for the ride to Besiktas.

Üsküdar is on Istanbul's "Asian side," as it's called; Besiktas is on
the "European side." Neither Europe nor Asia exist anywhere outside the imagination, of course. Traditionally we call each a "continent," though they are no more separate, geographically, than
Canada and the United States. A long time ago someone stood in,
say, Besiktas, pointed toward Üsküdar, and said, "That's Asia. It's
different from here." You can swim across the Bosporus when the
tides are right.

We leave for Europe in our little boat-taxi, called a *dolmus*—it
means "stuffed" or "filled." The boat-taxis that cross the Bosporus
putter slowly, tossed by the wakes of huge freighters plying between the Mediterranean and Black Seas. Both the Asian and
European sides of Istanbul rise steeply from the shore. Istanbul has
been the capital of three great empires, pagan, Christian, and

Muslim: Roman, Byzantine, and Ottoman. Now it wants to be part of a united Europe, since it knows that being outside of this new empire would leave it in the Third World, or whatever the not-powerful part of the globe is to be called....

At this point, though, neither of you is talking, because it is nighttime on the Bosporus and intensely pleasant to rock up and down on the creaking *dolmus* in silence. Dina smokes her cigarette, you close your eyes. This is your favorite place in all of Istanbul, a floating point between two imaginary continents, delicate, deliciously landless....

Remember Dina, traveling between Asia and Europe or vice versa on the *dolmus* that night: the way it creaked.

Remember eating grilled *palamut* when the *palamut* had just come into season and everyone at the waterside restaurants was eating it, the fishermen were out on the Bosporus in their small boats every day searching for *palamut*. Remember its luscious taste, the way you loved rolling the word in your mouth, *palamut, palamut.*

Remember glass after glass of tea with sugar in the day when it was hot and glasses of raki at night when it was cool.

Remember driving with your friend through Üsküdar one evening during a political campaign, the streets wildly decorated with the various parties' banners. "It's like a holiday!" he said. Turkish elections hadn't always been like holidays; they had also been times of fear and violence. Fear: the police stop you at an impromptu checkpoint, looking for terrorists or at least a few lire from intimidated drivers. (Checkpoints are most frequent before gift-giving holidays.) You watch your friend, a proud, sometimes arrogant man, affluent, well-known both in his own country and abroad, suddenly shake with fear as the police approach.

Remember the markets of Aksaray, with poor Eastern Europeans wandering around, giddy one minute, fearful of robbery the next. The signs said "Polish style," and you wondered: What is Polish style?

Remember listening to the Muslim prayer for the dead when a young friend of yours had just passed away, in another country: and how it touched you. If you forget a dead friend, does he die again? If you forget your ancestors do you lose time, or gain it?

Remember Dina on the drunken boat across the Bosporus at night, and the boat's creaking.

Remember eating anchovies in cornbread; and the former Roman cistern that's now a restaurant lit only with candles.

Remember. Everything can slip away, like a suicide over the gunwales on a quiet night. If you forget enough then other forces will take over your memory, buy it at a discount. The many people you've met will blend into one person, then disappear; "a thousand different faces become a single force." If you forget enough, then every place you visit will have been the same place, only better or worse. And you will have lost the taste of life.

In addition to travel, Scott L. Malcomson has written on subjects from AIDS to arms control. His work appears in such publications as The Village Voice Literary Supplement, Nation, *and* The London Review of Books. *He is the author of* One Drop of Blood: The American Misadventures of Race, Tuturani: A Political Journey in the Pacific Islands, *and* Borderlands: Nation and Empire, *from which this story was excerpted.*

Index

Index of Contributors

Recommended Reading

Arlen, Michael J. *Passage to Ararat.* St. Paul, MN: Hungry Mind Press, 1996.

Ash, John. *A Byzantine Journey.* New York: Random House, 1995.

Balakian, Peter. *Black Dog of Fate: An American Son Uncovers His Armenian Past.* New York: Broadway Books, 1997.

Balfour, John and Lord Kinross. *Europa Minor: Journeys in Coastal Turkey.* New York: William Morrow, 1956.

Brosnahan, Tom, Richard Plunkett, and Pat Yale. *Lonely Planet Turkey.* Oakland: Lonely Planet Publications, 2001.

Danziger, Nick. *Danziger's Adventures: From Miami to Kabul.* London: HarperCollins UK, 1992.

Darke, Diana. *Discovery Guide to Eastern Turkey and the Black Sea Coast.* London: Michael Haag Ltd., 1987.

Dodwell, Christina. *A Traveller on Horseback in Eastern Turkey and Iran.* New York: Walker and Co., 1989.

Feiler, Bruce. *Walking the Bible: A Journey by Land Through the Five Books of Moses.* New York: HarperCollins, 2001.

Fernea, Elizabeth Warnock. *In Search of Islamic Feminism: One Woman's Global Journey.* New York: Doubleday, 1998.

Freely, John. *Inside the Seraglio: Private Lives of the Sultans in Istanbul.* New York: Penguin, 2001.

Freely, John. *Istanbul: The Imperial City.* New York: Penguin, 1998.

Glazebrook, Philip. *Journey to Kars.* New York: Holt, Rinehart, and Winston, 1984.

Halliburton, Richard. *The Glorious Adventure.* New York: Star Books, 1927.

Howe, Marvine. *Turkey Today: A Nation Divided over Islam's Revival.* Boulder, CO: Westview Press, 2000.

Kaplan, Robert D. *Eastward to Tartary: Travels in the Balkans, the Middle East, and the Caucasus.* New York: Random House, 2001.

Kaplan, Robert D. *The Ends of the Earth: From Togo to Turkmenistan, from Iran to Cambodia, A Journey to the Frontiers of Anarchy.* New York: Alfred A. Knopf, 1996.

Kinzer, Stephen. *Crescent & Star: Turkey Between Two Worlds.* New York: Farrar, Straus, Giroux, 2001.

Krich, John. *Music in Every Room: Around the World in a Bad Mood.* New York: Bantam Books, 1984.

Lloyd, Seton. *Ancient Turkey: A Traveller's History.* Berkeley: University of California Press, 1989.

Malcomson, Scott L. *Borderlands: Nation and Empire.* New York: Faber & Faber, 1994.

Mango, Andrew. *Ataturk: A Biography of the Founder of Modern Turkey.* Woodstock, NY: Overlook Press, 2000.

Newby, Eric. *On the Shores of the Mediterranean.* Oakland: Lonely Planet Journeys, 1998.

Seal, Jeremy. *A Fez of the Heart: Travels Around Turkey in Search of a Hat.* Orlando, FL: Harvest, 1995.

Settle, Mary Lee. *Turkish Reflections: A Biography of a Place.* New York: Prentice Hall Press, 1991.

Shrady, Nicholas. *Sacred Roads: Adventures from the Pilgrimage Trail.* San Francisco: HarperSan Francisco, 1999.

Summerskill, Mimi LaFollette. *Aegean Summer: A Family Odyssey.* Middlebury, VT: Paul S. Eriksson Publications, 1990.

Tumpane, John D. *Scotch and Holy Water.* Lafayette, CA: St. Giles Press, 1981.

Valent, Dani, Perihan Masters, and Jim Masters. *Lonely Planet World Food Turkey.* Oakland: Lonely Planet, 2000.

Fiction and Poetry

Hiçyilmaz, Gaye. *Against the Storm.* Boston: Little, Brown, 1992.

Kemal, Yasar. *Anatolian Tales.* Translated by Thilda Kemal. New York: Dodd, Mead, 1969.

Pamuk, Orhan. *The Black Book.* Translated by Güneli Gün. New York: Farrar, Straus, Giroux, 1994.

Pamuk, Orhan. *The New Life.* Translated by Güneli Gün. New York: Farrar, Straus, Giroux, 1997

Star, Jonathan and Shahram Shiva, translators. *A Garden Beyond Paradise: The Mystical Poetry of Rumi.* New York: Bantam Books, 1992.

Tekin, Latife. *Berji Kristin: Tales from the Garbage Hills.* Translated by Ruth Christie and Saliha Paker. New York: Marion Boyars, 1993.

Acknowledgments

Thanks go to James and Larry for offering me this book, and for all of the support, wisdom, knowledge, humor, and patience they provided me with as we moved through the work. I've learned so much. Susan Brady and Christine Nielsen, since the first day, were so easy to work with, and I appreciate the ease and patience with which they answered each of my many questions. And my thanks go to everyone else at Travelers' Tales, as well: Krista Holmstrom, Jennifer Leo, Judy Johnson, Cynthia Lamb, and Keith Granger. I made such unbelievable friends in Turkey, and I wish I could thank each of them, because the memories they've given me run all through the making of this book. Anthony Cunningham kept me sane and laughing during my first year in Istanbul; he's an excellent guide, whatever the country or planet. Alan Mathison and Joanna Doggett deserve my thanks for their balcony over the Bosporus, for the fact that it was always open to me, and for so much more. And I want to thank Aysegül and Mali Tinay, who were never anything but warm, friendly, and funny. My family, as has always been the case, supported me in all the important ways; you merit much more than a simple thank you. And, finally, to Julie, my travel companion and love, thank you for everything: your encouragement, your understanding, and for all those meals you prepared while I worked late.

Frontispiece excerpted from "From Box to Box" by Rumi excerpted from *A Garden Beyond Paradise: The Mystical Poetry of Rumi*, Jonathan Star and Shahram Shiva, translators. Published by Bantam Books, 1992.

"A Dazzling Kaleidoscope" and "Ye Pipes, Play On" by Stephen Kinzer excerpted from *Crescent & Star: Turkey Between Two Worlds* by Stephen Kinzer. Copyright © 2001 by Stephen Kinzer. Reprinted by permission of Farrar, Straus and Giroux, LLC.

"Above the Ruins of Ephesus" and "In Cappadocia" by Mary Lee Settle excerpted from *Turkish Reflections: A Biography of a Place* by Mary Lee Settle.

About the Author

James Villers moved to Turkey in 1999. His welcome to the country—two weeks after he arrived—was a major earthquake that killed more than 10,000 people. Despite this shocking initiation, he stayed, spending more than two years there—teaching high school English in Istanbul, and traveling in and around Turkey. He has lived most of his life in California, but spent a year in France, and six months in Switzerland. He is a secondary school literature and drama teacher, with an M.A. in English from Sonoma State University. He now lives in the San Francisco Bay Area.

TRAVELERS' TALES

THE SOUL OF TRAVEL

Footsteps Series

THE FIRE NEVER DIES
One Man's Raucous Romp Down the Road of Food, Passion, and Adventure
By Richard Sterling
ISBN 1-885-211-70-8
$14.95

"Sterling's writing is like spit-fire, foursquare and jazzy with crackle...."
—*Kirkus Reviews*

LAST TROUT IN VENICE
The Far-Flung Escapades of an Accidental Adventurer
By Doug Lansky
ISBN 1-885-211-63-5
$14.95

"Traveling with Doug Lansky might result in a considerably shortened life expectancy...but what a way to go." —Tony Wheeler,
Lonely Planet Publications

ONE YEAR OFF
Leaving It All Behind for a Round-the-World Journey with Our Children
By David Elliot Cohen
ISBN 1-885-211-65-1
$14.95

A once-in-a-lifetime adventure generously shared.

THE WAY OF THE WANDERER
Discover Your True Self Through Travel
By David Yeadon
ISBN 1-885-211-60-0
$14.95

Experience transformation through travel with this delightful, illustrated collection by award-winning author David Yeadon.

TAKE ME WITH YOU
A Round-the-World Journey to Invite a Stranger Home
By Brad Newsham
ISBN 1-885-211-51-1
$24.00 (cloth)

"Newsham is an ideal guide. His journey, at heart, is into humanity." —Pico Iyer, author
of *Video Night in Kathmandu*

KITE STRINGS OF THE SOUTHERN CROSS
A Woman's Travel Odyssey
By Laurie Gough
ISBN 1-885-211-54-6
$14.95 — ★ ★ ★ —

ForeWord Silver Medal Winner
— *Travel Book of the Year*

THE SWORD OF HEAVEN
A Five Continent Odyssey to Save the World
By Mikkel Aaland
ISBN 1-885-211-44-9
$24.00 (cloth)

"Few books capture the soul of the road like *The Sword of Heaven*, a sharp-edged, beautifully rendered memoir that will inspire anyone." —Phil Cousineau,
author of *The Art of Pilgrimage*

STORM
A Motorcycle Journey of Love, Endurance, and Transformation
By Allen Noren
ISBN 1-885-211-45-7
$24.00 (cloth)
— ★ ★ ★ —

ForeWord Gold Medal Winner
— *Travel Book of the Year*

Travelers' Tales Classics

COAST TO COAST
A Journey Across 1950s America
By Jan Morris
ISBN 1-885-211-79-1
$16.95

After reporting on the first Everest ascent in 1953, Morris spent a year journeying by car, train, ship, and aircraft across the United States. In her brilliant prose, Morris records with exuberance and curiosity a time of innocence in the U.S.

TRADER HORN
A Young Man's Astounding Adventures in 19th Century Equatorial Africa
By Alfred Aloysius Horn
ISBN 1-885-211-81-3
$16.95

Here is the stuff of legends —tale of thrills and danger, wild beasts, serpents, and savages. An unforgettable and vivid portrait of a vanished late-19th century Africa.

THE ROYAL ROAD TO ROMANCE
By Richard Halliburton
ISBN 1-885-211-53-8
$14.95

"Laughing at hardships, dreaming of beauty, ardent for adventure, Halliburton has managed to sing into the pages of this glorious book his own exultant spirit of youth and freedom."
— *Chicago Post*

UNBEATEN TRACKS IN JAPAN
By Isabella L. Bird
ISBN 1-885-211-57-0
$14.95

Isabella Bird was one of the most adventurous women travelers of the 19th century with journeys to Tibet, Canada, Korea, Turkey, Hawaii, and Japan. A fascinating read for anyone interested in women's travel, spirituality, and Asian culture.

THE RIVERS RAN EAST
By Leonard Clark
ISBN 1-885-211-66-X
$16.95

Clark is the original Indiana Jones, relaying a breathtaking account of his search for the legendary El Dorado gold in the Amazon.

Travel Humor

NOT SO FUNNY WHEN IT HAPPENED
The Best of Travel Humor and Misadventure
Edited by Tim Cahill
ISBN 1-885-211-55-4
$12.95

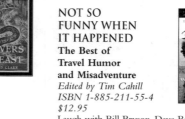

Laugh with Bill Bryson, Dave Barry, Anne Lamott, Adair Lara, and many more.

THERE'S NO TOILET PAPER...ON THE ROAD LESS TRAVELED
The Best of Travel Humor and Misadventure
Edited by Doug Lansky
ISBN 1-885-211-27-9
$12.95

★ ★ ★

Humor Book of the Year
— Independent
Publisher's Book Award

★ ★ ★

ForeWord Gold Medal
Winner — Humor
Book of the Year

LAST TROUT IN VENICE
The Far-Flung Escapades of an Accidental Adventurer
By Doug Lansky
ISBN 1-885-211-63-5
$14.95

"Traveling with Doug Lansky might result in a considerably shortened life expectancy...but what a way to go."
—Tony Wheeler, Lonely Planet Publications

Women's Travel

A WOMAN'S PASSION FOR TRAVEL
More True Stories from A Woman's World
Edited by Marybeth Bond & Pamela Michael
ISBN 1-885-211-36-8
$17.95

"A diverse and gripping series of stories!" —Arlene Blum, author of *Annapurna: A Woman's Place*

A WOMAN'S WORLD
True Stories of Life on the Road
Edited by Marybeth Bond
Introduction by Dervla Murphy
ISBN 1-885-211-06-6
$17.95

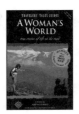

—★★★—

Winner of the Lowell Thomas Award for Best Travel Book— Society of American Travel Writers

WOMEN IN THE WILD
True Stories of Adventure and Connection
Edited by Lucy McCauley
ISBN 1-885-211-21-X
$17.95

"A spiritual, moving, and totally female book to take you around the world and back." —*Mademoiselle*

A MOTHER'S WORLD
Journeys of the Heart
Edited by Marybeth Bond & Pamela Michael
ISBN 1-885-211-26-0
$14.95

"These stories remind us that motherhood is one of the great unifying forces in the world" —*San Francisco Examiner*

Food

ADVENTURES IN WINE
True Stories of Vineyards and Vintages around the World
Edited by Thom Elkjer
ISBN 1-885-211-80-5
$17.95

Humanity, community, and brotherhood comprise the marvelous virtues of the wine world. This collection toasts the warmth and wonders of this large, extended family in stories by travelers who are wine novices and experts alike.

FOOD (Updated)
A Taste of the Road
Edited by Richard Sterling
Introduction by Margo True
ISBN 1-885-211-77-5
$18.95

—★★★—

Silver Medal Winner of the Lowell Thomas Award for Best Travel Book— Society of American Travel Writers

HER FORK IN THE ROAD
Women Celebrate Food and Travel
Edited by Lisa Bach
ISBN 1-885-211-71-6
$16.95

A savory sampling of stories by some of the best writers in and out of the food and travel fields.

THE ADVENTURE OF FOOD
True Stories of Eating Everything
Edited by Richard Sterling
ISBN 1-885-211-37-6
$17.95

"These stories are bound to whet appetites for more than food."

—*Publishers Weekly*

Spiritual Travel

THE SPIRITUAL GIFTS OF TRAVEL
The Best of Travelers' Tales
Edited by James O'Reilly and Sean O'Reilly
ISBN 1-885-211-69-4
$16.95

A collection of favorite stories of transformation on the road from our award-winning Travelers' Tales series that shows the myriad ways travel indelibly alters our inner landscapes.

THE WAY OF THE WANDERER
Discover Your True Self Through Travel
By David Yeadon
ISBN 1-885-211-60-0
$14.95

Experience transformation through travel with this delightful, illustrated collection by award-winning author David Yeadon.

PILGRIMAGE
Adventures of the Spirit
Edited by Sean O'Reilly & James O'Reilly
Introduction by Phil Cousineau
ISBN 1-885-211-56-2
$16.95

——— ✦ ✦ ✦ ———

***ForeWord Silver Medal Winner
— Travel Book of the Year***

A WOMAN'S PATH
Women's Best Spiritual Travel Writing
Edited by Lucy McCauley, Amy G. Carlson & Jennifer Leo
ISBN 1-885-211-48-1
$16.95

"A sensitive exploration of women's lives that have been unexpectedly and spiritually touched by travel experiences…. Highly recommended."
— Library Journal

THE ROAD WITHIN
True Stories of Transformation and the Soul
Edited by Sean O'Reilly, James O'Reilly & Tim O'Reilly
ISBN 1-885-211-19-8
$17.95

——— ✦ ✦ ✦ ———

***Best Spiritual Book — Independent
Publisher's Book Award***

THE ULTIMATE JOURNEY
Inspiring Stories of Living and Dying
James O'Reilly, Sean O'Reilly & Richard Sterling
ISBN 1-885-211-38-4
$17.95

"A glorious collection of writings about the ultimate adventure. A book to keep by one's bedside — and close to one's heart."   —Philip Zaleski, editor,
The Best Spiritual Writing series

Adventure

TESTOSTERONE PLANET
True Stories from a Man's World
Edited by Sean O'Reilly, Larry Habegger & James O'Reilly
ISBN 1-885-211-43-0
$17.95

Thrills and laughter with some of today's best writers: Sebastian Junger, Tim Cahill, Bill Bryson, and Jon Krakauer.

DANGER!
True Stories of Trouble and Survival
Edited by James O'Reilly, Larry Habegger & Sean O'Reilly
ISBN 1-885-211-32-5
$17.95

"Exciting…for those who enjoy living on the edge or prefer to read the survival stories of others, this is a good pick."
— Library Journal

Special Interest

365 TRAVEL
A Daily Book of Journeys, Meditations, and Adventures
Edited by Lisa Bach
ISBN 1-885-211-67-8
$14.95

An illuminating collection of travel wisdom and adventures that reminds us all of the lessons we learn while on the road.

THE GIFT OF RIVERS
True Stories of Life on the Water
Edited by Pamela Michael
Introduction by Robert Hass
ISBN 1-885-211-42-2
$14.95

"*The Gift of Rivers* is a soulful compendium of wonderful stories that illuminate, educate, inspire, and delight."
—David Brower, Chairman of Earth Island Institute

FAMILY TRAVEL
The Farther You Go, the Closer You Get
Edited by Laura Manske
ISBN 1-885-211-33-3
$17.95

"This is family travel at its finest." —*Working Mother*

LOVE & ROMANCE
True Stories of Passion on the Road
Edited by Judith Babcock Wylie
ISBN 1-885-211-18-X
$17.95

"A wonderful book to read by a crackling fire."
—*Romantic Traveling*

THE GIFT OF BIRDS
True Encounters with Avian Spirits
Edited by Larry Habegger & Amy G. Carlson
ISBN 1-885-211-41-4
$17.95

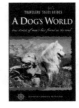

"These are all wonderful, entertaining stories offering a *bird's-eye view!* of our avian friends."
—*Booklist*

A DOG'S WORLD
True Stories of Man's Best Friend on the Road
Edited by Christine Hunsicker
ISBN 1-885-211-23-6
$12.95

This extraordinary collection includes stories by John Steinbeck, Helen Thayer, James Herriot, Pico Iyer, and many others.

THE GIFT OF TRAVEL
The Best of Travelers' Tales
Edited by Larry Habegger, James O'Reilly & Sean O'Reilly
ISBN 1-885-211-25-2
$14.95

"Like gourmet chefs in a French market, the editors of Travelers' Tales pick, sift, and prod their way through the weighty shelves of contemporary travel writing, creaming off the very best."
—William Dalrymple, author of *City of Djinns*

Destination Titles:
True Stories of Life on the Road

AMERICA
Edited by Fred Setterberg
ISBN 1-885-211-28-7
$19.95

FRANCE (Updated)
Edited by James O'Reilly,
Larry Habegger &
Sean O'Reilly
ISBN 1-885-211-73-2
$18.95

AMERICAN
SOUTHWEST
Edited by Sean O'Reilly
& James O'Reilly
ISBN 1-885-211-58-9
$17.95

GRAND CANYON
Edited by Sean O'Reilly,
James O'Reilly &
Larry Habegger
ISBN 1-885-211-34-1
$17.95

AUSTRALIA
Edited by Larry Habegger
ISBN 1-885-211-40-6
$17.95

GREECE
Edited by Larry Habegger,
Sean O'Reilly &
Brian Alexander
ISBN 1-885-211-52-X
$17.95

BRAZIL
Edited by Annette Haddad
& Scott Doggett
Introduction by Alex
Shoumatoff
ISBN 1-885-211-11-2
$17.95

HAWAI'I
Edited by Rick &
Marcie Carroll
ISBN 1-885-211-35-X
$17.95

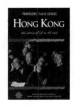

CENTRAL AMERICA
Edited by Larry Habegger
& Natanya Pearlman
ISBN 1-885-211-74-0
$17.95

HONG KONG
Edited by James O'Reilly,
Larry Habegger &
Sean O'Reilly
ISBN 1-885-211-03-1
$17.95

CUBA
Edited by Tom Miller
ISBN 1-885-211-62-7
$17.95

INDIA
Edited by James O'Reilly
& Larry Habegger
ISBN 1-885-211-01-5
$17.95

Destination Titles:
True Stories of Life on the Road

IRELAND
Edited by James O'Reilly,
Larry Habegger &
Sean O'Reilly
ISBN 1-885-211-46-5
$17.95

SAN FRANCISCO
Edited by James O'Reilly,
Larry Habegger &
Sean O'Reilly
ISBN 1-885-211-08-2
$17.95

ITALY (Updated)
Edited by Anne Calcagno
Introduction by Jan Morris
ISBN 1-885-211-72-4
$18.95

SPAIN (Updated)
Edited by Lucy McCauley
ISBN 1-885-211-78-3
$19.95

JAPAN
Edited by Donald W. George
& Amy G. Carlson
ISBN 1-885-211-04-X
$17.95

THAILAND (Updated)
Edited by James O'Reilly
& Larry Habegger
ISBN 1-885-211-75-9
$18.95

MEXICO (Updated)
Edited by James O'Reilly
& Larry Habegger
ISBN 1-885-211-59-7
$17.95

TIBET
Edited by James O'Reilly,
Larry Habegger, & Kim
Morris
ISBN 1-885-211-76-7
$18.95

NEPAL
Edited by Rajendra
S. Khadka
ISBN 1-885-211-14-7
$17.95

TUSCANY
Edited by James O'Reilly, &
Tara Austen Weaver
ISBN 1-885-211-68-6
$16.95

PARIS
Edited by James O'Reilly,
Larry Habegger &
Sean O'Reilly
ISBN 1-885-211-10-4
$17.95